THE CRIMEAN

BRIAN GLYN WILLIAMS

The Crimean Tatars

From Soviet Genocide to Putin's Conquest

HURST & COMPANY, LONDON

First published in the United Kingdom in 2015 by
C. Hurst & Co. (Publishers) Ltd.,
41 Great Russell Street, London, WC1B 3PL
© Brian Glyn Williams, 2015
All rights reserved.
Printed in India

The right of Brian Glyn Williams to be identified as the author of this publication is asserted by him in accordance with the Copyright, Designs and Patents Act, 1988.

A Cataloguing-in-Publication data record for this book is available from the British Library.

978-1-84904-518-6 *paperback*

This book is printed using paper from registered sustainable and managed sources.

www.hurstpublishers.com

For Eren "Pasha" Altindag, Yetkin Altindag, Feruzan and Kemal Altindag
and Ryan and Justin Williams

CONTENTS

Acknowledgements — ix
Prologue — xi

1. The Pearl in the Tsar's Crown — 1
2. Dispossession: The Loss of the Crimean Homeland — 9
3. *Dar al Harb:* The Nineteenth-Century Crimean Tatar Migrations to the Ottoman Empire — 19
4. *Vatan*: The Construction of the Crimean Fatherland — 33
5. Soviet Homeland: The Nationalization of the Crimean Tatar Identity in the USSR — 57
6. *Surgun:* The Crimean Tatar Exile in Central Asia — 89
7. Return: The Crimean Tatar Migrations from Central Asia to the Crimean Peninsula — 117

Notes — 161
Bibliography — 177
About the Author — 199
Index — 201

ACKNOWLEDGEMENTS

First and foremost I would like to thank the numerous Crimean Tatars who invited me into their simple stone homes in the settlements of the Crimea and greeted me with their people's legendary hospitality, despite their often tragic circumstances. In particular, I would like to thank Nuri Shevkiev and his wonderful wife Lilia and his children Emir and Elmaz for letting me live with them in their *samostroi* (self-built) home in the settlement of Marino near Simferopol. I still fondly recall the evenings gathered with the Shevkievs and Tatars from the surrounding houses eating homemade *cigborek* and drinking tea while collecting stories of the deportation, exile and return.

I would also like to thank Mustafa Dzhemilev for taking the time to grant me interviews during my stay. It was a real honor to get to know the "Crimean Tatar Mandela" who sacrificed so much to lead his people from exile to their homeland. I would also like to thank Lilia Bujurova, Izzet Khairov, Alie Akimov, Fevzi Yakubov, Abdullah Balich, Reshat Dzhemilev and Server Karimov for the time they took to grant me interviews.

In addition, I would like to thank my parents, Donna and Gareth, for encouraging me to travel the world as a young man and to respect other cultures. I would not be who I am today without their inspiration and guidance over these many years. I am also grateful to my wife Feyza Altindag for her support and patience with my obsession with the Crimean Tatars' history.

I also owe a huge debt of gratitude to my advisors at the University of Wisconsin who taught me Central Asian history, Uli Schamiloglu and Kemal Karpat. I would also like to say thanks to my colleagues at the University of Massachusetts-Dartmouth, Mark Santow and Len Travers, who provided me with the invaluable support I needed to produce this work. And as always I owe a huge debt of gratitude to my indispensable secretary, Sue Foley.

PROLOGUE

On the distant edge of Europe, where East meets West, Islam meets Christianity, and the world of the steppe nomad meets that of settled man lies the Crimean Peninsula. Since even before the classical era, when intrepid sailors from Greece arrived on its shores and interacted with the mysterious horse-riding peoples of the vast European plains who migrated to the Crimea's interior, this borderland has been an outpost of the nomads from the east. It has also been a preserve of nations, an ethnic time capsule and palimpsest of lost Eurasian races.

Located on the Black Sea shore of the Ukraine (whose name translates to "the Frontier" of the steppe in Russian), the Crimea has seen more than its share of conquering and migrating races. These races have, like waves coursing across the open steppes from the north and east, lapped up on its plains and cast their ethnic residue on the Crimea's genetic makeup.

It was here that the ancient Greek traders encountered the Scythian nomads, whose skill as horse-mounted archers gave birth to the legend of the half-horse, half-man Centaurs. After the Scythians came the nomadic Sarmatians, the Goths and Attila's Huns, followed by the Turkic Kipchaks (or Polovtsians, the "Men of the Plains" as they were known in Russian). But no nomadic race left as great an impact on the Crimea as the world-conquering Mongols. Storming across the Eurasian steppe from their home in distant Mongolia, the Mongols of Batu Khan (grandson of Genghis Khan) shattered the divided Russian principalities in the forests to the north and absorbed the vast hordes of Kipchak Turks of the south Ukrainian plains into their armies in the 1240s. The amalgam of pagan Mongols and Turkic Kipchaks then gradually converted to Islam and became known as "Tatars".

It was these horse-riding Turko-Mongol-Muslim Tatars that were to call the Crimea home until the present day. As the transcontinental Mongol world empire fractured and collapsed in the mid to late 1300s, the Tatars of the Crimea and surrounding steppes continued to dominate much of Eastern Europe. While the Mongols were ultimately expelled from China and the Middle East in the mid fourteenth century, in the southern Ukraine the Tatars were an anachronism that continued their horse riding ways for centuries.

Not even the liberation of Russia to the north from the Tatar Golden Horde in 1480 ended the power of the Crimean Tatars. By this time Khans (Genghisid rulers) of the Tatar Giray dynasty had established an independent Khanate in the Crimea and surrounding lands. The Tatar Khans of the Crimea, ruling from the fabled town of Bahcesaray ("Garden Palace") in the southern Crimean mountains, saw the rising power of Russia and made a far-sighted alliance with another up-and-coming power, the Muslim Ottoman Empire. This alliance helped the Crimean Tatars maintain their independence even as Ivan the Terrible's Russia inexorably expanded eastward across the vast forests of Siberia and down to the Caspian Sea, conquering the other Tatar remnants of the Mongol Golden Horde. Long after the Tatars of the Volga River region and plains north of the Caspian Sea had been absorbed into sixteenth-century Russia, the Crimean Tatars maintained their independence.

As the memory of the Medieval Mongols faded in other parts of the world, the Crimean Tatars continued to roam freely on the plains on the edge of a modernizing Europe. Riding on their rugged steppe steeds with their fur rimmed, spiked helmets on *chambuls* (raids for cattle and slaves), the Tatars of the Crimea continued their ancient ways and kept the Russians off the open plains of southern Ukraine for centuries. The Tatars of the Crimea were able to burn Moscow as late as 1571. Every year the Tatars would sally forth from their bastion in the Kirim ("the Fortress", the Turko-Mongol name which gives us the English word Crimea) to carry out vast slave raids into Poland, Russia and the Ukraine. Not even the modernizing Tsar Peter the Great could conquer the horse-riding Crimean heirs of Genghis Khan. In fact, the Crimean Tatars played a major role in the Turkish defeat of Tsar Peter's invasion of Ottoman Eastern Europe in 1711.

The incomparable Tatar horsemen also assisted the Ottoman sultans of Istanbul in their endless wars with the Christian West. The arrival of the Ottoman army in Eastern Europe was usually preceded by waves of mysterious Tatar horsemen, whom the Germans fearfully called "sackmen" and the Ottoman Turks admiringly called *akinjis* (literally "those who flow" over others' lands). The only sign Christian villagers had that the fast riding Tatars were coming was the urgent ringing of the *Turkenglocken* (Turk Bells) warning them of their impending arrival. While the main Ottoman army had to build bridges to cross rivers, the Tatar cavalry swam them. The hardy Tatars did not need cumbersome wagon trains to carry their provisions, they lived off the land and on bits of raw meat warmed beneath their saddle (hence the term "steak tartar" today). Covering vast distances at speeds that could not be believed, the Tatar outriders and skirmishers overwhelmed Austrian Habsburg positions and swarmed beyond Vienna, looting, enslaving Christians, and destroying small concentrations of troops. The arrival of the Tatar Khan for an Ottoman campaign was an occasion of much rejoicing for the Turks who considered his horsemen to be invincible.[1]

But the Tatars' days as outriders for the Ottoman sultans gradually came to an end, largely due to events bigger than themselves. In the late seventeenth century the Ottoman Empire had begun to weaken and lose its dominant role in Eastern Europe. By 1683, the Ottoman tide had crested at the walls of Vienna and had been repulsed by the Austrian Habsburg Empire. The reasons for the success of the Christians had much to do with their advances in military science, from the invention of bayonets and lighter rifles to more powerful cannons and navies, as the decline of the increasingly conservative and inward looking Ottomans.

To the north of the Crimea, Russia had also made tremendous strides towards modernization under Tsar Peter the Great and Catherine the Great (1729–1796). It was Catherine who was to ultimately defeat the Crimean Khans and their Ottoman allies in battle and conquer and annex this strategic part of the *Dar al Islam* (Realm of Islam) in 1783 (the year America's independence was recognized by Great Britain). The Ottoman sultan was said to have been devastated by the loss of his Crimean allies to the *Rus kafirs* (Russian infidels). As the horsetail standard of the Crimean Khans was replaced with the double head flag of imperial Russia, Europe's last Tatars lost their independence and became subjects of the "White Tsarina" of St. Petersburg. For the Russians, the conquest of the Crimea was seen as a God-ordained act of a civilizing Christian power, much as the white man's conquest of the Indians was in North America. It was this historic event that was to lead to the disintegration of the last independent Turko-Mongols of Europe under both the Russian Tsars and their successors, the Soviets. Under the Imperial Russians, the Crimean Tatars, whose ethnic origins went back to the eleventh-century Kipchaks and beyond to earlier south Crimean peoples, such as the Medieval Goths, Greeks and Italians, would begin to disintegrate as hundreds of thousands of the Tsarina's new Muslim subjects fled Russian repression to the sheltering lands of the Ottoman sultans/caliphs. The majority of the Crimea's Muslim Tatar peasants would ultimately leave the peninsula to partake in *hijra* (migration to preserve Islam from oppression by the nonbeliever) to the Ottoman Empire.

The Crimean Tatars, whose realm once extended from Romania through the southern Ukraine to the northern Caucasus, were brought to the point of extinction under Soviet leader Josef Stalin's genocidal policies. As the last of Europe's Medieval Mongols were ethnically cleansed by the Soviets in 1944 and deported to the deserts of Soviet Central Asia, the very name Crimean Tatar was wiped off the official Soviet map and virtually forgotten in the West. Hundreds of thousands would die under the Romanov Tsars and Soviet commissars in a tragedy that not only saw this people come to the brink of extinction, but presaged the later ethnic cleansing of Muslims in the Balkans by the Serbs in the 1990s.

It was only with the rise of the liberal Soviet leader Mikhail Gorbachev and the collapse of the Soviet Union in 1991 that the Tatars began to return *en masse* from their places of exile in Uzbekistan and elsewhere to the shores of the Black Sea to rebuild their community. Today, a small remainder of the the population—perhaps 250,000 in all—is struggling to recreate its identity in a place that was Slavicized and populated with Russians and Ukrainians during the half century of Stalin-imposed exile in Central Asia.

This work will analyze this journey over time and space, whereby the remnants of the Crimean Tatars were scattered across Eurasia, from the Anatolian and Balkan provinces of the collapsing Ottoman Empire after the Crimean War of 1853–56 to the deserts of Soviet Uzbekistan during the maelstrom of World War II. In so doing, it will trace the extraordinary process whereby this people, who had always defined themselves in ancient tribal and folk Islamic terms, gradually came to identify themselves as a modern *millet* ("nation") with links to a land they began to define as an *ata vatan* ("Fatherland"), in contemporary nationalistic terms. A thread that will be traced in this work is how the Tatars came to construct the Crimean Peninsula in the common imagination not as *Dar al Kufr* (the "Realm of the Infidel", which good Muslims should abandon to live in the *Dar al Islam*), but as the unique patrimony and "Motherland" of the Crimean Tatar nation.

It will also shed light on perhaps one of the most interesting, yet understudied, cases of the transformation of a pre-modern tribal-Islamic peasant people into a modern secular nation. It was this process of nationalization, territorialization of collective identity and modernization that saved the last of the

PROLOGUE

Crimean Tatars from complete extinction. This process allowed them to preserve their collective identity in the deportation years and begin a long national struggle to return from their Central Asian exile to the romanticized *Kirim Adasi* ("Crimean Island") to reconstruct their shattered community in post-Soviet Ukraine.

Today, as the Crimea undergoes its second conquest and annexation by the Russians following President Vladimir Putin's controversial seizure of the region in March 2014, the indigenous Tatars face an uncertain future in their natal land. As the most Russophobic population in the Crimea due to their long history of subjugation and displacement, the Crimean Tatars fear the worse. An understanding of their history of forced exile, genocide and revival as a nation puts their current fears in their proper historical context and helps explain their worries.

Map 1: Areas of Crimean Tatar concentration in Central Asia during the post-1944 deportation period.

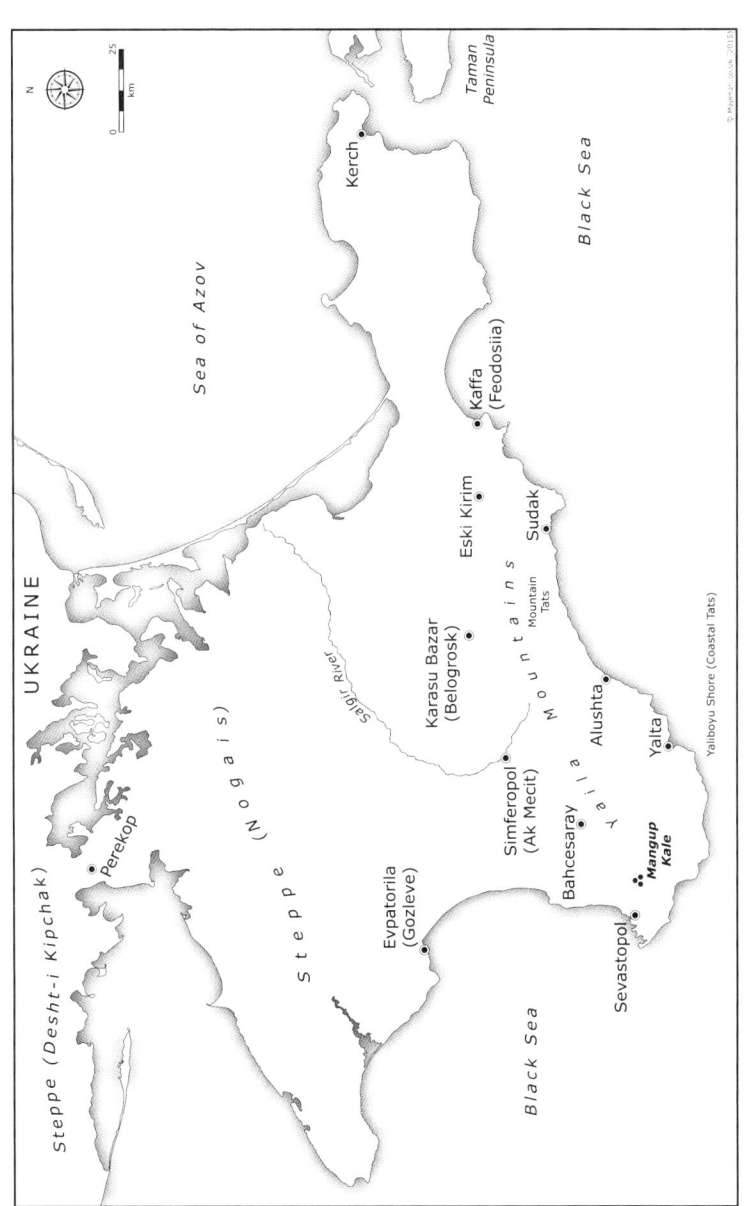

Map 2

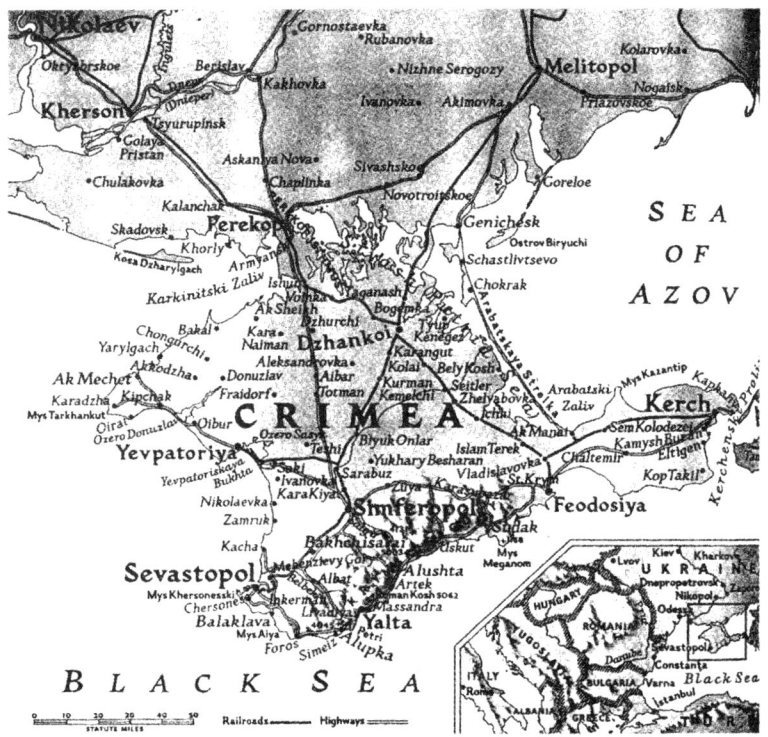

Map 3: Map of the Crimean Autonomous Soviet Socialist Republic featuring towns and topographic features with original Tatar names. Most towns were given Slavic names following the 1944 deportation of the Crimean Tatars.

1

THE PEARL IN THE TSAR'S CROWN

Following the Russian annexation of the Crimea in 1783, Tsarina Catherine the Great made a triumphant tour of her empire's latest acquisition on the shores of the Black Sea. As this was the era of the Enlightenment she brought in her entourage Western scholars to study the terrain, fauna, history, and ethnicity of this strange land and her exotic people. As the Tsarina's heavily guarded cavalcade made its way into the open plains of the southern Ukraine, which had long been denied to Slavic settlements by the Tatars, they encountered the last Eurasian nomads of Europe, the Crimean Tatar subgroup known as the Nogais. The Nogai Tatars lived in *yurts* (round portable tents) and migrated across the open plains with their flocks. It was the Nogais who had provided the Crimean Khans with swarms of hardy horsemen for their campaigns in the Caucasus, Russia and Eastern Europe. The once fearsome Nogais, however, seem to have rapidly lost their militaristic tradition soon after the Russian conquest.

In appearance, the Nogais of the south Ukrainian plains and the steppes of the Crimea's interior were Mongol and appeared to be the direct descendants of Genghis Khan's horsemen and earlier Turkic Kipchaks. The Nogais of the southern Ukraine steppes and the Crimea's northern two-thirds (an area known in Tatar as the *Chol*, the Plains) were ethnically distinct from the more Europeanized Tatars of the southern mountains and coast. One Russian visitor to the Crimean plains wrote of the Nogai subgroup:

> In these northern districts Tartars are chiefly met with who differ essentially from those inhabiting the southern coast, the former being rough, but kindly people, of the Mongolian type, mainly employed in the breeding of horses, sheep and

cattle, while those of the littoral, having in other days freely interbred with the Greeks and Genoese, are more refined in appearance and manner, and also more indolent, probably by reason of the more sunny and enervating climate.[1]

From the steppes of the Ukraine, which were already being settled by the first wave of Russians and Ukrainians at this time, the Tsarina's journey took her through the narrow entrance to the Crimea at Perekop and out onto the open plains of the northern portions of the peninsula. In appearance this flat, Nogai-inhabited *Chol* area was simply a continuation of the open steppes of the Ukraine and Eurasia. But as the Empress's party made its way south it encountered the south Crimean mountains known in Tatar as the *Yaila* (the Mountain Pasture). One contemporary nineteenth-century visitor to the Crimea recorded his first impression of his arrival to the southern mountains after crossing the Ukrainian steppes as follows: "Nothing can be conceived more gratifying, after an irksome journey over barren and uniform plains, than a view of the mountains, and a country presenting hills and beautifully variegated woods and occasionally intersected by the whimsical meanders of rivulets."[2] In the Yaila Mountains, the Russians found a second distinct Tatar sub-ethnic group known as the Tats. The Tats were less Mongol in their features and claimed to be the direct descendents of the Germanic/Scandinavian Goths as well as the ancient Greeks and Italians who had settled in this area since the classical Greek epoch and later become Islamicized or "Tatarized". One Western visitor to the Crimea wrote of the southern Tat-Tatars as follows:

> The Crim Tatars are divided into two classes, those of the plain and those of the mountains. Not only do these differ in habits and occupation, but in race; the former [the Nogais] are scattered over the steppe of the northern part of the peninsula, cultivating land and breeding cattle and horses, and building rude houses of unburnt clay. They bear on their visages the characteristics of the Mongols. The latter [the southern Tats] follow many industrial arts, are fond of gardening, cultivate tobacco, flax and the vine; and display the physiognomies of the Caucasian race. They have more beard than the others, and are above the middle height. They are supposed to be a mixture of races who have inhabited the Crimea, and resemble the Turks, or other Europeans, many of them having brown hair and fair complexions. They are refined in manner, and dignified in bearing, naturally polite and hospitable, honest in dealing, and frugal in eating.[3]

A nineteenth-century Russian account similarly stated:

> The Crimean Tatars should be divided into two groups, the mountain and steppe Tatars. The essence of the mountain people was intermixed with the ancient inhabitants of the Tauride [Crimea], with the Goths and the Greeks. They are in general of good height, slender and dark haired; their features are

regular, their physiognomy and carriage are expressive, they are free and generous in their treatment and in their speech they are thoughtful and sensible.[4]

In the Yaila Mountains, the Tat-Tatars maintained a local culture that had roots going back long before even the arrival of the eleventh-century Turkic Kipchak nomads and the later Mongols. For example, they celebrated festivals of spring and nature, such as *Tepresh, Derviza* and *Kedreles*, which were pre-Islamic in origin. On *Kedreles*, a distinctly Crimean festival with pagan and Christian roots celebrated on April 25—Orthodox St. George's Day—the venerated souls of the departed killed in battle (known as the *Aziz Shehitler*, the Great Martyrs) were remembered by horse racing, wrestling and the eating of specially prepared bread in open fields. The memory of Christian saints, also traceable to the ancient Greeks, Goths and Italians who lived on the Medieval coasts of the Crimea, survived in the names of Tatar villages and mountains such as Ai Vasili, Ai Gurzuf and Ai Danil (the villages of St. Vasili, St. Joseph and St. Daniel) or Ai Petri and Ai Todor (the mountains of St. Peter and St. Theodor).

Nowhere was the Tatar peasants' love of nature and the Crimean land more clearly on display than in the distinctive, vine-covered Tat houses, which had chimneys with nests built in them for nightingales. Of the mountain Tatars' houses, nineteenth-century traveler, Edward Clarke wrote: "The Tahtars delight to have their houses buried, as it were, in foliage. These dwellings consist each only of one story, with a low flat roof, beneath trees spreading immense branches quite over the whole building; so that a village, at a distance is only known by the tufted grove wherein it lies concealed."[5] Travelers also mentioned the southern mountain Tat-Tatars' habit of building their houses into the earth on the sides of terraced mountains. In his nineteenth-century account, F. A. Feodorov wrote:

> In the southern part of the Crimea, where the mountains are flat, the Crimean Tatars do not like to build their unique dwellings, instead they place them on the side of cliffs and fit them so they only have to build three walls, the fourth consisting of the mountain on which the home leans. By a similar means of construction, the Tatar village is always located on a mountain cliff and is situated in the form of an amphitheater. The roofs of the homes are flat, forming terraces and, as a result of their aversion to leakage, they are built in a most thorough fashion. The terrace forms for the Crimean Tatar almost the entire home; here they rest from work, here they greet guests.[6]

The lands inhabited by the terraced Tat-Tatar villages, which make up the southern third of the Crimean Peninsula, consist of a limestone coastal mountain chain. The chalky Yaila Mountains reach a height of just over 5,000 feet and have a gradual incline on their northern side before dropping off sharply on their southern front. The most prominent peak in the range, Cadir Dag (Tatar "Tent Mountain", 1,527 meters), dominates the central chain with its massive forested base and is the source of the Crimea's largest river, the northward flowing Salgir. Eighteenth-century Russians and Western explorers who entered the Yaila Mountains of the south found two large valleys, known as the Baidar and Sudak, carved into this chain, which impressed them with their beauty. One British explorer made a record of the Baidar Valley:

> The valley, upwards thirty miles in circuit, is an elegantly shaped oval basin, not deep, enclosed by finely wooded hills, and watered by two limpid streams. It is exclusively occupied by Tatars, who enjoy a degree of prosperity unknown to their co-religionists on the plains, owing to the productiveness of the soil. The villages, eleven in number, have a very pleasing appearance, being surrounded with orchards, and overtopped by enormous round-headed walnut trees. Possibly in extent, beauty, and fertility, the valley may be without rival in Russia.[7]

The Yaila Mountains had a gradual incline on their northern face before dropping off precipitously in steep cliffs along the southern shore. At these cliffs' feet lay a narrow strip of land, perhaps a mile in width at most, known in Tatar as the Yaliboyu (the Shore). It was in these two southern regions made up of the mountains of the south and the shore that the Crimean Khanate had its core. Here one found large coastal towns such as Kaffa, Sudak, Alushta and Yalta, as well as the capital of Bahchesaray and the city of Karasu Bazar.

In the shadows of Cadir Dag, the mountain Tat-Tatars used artificial irrigation to water their fields and bring this region to life. One nineteenth-century Russian visitor to the Crimea commented on the Tatars' irrigation skills as follows:

> Only in the mountains, and in particular in hot, rocky mountains such as those in the Crimea is man able to understand what water means for life...The Tatars search out springs as if they were gold and value them as if they were gold. They uncover every small wet place in the stonewalls and they work them little by little into a spring...The Tatar is the master of irrigation and channeling of water. Therefore he places great value and worth on irrigation. To build a fountain— that is the highest earthly virtue; the builders of the fountains consider it a requirement to place their name on them; on the fountain, as upon a shrine, you almost always find some scripture from the Qur'an inscribed.[8]

A Russian anthropologist wrote of the area's inhabitants: "Anthropologically, the south-coast Tatars, as far as can be judged from the meager material, are distinguished by a lack of Mongol characteristics."[9] We have other eyewitness accounts of these inhabitants who had become Tatarized over the centuries, written by Russian and Westerners who explored this region. According to one:

> Their faces are entirely European; white, straight and sometimes red and full of fire with shady eyelashes. Their children are especially close to our own. In them there is not a drop of Mongol blood. When you recall the customs of the south-coast Tatars; the freedom of their women, their celebration of several Christian festivals and memorials, and their love of settled occupations, one cannot but be convinced that the so-called Tatars are as close to the tribes of the Caucasus as we are.[10]

Another recorded the beauty of the Tats' homeland as follows:

> The true [mountain] barrier had now been passed which separates the great steppe over whose dead level of snow the cold north wind sweeps in the winter (producing a climate unusually rigorous for the latitude), from the warm and sunny regions of the south, into which we had just entered. On every hand were to be seen Tartar houses embosomed amidst mulberry and walnut trees, with the green tobacco leaf hanging to dry on the awning of trellis-work projecting in front; or villages picturesquely suspended to the side of the hill, the roofs of one row houses forming a terraced street for that above, and the whole tooling like a giant flight of steps. Far on in the valley shot up the tall poplar, here covered with thick foliage, and grown into a noble tree. Bright mountain streamlets, flashing into the light, were again concealed beneath the fringe of the myrtle and lime; and wide tracts were planted with the vine, on which hung the clustering grape; for the vintage had not yet commenced.[11]

In the secluded Tatar villages of the Sudak vicinity, where Russian settlement was initially rather limited, nineteenth-century visitors to the Crimea described a way of life that would have differed little from that existing on this coast for over two millennia:

> In every village the traveler, especially if he be not Russian, is received with the most affectionate care. Everywhere the best house, the most beautiful cushions and carpets, are placed at his disposal, and he is installed in a good apartment with coffee and *tchibouk* (pipe), in a way which can be appreciated only by those who know the inconveniences as well as pleasures of traveling in the East.
>
> At Toulouk, Kouz and Otouz, the Tatar dwellings, with their flat roofs, are raised against the hills which border the valley, and by this arrangement the inhabitants communicate generally by terraces of their houses. Nothing can be more picturesque than the appearance of these terraces on an evening: at the moment the whole population, men, women and children, are on the alert, and desert their dark chambers, where they seek refuge against the sun during the day, to install themselves on the roofs of the houses.
>
> The most agreeable animation succeeds the silence of the day, loud conversations are heard on all sides, and a very picturesque effect is produced by the various

groups who, still employed in household occupations, thus enjoy the coolness of the evening.[12]

Visitors to the Crimea also spoke in glowing terms of the former capital of the Crimean Khanate, Bahcesaray. Russian authors, and the odd Western visitor traveling to the valley city of Bahcesaray, found in this Muslim enclave (often described as the "Russian Alhambra") inspiration for Oriental Romanticism and musing of lost greatness in the form of the khan's palace complex. With its turban-capped marble gravestones inscribed in Arabic, latticed harem, falconry tower, Ottoman-style Khan Jami Mosque, and its numerous fountains (which were praised by such Russian poets as Alexander Pushkin), the Khan Saray (Khan's Palace) complex was the only remaining palace raised by the Tatar descendants of the Mongol Golden Horde. An early nineteenth-century visitor to the Crimea left the following account of this center of Tatar life in the Crimea as follows;

> The situation of Baghtchisarai is exceedingly picturesque, being overhung on the north side by a precipitous and fantastic mountain, and shut in on the other by one somewhat lower, on which we observed the ruins of two palaces, formerly occupied by some of the royal family. The houses are spread over the narrow valley, formed by these mountain-ranges, to a length of three versts, and are built of brick or wood, and covered with red tiles. With the exception of the shops, in which are manufactured and sold all the variety of small wares requisite for the support of Asiatic luxury, superadded to a few articles of necessary consumption, all the houses are surrounded with stone walls, and generally in front a wooden *piazza*, in which the inhabitants are fond of lounging for the sake of fresh air.
>
> The immense number of poplars rising from the orchards, around which the houses are built, greatly enhances the romantic beauty of the town. The inhabitants are well supplied with the finest water, by a small covered conduit running along one side of the principal streets, from which it is conveyed into the houses. With the exception of a few Greeks and Armenians, it is wholly populated by Tatars and Jews; and contains 9,000 souls. The Tatars are most numerous, and have not fewer than thirty-three mosques, three *medressas*, or schools of divinity, and a hundred and fifty *Mollahs*, who are attached to the mosques and schools.[13]

These eyewitness accounts of the customs, culture, economy and way of life found among the Crimean Tatars of Bahcesaray, the steppes, shore and mountains of the Crimean Peninsula are, however, among the last records of an ancient Black Sea culture that, to many nineteenth-century visitors, seemed to be dying out under Russian imperial rule. In spite of the bucolic nature of the initial descriptions of the Muslim peasants of the Crimean countryside provided by outsiders, many visitors to the region felt they were recording for posterity a people that was on the verge of disappearing. Meriel Buchanan's account is typical:

> Along the shores of the Black Sea, in green valleys, on rough rocky slopes little Tartar villages cluster, mosques with slender minarets, low-roofed houses, whitewashed or painted a faded salmon pink, children with solemn faces wearing stiff red and gold caps look up at one with enormous dark brown eyes, men whose features are more Greek than Asiatic smile and murmur a gentle greeting, while women peer at one curiously from dark door-ways of rough covered carts drawn with little shaggy horses decorated with blue beads to keep off the evil eye. All the radiance of the East lies about them, all the glamour of a race fast dying out and becoming extinct.[14]

In the decades following the Crimea's annexation, the Tatars' age-old way of life appeared to disintegrate as the Russian *pomeshchiks* (landowners), settlers and Tsarist officials moved into this peninsula and seized control of the Crimean Tatar peasantry's land.

The collapse of Crimean Tatar society was most clearly manifested in the extraordinary series of migrations this people made that saw the community gradually transformed into a Muslim minority in a Slavic sea. The Crimean Muslims had, since the time of the Russian conquest, reacted to the Slavic rule and influx by migrating in spurts to the lands of their historical allies and ethno-religious kin, the Ottomans. The pace of this migration accelerated in the nineteenth century, as more and more land belonging to Crimean communes and villages was expropriated by Russian magnates.

For all Catherine the Great's noble intentions, many aspects of Russian colonial policy towards the Crimean Muslims appeared to be causing many to flee their ancestral homes *en masse* in the decades after her death. As the size of the Muslim Tatar population dropped due to massive emigration, the Tatar remnant that remained in the peninsula faced the possibility of extinction as a separate ethnic group.

Nineteenth-century Russian colonial officials initially made little effort to understand the true causes of the decline and massive emigration of the Crimea's Muslim population, and Tsarist sources tend to ascribe their departure to "Islamic fanaticism" or "Oriental fatalism". These simplistic explanations hardly account for the phenomenon that saw an entire people, who were known for their tolerant frontier version of Islam, not their fanaticism, leave their home to undertake perilous journeys to the Ottoman provinces of Anatolia, the Caucasus and the Balkans.

A more nuanced analysis of the causes for the migrations points to, among other things, differing concepts of land ownership and property rights between the traditionally free Tatar peasantry and the new Russian landowners in the Crimea, who considered the local population to be little better than serfs. Contemporary sources also speak of a growing lack of respect for the Crimea's Muslim culture by the Russian colonial authorities.

Nineteenth-century visitor Edward Clarke was especially scathing in his description of Russian treatment of Islamic culture in the Crimea. In Bahcesaray, for example, Clarke reported "When the *mullahs*, or Tahtar priests, ascended the minarets at midday, to proclaim the hour of noon according to their custom, the Russian soldiers amused themselves by firing at them with muskets; and in one of these instances a priest was killed."[15] In another incident, this source describes the destruction of Islamic architecture and monuments in the coastal city of Kaffa by the local Russian authorities:

> We were in a Turkish coffee-house at Caffa, when the principal minaret, one of the ancient and characteristic monuments of the country, was thrown down with such violence, that it shook every house in the place. The Turks, seated on divans, were smoking; and when this is the case, an earthquake will scarcely rouse them; nevertheless, at this flagrant act of impiety and dishonor, they all rose, breathing deep and bitter curses against the enemies of their prophet.[16]

Clarke also mentions that, in the village of Karasubazar, the hallowed Tatar cemeteries, which played a key role in both Muslim ceremonies, such as *Kurban Bayram* and *Oraza Bayram*, and pre-Islamic festivals, were divested of their tombstones by the Russians for building purposes.[79] As their homeland was gradually transformed into a typical Russian province following waves of Slavic settlement, their land confiscated by Russian *pomeshchiks*, and their communal sense of Islamic identity threatened by newcomers who did not respect their culture, the Crimea's Muslim population increasingly abandoned the Crimea for the Islamic Ottoman Empire. Thus far little effort has been made to understand this process of emigration, but this work will now turn to an exploration its causes and results.

2

DISPOSSESSION

THE LOSS OF THE CRIMEAN HOMELAND

Scattered throughout the former Ottoman provinces—what is today Bulgaria, Romania and Turkey—are hundreds of thousands, if not millions, of descendants of those Crimean Tatars who migrated to these countries during the eighteenth and nineteenth centuries. While Tsarist officials often attributed these migrations to calls for *hijra* (migration from the land of the unbeliever to the land of Islam), Western, Turkish, Tatar and even non-official Russian sources make it clear that the Russia landlords contributed to this process by making life so unbearable for the Muslim Tatars in the Tauride Province, as the Crimea was known in the Russian imperial period, that they were forced to abandon their homeland. Part of the problem stemmed from the different conceptions of landownership of the Tatars and the new class of Russian *pomeshchiks*. Russian scholar E.I. Druzhinina has written:

> At the time of the annexation of the Crimea by Russia, free [Tatar] peasant-communes were still extant here. They jointly possessed pastures, hay making, forests and other lands considered to be the property of one or several *cemaats* [communities]. Land use was in no way regulated. Collective herds grazed everywhere. He who wanted to harvest grass could do so in any place and in any quantity.[1]

In light of the importance of Islam among the Crimean Tatars, it is not surprising that all aspects of ownership regarding the communal lands of the Muslim peasants were shaped by traditional Islamic notions of land and land use. According to Islamic law, the khans and the Tatar *mirza* nobility class could not claim the free peasantry as their serfs. For this reason the Tatar population of the Crimean Khanate had always remained free in comparison to peasants in Russia or other parts of Eastern Europe.[2] Local Muslim law also declared that all land designated as "wild or untilled" could be freely cultivated by Muslim farmers, and this contributed to the spread of the Crimea's agricultural lands.[3] In practice, the category of "wild lands" included any previously uncultivated areas that a farmer brought under cultivation. Qur'anic law also prevented Tatar landlords from claiming ownership over forests, springs, communal wells or fountains and wild pastures, which were deemed to belong to the *umma* (religious community) as a whole. The Crimean Tatars' labor obligations to their *mirza* landlords were also prescribed by Islamic law and ancient custom: these obligations were limited to the *ushr* (Qur'anic tithe) and *talaka* (corvée work on maintaining mountain canals, wells etc.).

By contrast, with the annexation of the Crimea in 1783, newly arriving Russian landowners began the gradual process of confiscating Crimean Tatar communal lands and demanding greater taxes and labor from the previously-free Tatar peasantry found in all three areas of the Crimea—the mountains, the plains and the coast. In the process, the Tatars' landownership traditions began to crumble.

For almost a decade the Tatars lived with the hope that the Ottomans would free them from their new Russian masters. But in 1792 the Ottomans signed the humiliating Treaty of Jassy with the Russians after losing the Russo-Turkish War of 1787–1792—fought primarily by the Ottomans to liberate the Crimea. This treaty officially recognized Russia's annexation of the region. When word of the treaty spread among the Tatars of the peninsula and surrounding areas, it caused considerable consternation. A mass migration of steppe Nogai Tatars to the Ottoman Empire began. Whole tribes migrated by land or sea to the Ottoman Empire to escape the Christian Russians, whose rule was now considered final. It is estimated that this migration consisted of roughly 100,000 Crimean Tatars from a pre-annexation population of 300,000.[4]

In this period, religion was still the primary basis for communal identification for both the Orthodox Russians and the Crimean Muslims. Many Russian officials, therefore, perceived the religious ties between the Tatars and Turks to be the main cause of this migration, considering it natural that the Crimean Tatar Muslims should desire to leave Orthodox Russia for the paramount nineteenth-century Muslim state. The Crimea was now part of the Russian *rodina* (homeland), which was still defined in terms of Orthodoxy by most Russians well into the nineteenth century. The Crimean Muslims were now suspect in this land. Others saw the existence of religious links to the Ottoman Empire by the Crimean Muslim community as a sort of betrayal or manifestation of "fanaticism".

In the Crimea, as in other parts of the pre-modern Islamic world, Islam functioned as more than just a religion for the Muslim Tatars. Islam provided the Crimea's Muslims with a moral, cultural, judicial, and societal framework, and shaped their views of themselves and their concepts of land and homeland. Alexandre Bennigsen's description of Islam's role in shaping Muslim collective identities, for example, certainly applied to the Crimean Muslims of the eighteenth and nineteenth centuries. According to Bennigsen:

> Islam itself is not merely a religion. It encompasses not only a corpus of directly religious beliefs and rites, but also a complex aggregate of cultural, psychological and social traditions, attitudes, and customs governing the whole way of life of the Muslim community. Its "rooting" in every level of society is certainly deeper than that of any other religion of the world, and many traditions, attitudes and customs of Islam are not contingent on the strict observance of the faith.[5]

Nineteenth-century Russian and Western accounts of the Crimea make repeated references to the Islamic basis of Crimean Tatar identity. The village mosque (often a simple, stone structure with a small minaret) served as the center of Tatar communal life and was one of the most visible outward symbols of a village's Muslim identity. Here the faithful came on Fridays to pray, to hear news of the outside world, and to exchange gossip. Village *mullahs* (the lower Islamic "clergy") performed life rituals here that were vital to the maintenance of the Muslim communal identity, such as marriages, funerals, sacrifices and circumcisions. They were held in great respect throughout the Crimean countryside. After living in the south Crimean city of Karagoss from 1816–1820, an English observer, Mary Holderness, mentioned, for example, that "The *mullah* is considered the head of every parish, and nothing of consequence to the community is undertaken without his counsel."[6] From such accounts, a picture emerges of an ethno-religious community whose society was firmly grounded in spirituality. Most sources agree that "In the Crimea, Islam was alive as a faith and held the allegiance of the Crimeans in practically all aspects of their life."[7] With the Russian conquest, the daily rituals of Islam became increasingly important markers of group and individual identity for the Crimean Muslims and were consciously used to distinguish the Tatar Muslims from the Russian or Ukrainian Christians. Considering the centrality of Islam in shaping the world view of the Crimean Muslim peasants in the eighteenth and nineteenth centuries, it is not surprising that the community also imagined itself to be part of the larger Muslim continuum, the *umma*. It was this macro identification (or an overlapping micro identification with a home village, tribe or valley) that provided the nineteenth-century Crimean Muslim with his or her primary source of personal identification

Among the divergent Crimean Muslim populations of the three separate zones of the peninsula there was, in fact, no over-arching, communal sense of *politicized* identity on the basis of ethnicity during this early period. Nor was there any political discourse stressing this people's unique claim to the Crimea as a national "Fatherland" or ethnicity-based patrimony. From the Russian perspective, the Crimean Muslims were considered a peasant *class* not a nation and the Crimea, far from being constructed as a Tatar homeland, was simply seen an undeveloped province in the Russian Empire.

This is not surprising when one recalls that the Western political ideology of nationalism—which posits that all ethno-linguistic groups with a shared history, culture and territory form a "nation" and have a "natural" right to a specific territory (defined variously as a national "Homeland" or "Fatherland")—was only just being formulated in Western Europe. The lack of ethno-national, political identification among the Crimean Muslims was certainly not unique in this East European Muslim context.

The Crimean Muslim peasants of this period also tended to view their community, and its links to land, in distinctly Islamic terms. This was never more evident than in the names given to the Tatar villages that dotted the Crimean Peninsula. Villages, such as Islam Terek (The River of Islam), Ak Mecit (White Mosque) Haji Bulat (Bulat the Pilgrim), Ak Sheikh (The White Sheikh, i.e. head of a dervish order), Ak Hoja (White Hoja) and Seit Elin (Saint Elin) were named for local mosques, Muslim religious figures or miracles associated with Crimean Islam. As in other parts of the Muslim world in this period, there was also a dualistic division of land between the *Dar al-Harb* (Abode of War) and the *Dar al-Islam* (Abode of Islam). The Hanafi school of Sunni Islam, to which the Crimean Muslims subscribed, was very clear on the obligations of the true believer in relation to these concepts. Islamic doctrine clearly stated that "the *Dar al-Islam* becomes the *Dar al-Harb* after conquest by unbelievers, if the laws of the unbelievers are enforced."[8] This was certainly the case in the Crimea where the *shariah* (Islamic law) courts lost their authority soon after the Russian conquest.

Having come to see a land as *Dar al-Harb*, Bernard Lewis states that "it was the duty of all Muslims, men, women, and children alike, to leave such territories, for it was against God's law for Muslims to remain under non-Muslim rule."⁹ The Muslim theologian Al-Wansharissi (died 1508) called on Muslims to emigrate from the land of the infidel to safeguard their beliefs and prevent the perversion of their faith. Living in such as place, this source claimed, might lead to such bad habits as marrying non-Muslims, adopting their customs and forgetting such important rituals as *namaz* (public worship), *zakat* (alms giving), *hijra* (pilgrimage to Mecca) etc. According to Al-Wansharissi, "a person who refuses to emigrate abandons the community."¹⁰ Islamic jurists in the Crimea would certainly have been aware of judicial precedents of this sort made throughout the Sunni Muslim world.

Far from articulating a unique ethnic right or claim to the Crimea as the eighteenth- and nineteenth-century Crimean Tatars' national Motherland, *Vaterland* or *patrie*, the widely accepted tenants of Hanafi Islam therefore seem to have actually dictated that the Crimean Peninsula (as a place where the laws of the unbeliever prevailed over *shariah*) was to be abandoned by all pious Muslims. In emigrating from the Russian *Dar al-Harb* to preserve their religious identity, the Crimea's Muslims were participating in a sanctified Islamic tradition known as *hijra* (religious emigration) established by the Prophet Mohammed himself.⁴⁶

Many devout Crimean Muslims must have felt that Russian settlement threatened the fabric of their traditional Islamic way of life. *Hijra* was increasingly seen as the most desirable option when economic and political conditions in the Crimea began to deteriorate. Muslims in other parts of the Islamic world during the nineteenth century were also facing this issue and Islamic jurists in both the heartlands of Islam and its frontiers were forced to negotiate with the unexpected intrusion of infidel rule in the lands of the *Dar al-Islam*. While the Ottoman *ulema* do not appear to have issued any *fetwas* (opinions or decisions based on Islamic law) calling for *hijra* from the Russian Empire, it is clear from nineteenth-century accounts that many village *mullahs* in the Crimea supported the idea. Turkish Crimean Tatar historian Hakan Kirimli eloquently sums up the nineteenth-century Crimean Muslims' perceptions of homeland, stating:

> The feeling of "temporary residence" in their own homelands was one of the most important factors which hampered the development of the notion of *patria* and territorially-defined nationhood in the modern sense among the Crimean Tatars. Notwithstanding the fact that the nostalgia of the Crimean Tatar emigrants, who obviously left the land of their ancestors involuntarily, lasted for generations as many of them continued to identify themselves with their origins, within the Crimea self-identification with the land and background hardly evolved during the nineteenth century, when existence in the

Crimea was apparently considered as living at the "wrong time and in the wrong place" due to extra-territorial allegiances of religion and culture which were still defined not in ideological but in vague traditional terms.[11]

These Islamic notions of land and community must not be seen as providing the Crimea's Muslim population with the sole catalyst for abandoning their home, but they certainly sanctioned (and even encouraged) emigration from the peninsula to the Ottoman Empire as a demonstration of Islamic piety. The Muslim Ottoman Empire was of course the natural destination for *muhajirs* (religious emigrants) during this period. In Tatar sources the Ottoman Empire was simply known as the *Memleket-i Islam* (Dominion of Islam), the *Memalik-i Mahrusa* (The Well Protected Realms) or *Devlet-i Aliye* (Exalted Realm). For most Crimean Muslims the sultan's realm was synonymous with the *Dar al-Islam*. Kirimli writes "Traditionally, the primary interest of the average Crimean Tatar in Turkey was the religious one, as this was the principle basis of his own self-identification. No doubt, the Ottoman Empire, as the seat of the caliph, held a certain mystical significance for him."[12]

For the nineteenth-century Crimean Muslim, the Ottoman caliph across the Black Sea was the "Defender of the Faithful", the "Shadow of God on Earth", and the "Vicar of the Prophet". Tremendous symbolic and spiritual importance was attached to him by the increasingly isolated Crimean Muslim enclave as Russian settlement progressed in the peninsula. As the loss of land to Slavic-Christian settlers increasingly disturbed the rhythms of the Crimean Muslims' patriarchal way of life, tales of the wonderful conditions found in the caliph's empire began to circulate among the repressed Tatar villages of the Crimea.

By the nineteenth century, informal, grass roots movements that were millenarian in nature had begun to periodically appear among the simple Muslim peasants in the Crimea. These popular movements often stressed nostalgia for the pre-Russian period and extolled migration to the lands of the caliph as a means of escaping the harsh reality of Russian rule. In many ways the *destans*, (laments and songs) of this period, are similar to the *zar zaman* ("difficult times") ballads of the nineteenth-century Kazakh bards who lamented the disruption of their nomadic way of life by Russian settlers and officials.

Songs and poems from the Crimea of this period often extolled the sacredness of the *ak toprak* (literally "white soil" or "white land") of the Ottoman Empire, a term with great religious symbolism for Crimean Muslims. For this religious community, the "white soil" of the sultan's empire was pure or blessed earth.[51] Sultan Abdulaziz (r. 1861–1876) was the first Ottoman sultan to actively present the empire as a haven for Muslims, a fact that is important to take into consideration when analyzing the massive post-Crimean War migrations of the Crimean Tatars to the region in 1860–61. One should also take into account the Crimean Tatars' long history of service in the Ottoman Empire and the sense of historical, ethnic and religious continuity a Muslim Tatar would have felt in the lands of the related Muslim Turks. Nineteenth-century Russian and Western sources support the notion that the Crimea's Muslim population had a certain sense of extraterritoriality based on religious notions of land that would have predisposed them to emigration. These accounts make it clear that there were certain societal factors operating *within* eighteenth- and nineteenth-century Crimean Muslim society ("fanaticism" in Russian parlance) that would have predisposed this pre-modern, religiously-defined populace to abandon their villages and homes if external factors compounded matters and created a hostile or untenable environment. The Russian confiscations of Tatar lands and displacement of the indigenous peasants from many areas of the peninsula provided just such an external stimulus.

That the Crimean Tatars did suffer from unprecedented dispossession of land during this period is beyond dispute. Contemporary Russian sources are replete with descriptions of the process that saw the Tatar peasants' land expropriated by landowning *pomeshchiks*, particularly during the nineteenth century. Many liberal Russian and West European observers sympathized with the Tatars' increasingly untenable position in the Crimea. In his insightful account, General Eduard Totleben, the Russian commander whose name was to be forever linked to the heroic defense of Sevastopol in the Crimean War, mentioned the Tatar peasants' massive loss of Crimean land, stating:

> The *pomeshchiks*, with the help of the local authorities, thus frequently appropriated for themselves, land belonging to the Tatars; on the state lands Tatar land was mortgaged without the knowledge of its owners. Proof of this can be seen in the fact that 30 years ago in the Crimea there were almost no landowners other than free Tatars and persons possessing gardens on the southern shore and in the river valleys; now, however, the greater part of the land in the Crimea belongs to the *pomeshchiks* and the Tatars living on it have been practically turned into serfs.[13]

Nineteenth-century Russian writer G.I. Levitskii pointed out the lack of clear land tenure laws as the cause of the Crimean Tatars' plight:

> In no other place can one find such ugly, bare force, and willful inhuman cruelty as in the duties on the departing Tatar population in the Crimea. The lack of clarity and the disorder prevailing in this region surpasses belief. The owners, officials and administrators of state properties, the local village authorities and land police, from small to big, scourge without halt the poor Muslim population

of this region and drive it to despair. They have found no succor and have been driven into poverty.[14]

This source also stated: "It has been said that no other people, not even our Russian population, could have endured without murmur or obvious resistance the ten-score insults and injustices endured by the Tatars."[15] Another nineteenth-century visitor to the Crimea reported that the nomadic Tatars of the steppes were particularly vulnerable to land confiscation and displacement. According to this source:

> Since the Russians have taken possession of the Crimea, the Tatars have given up a portion of their land—and that generally the best—to foreign settlers...Wherever a spring gushed forth from the ground, the prospect was more pleasing and verdant. But such fertile spots—real oases—are of no service to the Tatars, the original owners of the Crimea, for, as they had no permanent residence, the Russians declared it to be unwanted land and seized it.[16]

The Tats of the south also suffered from land confiscation according to Totleben who claimed:

> Many forests, through inheritance or purchase, belonged to Tatars living on state lands, and they used them at their discretion. When the ministry of state property, however, established guardianship over the forests with the aim of preserving them, the Tatar owners suddenly lost the right to use their property—because they lived on state land—and in this fashion they, together with their property, became the property of the state.[17]

While it was the village commune of the Tatar peasant class that suffered most from increased exploitation and land confiscation, it must also be mentioned that the Crimea's extensive *vakif* (religious endowments of land held in mortmain) states were also expropriated at a steady pace during the nineteenth century. In 1783, *vakif* estates in the Crimea consisted of 460,000 hectares of land, but by 1917 only 100,000 hectares of this remained.[18] The loss of this important community fund, which had for centuries supported *mektebs* (schools), *medreses* (seminaries), mosques, fountains, dervish hostels and other cultural institutions in the Crimea, took a heavy toll on the nineteenth-century Crimean Tatars' intellectual development. Of much more pressing concern for the average Tatar farmer, however was the loss of this vast communal reserve of workable land associated with *vakifs*.

It should be stated that the Tatar *mirzas* who had been granted *dvorianstvo* (nobility) status by the Russians did not defend their co-religionist Tatars from this process of confiscation. On the contrary, far from serving as national leaders, they identified with the Russian nobility and even joined them in confiscating land. One nineteenth-century Russian account describes a certain Aga Celebi who threw peasants of his land as follows:

> Examples of the expulsion of Tatars, in which nothing is spared, are seen by us in the Crimea frequently; people are driven from the cottages built by their forefathers without any compassion in winter, in the cold frost. This, for example, recently occurred in the Feodosiia district. *Aga* Celebi expelled all the Tatars living and working on his land as a result of their unwillingness to fulfill his demands of increased work requirements. As recently as a few months ago one Russian landowner expelled an entire Tatar village from its land in Simferopol.[19]

All accounts then seem to point to a tremendous loss of land by the Crimea's Muslim population during the nineteenth century. It is not surprising that this, combined with the Crimean Tatars' pre-modern sense of religious attachment to land, led to the mass emigration of the Crimea's indigenous Tatar population in the mid-nineteenth century. While the Crimea's Tatars had never been known for their fanatical version of Islam, many traditionalist Muslims of the peninsula had begun to see their loss of land in apocalyptic terms as demonstrated by their songs from the era. Much of the Crimea's Muslim population had, by the mid-nineteenth century, come to the conclusion that their economic and spiritual salvation lay not in Christian Russia, but in the Muslim Ottoman Empire. In retrospect, it should not have come as a surprise to the Crimea's rulers that even the smallest of sparks would set off the flame of mass migration among this unstable and increasingly displaced community.

Such a catalyst came in the form of one of the most costly of Europe's nineteenth-century conflicts, the Crimean War of 1853–6. With the allied French, English, Sardinian and Ottoman invasion of the peninsula and the bloody reduction of the Tsar's proud naval bastion at the Crimean port of Sevastopol, the Crimean Muslims' position was, in the words of their *destans*, "to go from bad to worse". For many Russian military officers, the distrusted Crimean Muslims were to become synonymous with the hated Ottomans. There was in many circles in St. Petersburg a desire to find a scapegoat for the empire's humiliating defeat in the Sevastopol campaign. The Crimean Tatars, whose sympathy for Istanbul was well known, soon fulfilled this role. Their fate was thus, in many ways, linked to the bodies of thousands of Russian soldiers that lay buried in the rubble of the ruined port of Sevastopol. From this time forward, Russian officials, from the lowest Cossack officer to the Tsar himself, would see in the Crimean Tatars a distrusted race to be expelled from the lands of Holy Russia.

3

DAR AL HARB

THE NINETEENTH-CENTURY CRIMEAN TATAR MIGRATIONS TO THE OTTOMAN EMPIRE

In 1853, the historic rivalry between the Ottoman and Russian Empires again flared up and led to open warfare. In time-honored fashion, the Russian army invaded the Ottoman provinces of Rumelia (Turkish, *Rum-eli*, "the Land of Rome", the truncated European sections of the Ottoman Empire found in the Balkans). In the first year of the war the Russian army spread fire and sword through many Muslim villages of the region of the Ottoman provinces that would later form the independent states of Romania and Bulgaria. This destruction soon spread south of the Danube River to the coastal plains of Dobruca inhabited by the Crimean Tatars (predominately Nogais), who had fled the Russian advance into their steppe homelands to the north.

Fearing an increase in Russian power in the strategic Bosphorus Straits at the expense of the enfeebled Ottoman Empire, France, Britain and Sardinia joined Sultan Abdul Mecid in his struggle with the Russians. The Allies' combined army quickly went on the offensive and decided upon an attack on one of Russia's most vulnerable spots, the Crimean Peninsula. Thus was born the Crimean War, which has been studied endlessly—largely as a result of the unprecedented number of casualties suffered on both sides during the conflict. While there has been considerable research on the role that disease, poor sanitary conditions and the increasingly effective modern weaponry of the mid-nineteenth century took on the combatant nations, little attention has been devoted to the impact this war had on the indigenous population inhabiting the theater of conflict. That this conflict was to have dire results for the Crimean Tatar peasants who became caught up in this, the first hot conflict of the Russian and British struggle for power in Eurasia known as the "Great Game", was to be seen almost from the start of the Crimean invasion.

The allied operation in the Crimea began with an amphibious landing in the broad Kalamita Bay off the shore of Evpatoriia (still known to the Crimean Muslims by its old Tatar name, Gozleve) on the western coast of the Crimean Peninsula. Here, the British and French soldiers came into contact for the first time with the remnant of the once numerous Tatar inhabitants of the northern coasts of the Black Sea. The following description of the initial meeting between the English and the indigenous Muslim population is typical of the wary, but often cordial, greeting the Allies appear to have found among the Crimean Tatars, whose villages presented a backdrop for some of the worst fighting in nineteenth-century Europe:

> When the people of the neighboring district came to see the strength of the armies descending upon their coast, the headmen of the villages began to present themselves at the quarters of the Allies. The first of these deputations was received by Lord Raglan in the open air...They wore the pelisse or long robe, and, although their headgear was black lamb-skin, it was much of the same shape as the Turkish fez. They spoke with truthfulness and dignity, allowing it to appear that the invasion was not distasteful to them, but abstaining from all affection or enthusiastic sympathy. They seemed to understand war and its exigencies; for they asked the interpreters to say that such of their possessions as might be wanted by the English army were at Lord Raglan's disposal.[1]

As the Allies commenced their partial occupation of the southwestern Crimea and the long siege of the naval bastion of Sevastopol, there were many such contacts between the invaders and the Tatars who were densely settled in this region. For the most part, however, the wary Crimean Muslim peasants, having had considerable experience with armies in the past, greeted the invaders with reserved caution. To prevent such contacts or collaboration with the invaders, several Russian officials and generals proposed the expulsion of the entire Crimean Tatar population from the peninsula. But the Russians lacked the logistic means to transport hundreds of thousands of civilians from the Crimea in a time of war, so nothing came of the plans.[2] While this immediate threat to the Crimean Tatars had been removed, they faced a new danger in the form of Cossack *sotinas* (squadrons) sent to patrol the peninsula's Muslim villages during the siege of Sevastopol. It should be mentioned that the Cossacks, who earned a reputation for their pogroms against Russian Jews of the Pale region in the nineteenth century, also had a deep-seated antipathy towards their historical enemies, the Muslims. For centuries the Cossacks had loyally guarded the Tsar's frontiers against the inroads of Muslim peoples, such as the Turks, Bashkirs, Tatars, Chechens, Kazakhs and Circassians, and warfare against Muslims was ingrained in this frontier people's culture. It is not surprising that the Cossack units assigned to guard the approaches to the allied-occupied Evpatoriia district took advantage of this opportunity to plunder their traditional enemy.

General Totleben, one of the Russian commanders in charge of the defense of Sevastopol, seems to have looked upon the attacks of the Cossack military units (headed by an official identified only as Maksimov) on the Crimea's civilian Tatar population with some distaste. In his article on the Crimean Tatar emigration, this uniquely qualified eyewitness source wrote:

> Maksimov, with the Cossacks, began to punish and rob the villages of the Tatars and raped women, in the village of Tshei they flogged to death 7 men and announced that with the arrival of the Russian army all Tatars would be killed. At that time the proclamation of Marshall St. Arno [St. Arnaud, the French commander] promising complete protection was read and 20,000 Tatars of the Evpatoriia district went over to the allies.[3]

Other contemporary Russian sources support Totleben's account of events in the Evpatoriia district during the Crimean invasion. In his account, G. I. Levitskii claimed:

> During the course of the recent war, Cossack patrols moving through the district arbitrarily seized unfortunate Tatars under the pretext that they intended to go over to the enemy and forced them to pay ransom and, if they refused, they were handed over to the command as deserters and traitors…Therefore at the present there are many Tatars in the provinces of Orlovsk, Kursk, Poltava, Ekaterina and Kherson [mainland Ukraine] who are entirely innocent.[4]

During their attacks on the Tatar villages of the Evpatoriia district, the Don and Ural Cossacks also drove off the local Nogais' cattle and raided their *yamas* (underground grain storage bins). In addition, Cossack patrols arrested and deported any Tatars who left their village to collect water. In his nineteenth-century account, Evgenii Markov claimed "If a group of 20 Tatars gathered they were fired upon. This was also a betrayal. The Cossacks so loved this idea that they looked upon the entire Crimea as upon traitors. Under this mandate, they drove away herds of sheep, burnt down whole villages and even the farms of *pomeshchiks*."[5]

As a result of these depredations, thousands of Tatars from the predominately Nogai-inhabited Evpatoriia district fled to the Allied-occupied city of

Evpatoriia seeking sanctuary. A contemporary Russian source describes this panicked flight to escape the Cossack marauders and claims "Fearing most of all the pursuit of the Cossacks, whole Tatar villages moved to Evpatoriia and its environs and died there in droves from starvation and lack of housing."[6] As many as 20,000 Crimean Tatars were later evacuated by the departing allies once the war was over. This led many Russians to conclude that the entire Tatar population of Crimea were traitors.

According to contemporary sources, after the war, Russian land speculators began circulating rumors among the frightened Crimean Muslim peasantry that the Russian government intended to expel the Crimea's Tatar population to the Orenburg district of Siberia for wartime treachery.[7] Their intent was to scare the passive Tatar peasantry into emigrating and so freeing up their lands for purchase at base prices. Such rumors certainly destabilized this war-stricken community in the years after the Crimean War and also led to a retroactive debate in Russian circles concerning the level of the Crimean Tatars' traitorous activities during the war.

The Tatar collusion with the Allied invaders in Evpatoriia appears to have actually been of a rather limited nature. Mark Pinson claims that during the Crimean campaign some of the Tatar refugees in Evpatoriia assisted the Allies in constructing defenses for the city during the English and French occupation of the port.[8] Few could deny that this refugee element had come to tie its fate to that of the invading Allies, not the Tsarist government, which was represented in the Crimea by plundering Cossack squadrons. Having provided perhaps the most in-depth analysis of the reported incidents of Crimean Tatar betrayal during the war, Levitskii concluded in his nineteenth-century account "All these accusations were insufficient to censure an entire people."[9]

In the aftermath of the Crimean War, there was nevertheless a feeling among government circles that the Crimean Tatars had somehow played a role in the Russian defeat in the conflict. It is interesting to note, however, that Russian peasants actually living in the Crimea after the war were of a different mind. A nineteenth-century visitor to the Crimea provides the following anecdote, which relates his discussion with Russians in the Crimea after the war:

> Here [in the Crimea] I did not meet one long-time inhabitant who did not scorn with all his heart the mean censure of the Tatars which resulted in such a disaster for the entire region...Again one may ask "Is this really a voluntary betrayal of the government?" Even in the very places of the [enemy] landing, the Tatars remained quiet and faithful. One *pomeshchik* known to me, on the day of the landing, arrived at his estate located not far from Burliuka and ordered the hay and grain to be burned upon the first approach of the enemy. The Tatars

placed their hands on their hearts and promised to execute the order. The enemy arrived and the hay was burnt. There are your traitors! However, even if the Tatars finally really did engage in betrayal, they should be absolved. One would need to be a true follower of Allah and a fatalist to quietly endure that which was done to this poor people during the campaign.[10]

For the most part, the unarmed Tatar peasants appear to have been little more than spectators to the massive battles between modern armies that surged over the southwestern sections of their homeland. The vast majority of Tatars followed the Crimean *mufti's* edict ordering them to "be faithful to the Tsar and homeland."[11] Regardless of the facts, rumors of the Crimean Tatars' "mass betrayal" reached the ears of the Tsar himself. As news reached St. Petersburg that some fearful Tatar peasants had begun to emigrate in the years after the war, Tsar Alexander II sent word to the Crimea stating "It is not appropriate to oppose the overt or covert exodus of the Tatars. On the contrary, this voluntary emigration should be considered as a beneficial action calculated to free the territory from this unwanted population."[12] When news of the White Tsar's declaration reached the Tatar villages of the Crimea, Totleben claims "The Tatars accepted this as a forced measure of eviction, concluding that they had forever lost the favor of the Tsar."[13]

As all these events were happening, the Russians conquered the northern flank of the nearby Caucasus Mountains after defeating the Dagestani Avar holy man, Imam Shamil, and his defensive mountain jihad. The Russians then began to expel the entire race of Circassians, an ancient mountain people living in the northwestern Caucasus, to the Ottoman Empire. Hundreds of thousands of Circassians would die in this brutal conquest and expulsion that was to take on genocidal proportions.[14] By the spring of 1860, panic had begun to spread among the Muslim population of the Tauride Province. Unsettling rumors spread among the Tatar villages claiming that the Tsar would soon be giving the Crimean Tatars the same choice he had given the defeated Circassians: removal to the interior provinces of the empire or deportation to the Ottoman Empire. In early 1860 the *Buyuk Goc* (Great Migration) spread from the Caucasus to the Crimea and the peninsula's Muslim population began selling its possessions to earn enough capital to survive the journey to the Islamic Ottoman Empire. There appears to have been a mixture of sorrow and joy in the Crimea as the oppressed, and increasingly landless, population of Crimean Tatars began preparations to leave for the blessed soil of the Ottoman caliph.

As the Tauride Tatars began their preparations for departure, bewildered Russian officials were quick to describe this emigration as an obvious manifestation of religious fanaticism. An official in 1860, for example, wrote "The administration of the time was convinced that the emigration of the Tatars was evoked by the Mohammedan clergy which, in every way, agitated for emigration and assured the ignorant masses that the *mirzas* had sold them to the Russian government which intended to forcefully convert them to Orthodoxy."[15]

To an extent this viewpoint was correct: as had been the case with the Caucasian peoples, there certainly were undertones of religious migration, or *hijra*, in this emigration movement that appeared in 1860 among the Tauride Muslims. One must not, however, overlook the Crimean Tatars' oppressed situation in the empire, which stemmed from their loss of land to *pomeshchiks* or their suffering during the Crimean War. These events certainly contributed to calls to abandon their Crimean hearth for the Ottoman Empire.

The migration movement in the Crimea appears to have begun in the Ak Kogekskii, Apskii and Aikish counties of the Feodosiia (Kaffa) district and soon spread into the steppes towards Evpatoriia, Simferopol and Perekop.[66] According to a nineteenth-century Russian eyewitness:

> The emigration began in spring of this year. The Tatars as early as winter had decided to abandon the Crimea and they moved to sow and apply for jobs by no later than April 15. From this date the movement became clearly noticeable. At first a solitary wanderer, then a family, and finally a commune aimed for Turkey, selling their belongings, throwing that which could not find a buyer onto the steppe or into a marsh. The emigration grew not by the day, but by the hour.[16]

By the summer of 1860, "the movement flared up like a steppe fire, moving from district to district, it became out of control like an avalanche."[68] A Crimean landowner of this era describes the departure of the Crimean peasants of his estate as follows:

> I am not able to recall this event, which reminded me of the expulsion of the Moors from Spain, without sorrow...having fixed a day for departure, a chosen person left for the nearest port city, where a steamboat or sailing vessel had been selected in advance. Finally, they all departed and immediately there was silence in the village where the day before hundreds of voices had been heard. Sending off the inhabitants on our land, from the village of Kopurchi, to Evpatoriia, I was a witness to the following scene; as the carts left the village and passed the cemetery, everyone took a handful of soil from the graves of their relatives which was carefully placed in a towel.[17]

As the summer of 1860 waned, the pace of emigration from the Tauride Province accelerated and whole districts began to empty, especially in the Nogai-inhabited steppe districts of Evpatoriia, Perekop and areas to the north of Simferopol. From throughout the steppes the Nogais began to gather around Sarabuz (north of Simferopol) and to make their way to the Crimea's ports. The majority of these were "devastated peasants dressed in rags".[18] The Russian government initially made little effort to halt this migration; it aligned neatly with the wishes of the highest authorities. A governmental official sent from St. Petersburg to the Crimea to assess this migration traveled through the Crimean Tatar countryside declaring that the Tatars were unproductive and untrustworthy peasants who were to be encouraged to emigrate.[19]

Throughout the Crimea, other Russian officials similarly encouraged the peninsula's Muslim population to emigrate from the empire. Russian officials in the city of Evpatoriia, for example, publicly announced Tsar Alexander's decree on the desirability of the Tatars' departure to the accompaniment of drums in the town square.

As the emigration movement snowballed, however, the local administration's attitude towards the departure of the Muslim peasantry began to change. It soon became apparent that the Crimea's Muslim population was not emigrating in the thousands, but in the tens of thousands. Russian *pomeshchiks* in particular became seriously alarmed when whole estates lost their tax paying peasants. The government itself became concerned when entire tax paying villages and productive districts began to lose their hardworking field hands. With the departure of the Crimea's agrarian work force, land value in the region plummeted and many Crimean *pomeshchiks* faced the daunting prospect of financial ruin as a result of the very exodus they had themselves initially encouraged.

Towards the end of the summer of 1860, the Crimean *pomeshchiks* summoned an urgent all-Crimean meeting in Simferopol to discuss this problem that few had foreseen. According to a contemporary source, the Crimean magnates came to the conclusion that the emigration of the Tatars "was costing the state close to 300,000 meek, gentle, submissive, tax-paying subjects. As to the region itself, in the end it will be forever devastated. The Tatars are the only working force in the peninsula."[73] The following account of this meeting of Crimean landowners shows how sharply the position of this class towards the Crimean Tatars had changed:

> On August 1860 a special, extraordinary meeting of Crimean *pomeshchiks* was held. There was only one question on the agenda—how to prevent any further Tatar departures. Many tears were shed here concerning the exit of the Tatars who had been treated as "slouchers" and "idlers" by these very *pomeshchiks*. There were bitter arguments as the *pomeshchiks* blamed one another for exploiting the peasants.[20]

Motivated by the pragmatic goal of preventing their own financial ruin, the powerful Crimean *pomeshchiks* sent an urgent message to St. Petersburg calling for a halt to the issuing of emigration passports to the departing Crimean Tatars. Fear that the emigration movement would spread to the Volga Tatar region also rose at this time and the Russian government saw the continued migration of its Crimean Muslim subjects as a real threat.

It is also interesting to note that Russian officials in the Crimea felt that the religious motives for the Tatar migration were so real that they made an effort to prove that there was no verse in the Qur'an calling for the emigration of Tatars from the Russian Empire.[70] As the Russian government's policy towards the Crimean Tatars changed, albeit for purely economic reasons, Crimean officials began, at last, to analyze the causes of this mass migration of the hardworking Crimean Muslim class, whose value they appear to have underestimated.

By the winter of 1860, the rate of migration had tapered off due to the poor conditions associated with traveling across the stormy Black Sea during this season. By the spring of the following year the Russian government had reversed its stance on the issue of the Crimean Tatar emigration and had canceled the issuance of passports to the Muslim population. Although the migration continued in 1861, this movement was much smaller than that of the previous year (only 11,000 departed in 1861) and soon came to a halt. The decision to halt the migration was taken in order to protect "the landowners of the southern shore and, in particular the great princes of the Tsarist administration and the governor himself who feared the migration movement would spread from the steppes to their valued estates on the southern coast."[76]

When calm again returned to the Crimea in late 1861, stunned Russian officials came to the conclusion that the mass emigration of the previous year had cost the Tauride Province 200,000 tax paying-peasants: a full two-thirds of its Tatar population of approximately 300,000. It was only by preventing the departure of the south-coast Tat Muslims that this important agricultural element had not participated in the general emigration which had begun to spread to this region in the fall of 1861. It is ironic that a Crimean Tatar presence in the Crimean *Dar al-Harb* (which later provided the seed for the rise of a Crimean Tatar national identity in the twentieth century) may have thus been forcefully maintained by Russian *pomeshchiks* for strictly economic reasons.

In the aftermath of the Great Migration of 1860–61, Crimean officials began to look for the underlying causes for this movement, which had already begun to have a devastating impact on the peninsula's economy. Totleben recorded his findings on the subject after interviewing departing Crimean Muslims and left the following account:

To the question of "Why are you leaving?" the Tatars answered: "I don't know" ... "It is necessary to go"... "The *pomeshchik* is bad" ... "If they permit us to go, it means go" ... "If one goes we should all go" ... "The district has been hurt" ... "The Tsar is far off, but the sky is higher". A kind-hearted elder said to me "We have eaten Russian bread for 60 years, God give health to the Tsar."²¹

As in the past, there was interest among Russian officials in the role that religion had played in the Crimean Muslims' decision to leave the Russian Empire for the Ottoman Empire. In his article on the emigration, Vol'fson stressed the religious factor as a motive for the Tatar migrations. According to this account:

A wide agitation took place among the Tatars with the assistance of the Muslim clergy of Turkey. They spread false rumors that the Sultan had raised new cities to which he invited all worshippers of Mohammed, that the Sultan would give the best land without rent fees to settlers, when necessary he would give a pair of oxen and a horse to be paid for over a 10 year period, that there was free land in Turkey sufficient for 300,000 people, that a day's wages there was 3 rubles, that every settler would receive 14 kopecks a day for a year etc. The Turkish agents were well dressed, with large amounts of money in their pockets, and circulated among the cities and countryside relating how "wonderful" and "blessed" life was in Turkey. The agitators were helped by the *mullahs* who speculated on the religiosity of the ignorant Tatars. The "infidels are robbing you," they said "it is not necessary to endure this any longer, God himself has led you to resettle in Turkey." Leading the drive to *hijra*—the arrival of the messiah [sic]—the *mullahs* declared that all those who did not desire to emigrate to Turkey were "unbelievers".²²

Russian officials were convinced that there were internal factors operating within the Crimean Muslim community causing the strange departure of the majority of the Crimea's Tatar population (millenarian movements calling for *hijra* to the lands of the caliph, i.e. "fanaticism"). Markevich states "The agitation of the Turks certainly played a role in this emigration and appeals in the name of the caliph under the *Sancak-i Serif* [Banner of the Prophet]."²³ The great twentieth-century Crimean Tatar poet Hamdi Giray described these internal calls for migration in his work entitled *Hicret (hijra)*. Giray has a Crimean *mullah* proclaim "There is no life for Muslims here in this land anymore! It is time to move to the *Ak Toprak* [White Soil of the sultan]!" while the common folk cried "It is Allah's will. It is the end of the world (*Ahir Zaman*). It is our *kismet*."²⁴

A contemporary of the events, Haji Murat Ibrahimbeili, however, remarked that "The propaganda of Turkey and England would not have been effective in influencing the intelligent population if there had not been internal socio-political causes, which produced dissatisfaction among the masses of people. Tsarism took away land from the local inhabitants, evoking sharp dissatisfaction among them."[25] A Russian landlord of the period points to the same multi-causal roots for the Crimean Tatars' migration even while describing the role of religious figures in calling up this *hijra:*

> From the start of Spring, Turkish emissaries, *mullahs* of course, inundated the Crimea and preached among the mosques of all of its cities and villages on the necessity of Muslims to migrate under the banner of the Turkish sultan since, they added, this was declared in the Qur'an. The soil for this propaganda was, however, incredibly fertile. The steppe Tatars were actually horribly oppressed; more than feudal slaves in times past.[26]

Totleben concurred and stated "It is obvious that all these preceding causes and the totality of the circumstances were enough, in a short period of time, to incite the entire population, without the excitement of fanaticism to which many solely ascribe the migration."[27] After experiencing the devastation of the Crimean War and three-quarters of a century of land confiscation, the reports from friends and kin in the idealized lands of the Ottoman caliph would have provided a most powerful incentive for many oppressed mid-nineteenth-century Crimean Muslims to abandon their Russian home for the opportunity to live in the *Dar al-Islam*. For these nineteenth-century *muhajirs*, the Ottoman Empire had become an "imagined homeland" and the *umma* an "imagined community". Tens of thousands of Crimean Muslims sold their possessions and followed their *ak sakals* (literally the "white beards", village elders) and *mullahs* in a migration that combined both the hope of preserving their community's religious identity and finding salvation in socio-economic terms in the *ak toprak*—the white lands of the sultan.

The *muhajir destans* (religious-emigrant ballads), which became an integral part of nineteenth-century Crimean Muslim culture, are replete with the imagery of Islam and reflect the influence of religion in many Tatars' decision to emigrate. Throughout the nineteenth-century, Crimean Tatar *kedays* (traveling bards) sang of the sorrow of migration and their songs captured the panic that swept the Crimean countryside during this dark period. Ballads from this genre also speak of the veneration the simple Crimean Muslim peasants felt upon arriving in the minaret-studded skyline of Istanbul, the sprawling capital. For the nineteenth-century *muhajir*, the first sight of the sultan's Topkapi Palace dominating the bay of Istanbul's Golden Horn, with the towering minarets of the Sultan Ahmed Mosque (the Blue Mosque), the Suleimaniye

Mosque and Hagia Sophia as a backdrop, would have had considerable religious symbolism. Nineteenth-century accounts similarly report that Circassian immigrants arriving in the sultan's lands in Syria removed their shoes before walking on the holy soil of this region. Many Crimean *muhajirs* would have had a comparable feeling of spiritual awe upon arriving on the "white soil" of the Ottoman caliph.

The Crimean Tatars and other Russian Muslims were not alone in migrating to the core of the Ottoman Empire during this period. Tens of thousands of Bosniaks (Bosnian Muslims), Albanians, Balkan Turks, Pomaks (Bulgarian Muslims) and Muslims from lands occupied by European powers, such as Algeria and Tunisia, also migrated to the heartland of the Ottoman Empire.

The *muhajir destans* from the nineteenth-century Crimea, with their apocalyptic tone, are very similar to songs from the Muslim Balkans after 1876. These songs of departure evoke the sorrow of leaving traditional homelands that are symbolically consumed by fire and disaster with the arrival of Christian (Serbian, Austrian, Romanian, Bulgarian etc.) rule. In the Crimean context, the *destans* also speak of the sorrow experienced by simple Crimean Muslim peasants who felt compelled to leave behind their villages, farms and hereditary stone houses, which had been passed on from generation to generation. The following *destan*, collected from Crimean Tatars by an early twentieth-century Russian anthropologist, is fairly typical of the *muhajir destan* genre and clearly demonstrates the importance of Islam in nineteenth-century Crimean migrations to the Ottoman Empire:

> Let me tell you about the situation in the Crimea, Neither young women nor young man remains in her, They all burn with the longing to migrate to the Islamic lands, Look down on us God, we are leaving the Crimea!
>
> What a wonderful climate is in the Crimea!
> But strife is not solved in her according to the *shariah* [Qur'anic law] Why does the *Padishah* [Sultan, i.e. Tsar] accuse us of rebellion? Look down on us God, we are leaving the Crimea!
>
> At one time they continually took passports,
> The officials benefited, but the people were ruined,
> All Muslims, without exception hurry to acquire passports,
> Look down on us God, we are leaving the Crimea!
>
> The well-to-do acquire passports without hindrance,
> The poor people are driven to despair,
> The mosques and *medreses* [seminaries] are boarded up,
> Look down on us God, we are leaving the Crimea![28]

Many of the popular songs of migration that were sung by both the diaspora groups of the Ottoman Empire and those that remained in the Russian Empire are named for the home village of the *destan's* author. Songs of this sort provide insight into the nineteenth-century Crimean Muslim emigrants' sociology and give a unique insight into their motives for leaving the peninsula. The following *destan*, written by an emigrant from the village of Soguk Su (Cold Water) in the southern Crimea, became particularly popular in Anatolia among emigrants who, having migrated to the Ottoman Empire, found themselves longing for the *yeshil ada* (green isle) of the Crimea. While the loss of rhyme in the translation certainly detracts from the ballad's poignant symbolism, its message of longing for the Tatars' home villages is clear:

> We are setting off on a voyage, having left behind our village, We know not what we do and we find ourselves lost! Soguk Su is famous for its cleft cliffs; Truly my love, our village was left in vain!
>
> When the wind blows strongly, the leaves blow from the trees; We were not able to take a handful of soil from our village! We are setting off, forsaking our village and watching the clouds; With whom will we frolic as the flowers have been scattered?
>
> We do not want to leave, but the *pomeshchik* said "depart!"
> If we happen to die on the sea, our bodies will be devoured by fish!
> In Soguk Su there are five apple orchards,
> Never before was there such sadness!
>
> Soguk Su's orchards stretch for 100 versts,
> From the village abandoned by us, we set off with 100 rubles!
> When we sat on the ferry, we were in a panic,
> And now we are no longer fit to live in the Crimea!
>
> Soguk Su's fountain...the sea and the ocean, Let our name remain and call us emigrants! Glory to the mosques and minarets of Istanbul, Upon embarking on the ferry my head spun;
>
> Friends, my sister remains in the Crimea!
> The fruit in the garden of the Count is ripening early,
> And a fire has descended on the Crimea![29]

After 1861, those Crimean Tatars who remained in the Tauride Province, which was described among the Ottoman Tatar diaspora as "a land of fire", increasingly found themselves a minority in their own homeland. From a demographic perspective the century-long advance of Slavic settlers into the southern Ukraine at the expense of the indigenous Turko-Muslim population had made a great step forward with this migration. The Crimean Tatars would never again be a majority in their traditional hearth and the Crimea's plains had been opened up for Slavic colonization.

With the departure of the bulk of the Crimea's Nogai inhabitants, the majority of Tatars remaining in the homeland were concentrated in the Yaila hills and mountains of the southern Crimea and along the southern shore. Hundreds of steppe villages had been abandoned in the Great Migration and Crimean Tatar life was now centered in small terraced coastal villages, such as Gurzuf, Uskut, Tarak Tash, Kizil Tash, Yalta, Alupka, Alushta, Derekoy, Gaspra, Buyuk Lambat, Soguk Su, Simeiz, Sudak or smaller villages in the Yaila hinterland.

As the stunned remnant Tatars living in the Crimea's south surveyed the transformation of their home following the exodus of 1859–61, they saw a land that had been fundamentally changed. The Crimea was now a Russian land, Russian was the language and culture of the towns, bureaucracy and, increasingly, of the countryside as tens of thousands of Slavic peasants from the neighboring mainland provinces of Ekaterinoslav, Kursk, Poltava, Chernigov, Kharkov and Voronezh filled the places vacated by the Nogai emigrants. In addition to the influx of simple Slavic peasants, the Russian elite built pleasure palaces on the coast and the royal Romanov dynasty itself had a palace erected at Lividia on the outskirts of the Tatar village of Yalta.

In the face of this settlement movement, the unstable Muslim community of the Crimea continued to find ways to define itself in traditional Islamic terms and to look to the Islamic Ottoman Empire for salvation. After 1861, the Crimea's remaining Muslim population continued to live in fear in their Russian homeland and to await the issuing of every edict by the White Tsar with growing apprehension. In this environment, any decree from the government could spell the end of Islam in the Crimea and impel the faithful to emigrate to the Ottoman Empire to preserve their way of life and their religious identity.

But it was from this unstable community of devout and increasingly inward looking Muslims that an indigenous nationalist movement developed that was to gradually come to define the Crimea not as *Dar al Harb* to be abandoned by good Muslims, but as a *vatan*—a homeland for the Crimean Tatar nation.

4

VATAN
THE CONSTRUCTION OF THE CRIMEAN FATHERLAND

While the identity of the Crimean Tatars of the nineteenth century was largely shaped by an inward-looking, traditionalist Islam that led to *hijra*-emigration to Muslim Turkey, it was nationalism, a Western "Christian" socio-political construct, that was to shape this people's identity in the succeeding century. In one of the most remarkable social transformations in East European history, the small, dying Tatar-Muslim ethnic group of the Crimean Peninsula underwent a socio-political revival that was to completely alter its conceptualization of itself as a community and, in the process, to reshape its connection to its native land. In the span of a lifetime this politically apathetic, religiously-defined people was to evolve into one of the most secular, politically mobilized nations in the world. With this transformation came a concomitant territorialization of the Crimean Tatar communal identity, as the Crimean Peninsula came to be constructed as a *"vatan"* by an indigenous Tatar intelligentsia.

Ismail Gasprinsky: The Father of the Russian Turkic Nation

In the case of the Crimean Tatars, the imagining of the Crimean Peninsula as a homeland and the Crimean Muslims as a nation was closely linked to a cultural reform movement begun by the great educator and writer Ismail Gasprinsky (1851–1914). While Gasprinsky was not himself a narrowly focused nationalist entrepreneur, his work laid the social foundation for the forging of a narrow Crimean Tatar national movement in the Russian Empire.

In dealing with a man of Gasprinsky's stature there are, of course, bound to be differing historical interpretations and, not surprisingly, these often pit Soviet accounts of Gasprinsky's life against Tatar accounts. Ismail Gasprinsky (or Gaspirali, the Tatar version of his name), the first Crimean Tatar of any real significance in Crimean history since the reign of the last Khan, Shahin Giray, was born into a lower class *mirza* family in the village of Avcikoy (Hunter's Village), Bahcesaray district, in 1851.

Growing up in this slightly privileged household enabled the young Gasprinsky to attend the Zinjirli *madrasa* (seminary) in Bahcesaray and the prestigious Voronezh military academy in Moscow as a teenager. This, and later experiences, such as spending time learning under the Pan-Slavist Ivan Katkov and working for the great Russian author Ivan Turgenev in Paris, as well as travels to the modernizing Ottoman Empire of the late nineteenth century, exposed the young Gasprinsky to a changing, modernizing world. This was a world with which most of his simple Crimean Tatar compatriots were unfamiliar. Most importantly, these experiences convinced Gasprinsky that his moribund people, and indeed all Turkic-Muslim groups in the Russian Empire (such as the Azerbaijanis, Volga Tatars, Kazakhs, Uzbeks, Kirghiz, Turkmen etc), were in need of reform as a means to cultural rejuvenation and socio-economic salvation.

Gasprinsky felt that "his people" (a term which he gradually applied to all Turkic-Muslims in the Russian Empire) were dying in a cultural sense under the stifling stranglehold of reactionary, conservative Islam. This folk Islam kept the Russian Turkic Muslims from adapting to the new world that their Russian countrymen were constructing. It had also led to the mass emigration of his own Turkic "sub-tribe", the Crimean Tatars, to the Ottoman Empire.

In this respect Gasprinsky was not alone. A reformist movement had begun among the Volga Tatars at this same time led by Shihab al-Din Marjani (1815–1889), who showed Russian Muslims that modern science was compatible with Islam, and Abd al-Qaiyum al-Nasiri (1825–1902), who taught that the Tatar vernacular language could be used in secular/lay writing in addition to the holy script of Arabic. Along with Gasprinsky, these and other Volga Tatar modernists made the comparison between the cultural progress of Western Christian nations and the decaying condition of Muslim life in Russia. They concluded that some borrowing from, and accommodation with, Western ideas was necessary for the very survival of their community.

For his part, Gasprinsky saw the Russian Muslims' inward looking, traditionalist educational system as the main barrier to his people's accommodation

VATAN: THE CONSTRUCTION OF THE CRIMEAN FATHERLAND

with Western progress and modernization. Gasprinsky once commented that "it is an indisputable fact that the contemporary Muslims are the most backward peoples. They have been left behind in virtually every area of life by Armenians, Bulgarians, Jews, and Hindus."[1] With the aim of improving his people's educational status and introducing them to modern culture, in 1884 Gasprinsky embarked on an ambitious program of educational reform that was to completely reshape Muslim education in the Russian Empire and beyond. Gasprinsky, and a growing number of like minded associates, opened a series of New Method (*Usul-i Jadid*) schools in the Crimean Peninsula that were to spread throughout the Russian Empire and revolutionize the outdated educational system of the Islamic *mektebs* (primary schools) and *medreses* of Russia.

Gasprinsky's followers who sought to modernize their atrophied Turkic Muslim society took their name, *Jadids* (Modernists), from the term *Usul-i Jadid*. By the time of Gasprinsky's death he would have the satisfaction of knowing that more than 5,000 of his New Method schools, with their revolutionary modern curriculums, had been established throughout the Russian Empire.

In addition to this remarkable achievement, in 1883 Gasprinsky started the first newspaper in Crimean Tatar history, known as *Tercuman* (the Translator), which became widely read by Muslims throughout the Russian Empire. In the pages of his paper, Gasprinsky patiently opened his readers' minds to the greater world, subtly attacked religious obscurantism, fought for the liberation of women in Muslim society, and called for greater cross-cultural sharing and contacts between the Russians and the Empire's large Turkic-Muslim population.

In both of these endeavors Gasprinsky and his *Jadid* supporters had to walk a fine line to avoid offending the sensibilities of the conservative Islamic *ulema* (clergy), which still exerted considerable control over the Muslim peasantry of the Russian Empire. The reformers also had to make sure they did not offend the government's censors. This second task was made easier by the fact that Gasprinsky did appear to have a genuine appreciation for Russia and its people's culture. Throughout the pages of his newspaper Gasprinsky called for rapprochement (*sblizhenie*) between the Muslims of the Russian Empire and the Russians, and his work can hardly be described as anti-colonial (that is, anti-Russian) or militantly nationalistic. In a typical article, Gasprinsky wrote "The Russian, thanks to his fortunately composed character lives as "his own" and "as a native", not only among us Crimeans, but also as we have the opportunity to observe, in both the Caucasus and Central Asia. Therefore, thank God, amongst our Muslim peoples there is no feeling towards the Russians other than goodwill."[2] Gasprinsky's admiration for things Russian (i.e. modern) went so far that, on one occasion, he claimed "There are those who say that I am more of a Russian than is a Muscovite."³

Seen in this light, Gasprinsky's contemporary critics, most of whom were conservative *mullahs* defending the old order, considered this enlightener to be nothing more than a dangerous emissary of Russification. Gasprinsky's revolutionary efforts were constantly bedeviled by those conservative Muslims who saw in this Russified Tatar and his plans for rapprochement with the Russians a threat to their conservative Islamic identity. He was called everything from a Russophile to a heretic by his Muslim critics.

Interestingly, Gasprinsky was also rejected by the first generation of Turko-Muslim nationalists, who subsequently emerged in the Russian Empire on the eve of the empire's collapse during World War I, for not being revolutionary enough. Gasprinsky's cautious stand against revolutionary political movements calling for autonomy and national independence resulted in his being labeled a "lackey of the autocracy" by those later nationalist revolutionaries who subsequently disdained his desire to work within the Tsarist system for the betterment of his community.⁴ This new generation of overt Turkic nationalists was not willing to work with the Russian authorities and considered Gasprinsky's earlier educational process to be too tame.

Regardless, with the outbreak of the First World War and the upheavals this would entail for Russia, the Crimean Tatars, and, indeed, all the empire's Turkic Muslim groups, the legacy of Gasprinsky (who died in 1914) was to be felt from the Crimean shores to the Tien Shan Mountains of Central Asia. In order to fully appreciate Gasprinsky's role in beginning the process of forging a modern Crimean Tatar identity via his work on education and literature, a background assessment of the world in which he began his efforts is necessary. As should be apparent from the previous chapters on emigration, one must, in particular, take into consideration the role that conservative Islam played in shaping the communal identity of the late nineteenth-century Crimean Muslims. Most importantly, the role of traditionalist Islam in preventing modernization among them should be mentioned. Few Crimean Tatars in this era were willing to learn from the Russian unbelievers, even fewer were willing to send their children to schools established by the Russian government in order to educate Muslim children. Borrowing from the Russian unbelievers in any way shape or form was considered *bid'at* (religiously forbidden innovation).

During his youth, Gasprinsky could hardly have failed to witness outward manifestations of the Crimean Muslims' traditional religious identity. In 1874, fourteen years after Gasprinsky's birth, thousands of Crimean Tatars

VATAN: THE CONSTRUCTION OF THE CRIMEAN FATHERLAND

had again demonstrated their religious devotion by emigrating from the Russian Empire to preserve their religious identity from the "contamination" of serving in the Tsar's Christian army.[5] Any perceived threat to this religious foundation of the Crimean Muslims' identity was feared in the Crimea of Gasprinsky's youth.

The massive Tatar migrations to the Ottoman Empire, which brought this people's unique culture and identity close to extinction had, in part, been caused by the Crimean Muslims' traditional Islamic world view. To make matters worse, the conservative *mullahs*, the self-appointed guardians of the *ancien regime*, refused to countenance changes or improvements that might benefit the lot of those who remained in the Russian Empire if these innovations came from the *Urus Kafirs* (Russian infidels). In doing so, these gatekeepers of the Crimean Muslim morality stifled their people's educational development in particular.

A nineteenth-century account of the Crimean Tatars' literature, for example, pointed out the Crimean Muslims' lack of acceptance of any book other that the *Qur'an*. This source stated "There is scarcely anything among them worthy of the name of literature. There is not one living Mohamedan author in the Krimea, and when I have mentioned this to the *effendis* (religious scholars) they give as their excuse that everything worthy of being written is contained in books already in their hand."[6]

The Crimean Muslims' *mekteb* and *medrese* educational system was extremely calcified and produced students who, after years of schooling, could recite the *Qur'an* and *Hadiths* in Arabic (without having actually learned Arabic) but were capable of doing little else. A Westerner who visited the Turkic peoples of the Russian Empire noticed the lack of national identity among these Muslims which resulted from this atrophied Islamic education and claimed "locked in on all sides by Russians, the Russian Turks are no longer a people; religion has, for them, necessarily stepped into the place of nationality."[7]

It should come as no surprise that a Crimean Tatar such as Gasprinsky, who had studied in a modern Russian *lycee*, lived in Paris and the reforming Ottoman Empire, and traveled in the literary circles of Russia, should be horrified by the state of affairs extant among his Turkic-Muslim kin in the Crimea and other parts of the Russian Empire. Having himself accessed Western civilization via a Russian education and the Russian language (while carefully maintaining his Islamic-Tatar identity), it is also not surprising that Gasprinsky saw the introduction of modern culture as a panacea to cure the ills of Russian

Muslim culture. Gasprinsky appears to have felt that, in the long run, allowing the conservative *mullahs* to maintain a monopoly over the Russian Muslims' education would lead to a breakdown of their society. As the Russians continued to progress he felt the backward Tatars and other members of his imagined Turkic-Islamic nation would be left even further behind on every level.

This awareness put Gasprinsky in the unenviable position of confronting many of the Crimean Muslims' traditional ways of looking at the world. As the popularity of Gasprinsky's modernist schools spread after 1884 (based on the simple fact that his students learned how to read and write, whereas graduates from eight years of study in a traditional *medrese* usually could not), he found himself perpetually battling with the conservative *mullahs* who considered his schools to be a heretical threat to the Crimean Muslim community's identity. One *mullah* who represented the *Kadimist* (traditionalists) viewpoint, went so far as to declare "whoever believes in God and Muhammed must be an enemy of the modernists. For them the *shar'iah* demands the death penalty."[8]

It was these staunch critics of Gasprinsky who were to begin a campaign to paint him as a Russian agent bent on Russifying the Crimean Muslim people. Ironically, while he was feared by Islamic traditionalists on the one hand as a Russifier, many in Russian officialdom also considered Gasprinsky a threat, believing that he might be one of those Muslims who would "strive to use all the advantages of Russian culture to defend their own nationality."[9] Russian officials who worked closely with the traditional Muslim clergy appear to have had tremendous distrust of Gasprinsky and his reforms, which they felt had the potential to threaten the status quo among the empire's politically apathetic Muslim groups. Seen in this light, Gasprinsky's efforts to reform and modernize his own people through the vehicle of Russian culture hardly make him a "minstrel of Tsarism". Rather, Gasprinsky appears as a modernist who sought to preserve his people by utilizing that which was contained in the comparatively advanced culture of Russia that might benefit his own Turko-Muslim people.

In spite of resistance from both the conservative Muslim clergy and the suspicious Russian authorities, scores of young Crimean Tatars enrolled in Gasprinsky's schools and a whole generation grew up on the eve of the Russian Revolution exposed to modern classroom subjects such as geography, history, science, and literature. Education became so important to this new generation that the saying "To see a school is the joy of man" (*mektep kormek insana devlettir*) is still a popular Crimean Tatar proverb.

In the process of breaking out of their traditional confines through education, many young Crimean Tatars had, like their master, come to the conclusion that "The traditional means of societal self-preservation, i.e. mass emigration or desperate isolation in a shell of obscurantism, had actually accelerated the process of dissolution."[10] This realization was an important first step in breaking down defensive Islam as the defining marker of Crimean Tatar identity for this new generation that was to begin to see itself in modern, secularist terms.

Gasprinsky's Tercuman *as a Vehicle for Creation of a "Turkic Nation"*

Gasprinsky's groundbreaking work in educational reform was matched only by his original work in publishing the Crimean Tatars' first newspaper, *Tercuman*. The impact of this innovative step for a community that had, in most cases, only been exposed to the *Qur'an* cannot be overestimated. The novelty of the idea of printing a publication for the Crimean Tatars can be seen in Gasprinsky's claim in 1888 that "even a short time ago there were very few Muslims who could tell you what a newspaper was, and if they were aware of the periodical press, the odds were that they would regard it as the work of the devil, to be avoided by all true believers."[11]

Crimean Muslim peasants who gathered before the village mosque to hear young students read aloud from the pages of *Tercuman* were, for the first time, exposed to events taking place beyond their immediate world. In the pages of *Tercuman*, Gasprinsky wrote of technical inventions in the United States of America, wars in the Balkans, the modernization of Japan, reform in the Ottoman Empire, the spread of European colonialism in Asia and Africa, the growing movement for women's rights in the West etc. While much of *Tercuman's* coverage was thus international, the majority of his paper's articles were devoted to Gasprinsky's own widely defined nation, the Turks of the Russian Empire.

Herein lies an important distinction between Gasprinsky and later Crimean Tatar nationalists. Gasprinsky believed that his nation was not restricted to the small community of approximately 200,000 Turkic Crimean Tatars living in the peninsula at the end of the nineteenth century, but the greater Turkic nation of millions. His program was in its nature Pan-Turkist and he aimed to unite the scattered Turkic-Muslim peoples of the Russian Empire through his paper. He was inspired in this endeavor by Pan-Slavism and state building in countries such as Germany or France that, over time, coalesced around a chosen central dialect and united to form a nation.

Gasprinsky actively promoted his motto "Unity in Language, Thought and Deed" (*Dilde, Fikirde ve Iste Birlik*) by means of a Turkic language that he created for his paper known as *Turki*. Gasprinsky's language, known in the Crimea as *Orta Turk Tili* (the Middle Turkish Language), was based on a simplified Oghuz Turkic dialect (basically Oghuz Ottoman without its complex Arabic, Persian and court Turkish grammar) with a large component of Kipchak Turkic vocabulary. This hybrid language, which combined the two great Turkic languages of Kipchak and Oghuz, was designed to connect the Kipchak-speaking Nogais, Volga Tatars, Kyrgyz and Kazakhs, with the Oghuz speaking Turkmens, Azerbaijanis, Crimean Tats and Ottoman Turks. Gasprinsky's ambitious objective was to unite "the boatman of the Bosphorus with the cameleer of Kashgar."[12] On a narrower basis, this language would also unite, for the first time, the Nogai-speaking Tatars of the Crimean steppe with the Oghuz-speaking Tat Tatars of the Crimea's southern coast.

It should be stated here that Gasprinsky's calls for linguistic and cultural unity among the Turkic peoples of the Russian Empire did not have an overtly political tone. Had they done so there is little doubt that his newspaper, the longest running Muslim periodical in the empire's history (1883–1918), would have been shut down by Russian censors. Even without this threat, however, it can hardly be doubted that Gasprinsky, who felt that the empire's Muslims benefited from the modernizing influences of Russian rule, was adamantly opposed to confrontation with the Tsarist regime.

Seen in this light, it is not surprising then that, by the twentieth century, Gasprinsky had also come out against the rise of narrowly focused nationalist movements among the various Turkic peoples of the empire that his work helped spawn. Gasprinsky felt that these narrowly-defined nationalist movements threatened the unity of the greater Turkic nation which would stretch from the Kazakh steppe to the Crimea. On many occasions Gasprinsky spoke out against the danger of "narrow nationalism" and "particularism" which he felt was unnecessarily antagonistic towards the Tsarist regime and detrimental to the Turkic nation's unity. In a typical comment Gasprinsky opined that, "Although the Turks who were subjects of Russia are called by the name 'Tatar', this is an error and an imputation...Those peoples who are called by the Russians as 'Tatar' and by the Bukharans as 'Nogay' are in reality, Turks."[13]

As the Russian Empire began to descend into chaos on the eve of the Russian Revolution, Gasprinsky's notion of a Turkic nation, however, began to appear Utopian. The Kazakh shepherd on the Chinese border had very little in common with the Crimean Tatar farmer on the south Crimean shore and few but a dedicated coterie of Pan-Turkist intellectuals ever imagined themselves as belonging to a larger "Turkic nation".

VATAN: THE CONSTRUCTION OF THE CRIMEAN FATHERLAND

In addition, most Russian Turks would have had difficulty in imagining a Turkic homeland of such a large and amorphous nature. There was little territorial identification with a widely-defined Turkic homeland known as *Turan* or *Turkestan* among the Turkic masses of the late nineteenth century in Russia. As revolutionary movements for change swept through the Russian Empire after 1905, the idea of a broadly-defined, Turkic nation had little appeal to a new generation of Russian Muslims who saw their fate increasingly linked to their more immediate territories. It was these localized, micro territories that would come to be constructed in the common imagination as national "homelands". In this respect, Gasprinsky can hardly be considered the "founding father" of a narrowly-defined Tatar nation of the Crimea; he was, on the contrary, opposed to such a micro development.

The importance of Gasprinsky's ideas in shaping later nationalist identity formation among the Crimean Tatars, and other Turkic subjects of the Tsar, should not, however, be underestimated. While Gasprinsky's nation was Islamic, this community was, for the first time, to be based on Turkic ethnicity and language, not religion. With the gradual loss of Islam as the sole marker of group identity by the Turkic peoples of the Russian Empire (in part a direct result of Gasprinsky's challenge to the Islamic old order through his widely diffused New-Method schools and newspaper), it was language and ethnicity that came to play the defining role as markers of group identity for many Turkic Muslims in Russia. By 1917 the Tsar's Muslim subjects (especially the elite) increasingly began to define themselves as ethnic Azerbaijanis, Kazakhs, Volga Tatars, or Crimean Tatars, for example, firstly, and Muslims secondly.

In the narrower Crimean context, Gasprinsky's newspaper (which is described by Edward Lazzerini as a "revolution in communication") played the important role that Karl Deutsch ascribes to print press in his classic work *Nationalism and Social Communication*. Namely, it enabled members of the Crimean Tatar ethnic group to identify with other members of their community who they would never actually meet (i.e. the nation) and to see themselves in relation to other groups on the basis of ethnicity.[14] Gasprinsky's reforms also had the effect of de-legitimizing the old order, which was based on conservative Islam, as can be seen from this report from the Russian police chief of Bahcesaray in the early twentieth century:

> Over the previous period, the police-meister was persuaded that an essential, radical change in the customs and communal way of life of the inhabitants of Bahgesaray had taken place. The influence of the clergy had gradually weakened. The youth were already critical of the old customs, *mullahs* attended theater

performances, they took photographs, they were able to sit at one table with the Christians when they would not have done so earlier. They even sought to send their children after the *mekteb* to Russo-Turkish schools...The customs of the city-dwellers had changed so much that, in the coffee houses, they began to read Russian newspapers in order to attract customers.[15]

Gasprinsky and the Issue of Migration to the Ottoman Empire

In addition to his work establishing ethnicity, as opposed to religion, as the primary marker of group identity for the Crimean Tatars and other Russian Muslims, Gasprinsky also contributed to the forging of the Crimean Tatar nation by working tirelessly to halt migration to the Ottoman Empire. Gasprinsky believed that these harmful migrations were the direct result of the very Islamic backwardness he was laboring to overcome. He spoke out against them on many occasions. As early as 1883 Gasprinsky began his attacks on the migration of "the local Tatars" to the Ottoman Empire writing:

> Having learned of the imposition of war duty, they are selling their movable and immovable property and migrating to Turkey. There is harm in this, since people frequently forget that there is no land where they can live with only happiness. The Crimean Muslims in general would not leave for Turkey if they were able to foresee their sad fate in this alien land.[16]

Gasprinsky blamed these migrations, in part, on the policies of the Tsarist government in the Crimea and claimed that "the government, and behind it the local authorities, did not have a clear, defined position on the emigration of the Crimean Tatars, therefore, this emigration was at one moment encouraged as desirable, then held back as a harmful one."[17] In an article titled "Permanent Emigration" Gasprinsky estimated that somewhere between 1,000,000 and 1,200,000 Crimean Tatars had left the Crimea between its annexation and the year 1902, and this was seen as an irreparable loss to the entire Turkic people of Russia.[18]

When a new move towards migration to the Ottoman Empire broke out among the Tatars in the Crimea in 1902, an alarmed Gasprinsky began a regular series of articles entitled "On Migration". In these articles he fought to prevent the departure of his Turkic countrymen to the lands of the sultan. In issue after issue Gasprinsky gently spoke out against migration, and repeatedly informed his simple audience of the pitfalls associated with migration to the Ottoman Empire. In a typical article from this period Gasprinsky wrote:

> Last year in a series of articles we proved to our countrymen all the absurdity and disastrous nature of emigration to Turkey...The results of this rashness are now

becoming apparent to all. Hundreds have written reporting the deaths of whole families and massive illness among emigrants. As the living witnesses to the calamities, those having the possibility to return to the Crimea arrive with every steamship, having grown older over the year and, of course, having been ruined. The victims of the emigration mania are so eloquent that seeing and listening to them is heartbreaking. There is a hope that the emigration, which is already calming down, will die permanently. Thank God since there were no causes for emigration and there still are none. It is necessary to simply sit down and engage in work with zeal.[19]

In another article from May 1902 in the series "On Migration", Gasprinsky appears to show exasperation towards the decision of Crimean Tatars to abandon their homeland for the Ottoman Empire as follows:

> We have heard rumors that in one or another Tatar village people are selling their land and cattle, having in mind resettlement in Turkey. If this is true, then we must pity these people for they know not what they do. To leave one's homeland one must have some sort of reason, to go to a new place one must have true, exact knowledge of that place, otherwise it will not be resettlement but senseless wandering. Any senseless, unfounded move will lead to poverty, destruction and ruin.
>
> We do not at this time wish to go into the living and working conditions of our people in Turkey, but wish to caution those inclined to wander to do the following; do not sell anything, do not undertake anything until it is positively known that the government will allow resettlement; a passport to travel abroad costs 10–15 rubles and therefore it does not make much sense to waste such a huge sum…You will just be throwing your money away.
>
> Those who exhaust their means will live in poverty there and then live in poverty here, as often happens when they return to the Crimea. Everyone should think twice before selling everything and setting off on an unknown journey with children and elderly. There is no land of milk and honey over there. Anywhere and everywhere one must work diligently, skillfully and untiringly for his daily bread. The rules of life are the same in the Crimea as they are in Turkey and in Japan.[20]

For those who were tempted to disregard his advice, Gasprinsky offered the following cautionary tale:

> Here is an evident fact: not long ago the relative of the famous master Selim Usta, Maksumadzhi Khalil, left from Bahcesaray. He [Selim Usta] received a tearful letter, which he conveyed to the editor. The emigrant complains that no one remained in Constantinople, and that they were transported to the Asiatic side [of the Bosphorus]. Here they left them without any assistance, letting each get settled as he was able and capable. As to requests for allotting land, the local authorities require an acceptance certificate for resettlement. Those who do not possess such a certificate are coldly asked—"Were you really driven from Russia or is perhaps someone calling you here?"

The aforementioned Khalil states further that emigrants on the steppe set up tents from torn felt, clothing and other trash. Thank Allah, that the warm spring sun allows such an existence, otherwise death would arrive soon.[34]

In a 1902 article entitled "Friendly Advice", Gasprinsky used a traditional Crimean Tatar narrative technique and created a hypothetical discussion with an "Ali-Jaffer" in an appeal to his audience to think carefully when considering their decision to emigrate:

> My dear friend Ali-Jaffer, you have decided to resettle in Turkey. You have decided this is what you want to do; and God be with you! May God grant you everything good. But permit me to be to you a sincere friend who frequently prays for your well being and weeps over your fate—since you are a good, simple man take this brotherly advice.
>
> Dear Ali-Jaffer, you may depart now, you may leave in spring or next year—you are allowed to go; nobody will detain you—but do not hurry in this fashion, Allah does not love haste. At present it is winter, and cold; the earth is covered with snow and here you are preparing to go somewhere. Everything living is in its burrow; all things living are hiding from the frigidity and cold. Who is driving you my dear, that you throw yourself with your family and baby in this cold time on a journey across the stormy sea? Why my dear, do you subject the children of your blood to the misery of a winter voyage? Consider, will it not be a sin to subject them to such suffering? After winter comes spring; after the cold comes warmth. Once you have decided to abandon the blessed Crimea, would it not be better to prepare to travel in the spring, when it will be warm, and then proceed on the road you will travel? Surely now, you will not see the land on which you dwell for it is covered with snow.
>
> Brave Ali-Jaffer, remember your distant ancestors were brave knights, the praise of whom resounded half way around the world, your close fathers were universally known as honest, kind, patient people, worthy of a better fate and greater fortune. Do not throw your little ones into the embraces of the cold, or even perhaps starvation. It is true that God will provide for everything, but remember the children and the family, He has entrusted them to us.[21]

While the causes for the migration movement of 1902 may have been related to the Crimean Tatars' perennial difficulties in Russia (the land issue in particular), one source points out that there was also calls for *hijra* at this time from religious figures in the Crimea. A Sheikh Haci Bekir Effendi from the Bahcesaray district had in fact declared that *"hijra* was required of true Muslims" and that "Muslims could no longer remain here now."

One of Gasprinsky's cohorts, who was to become a leading Crimean Tatar nationalist, Seyit Abdullah Ozenbashli, attacked this movement for *hijra* with a new language that sounds increasingly nationalistic in a late 1902 article. In the writings of Ozenbashli, the Tatars' traditional impulse to emigration was to be confronted for the first time by a proponent of a new world view which saw the abandonment of a people's "Fatherland" as anathema. Ozenbashli's tone is also much harsher than Gasprinsky's fatherly coaxing and his article implies that abandonment of the Crimea is a betrayal of the nation (*millet*) and countrymen (*ihvan*). In essence, Ozenbashli's article is a nationalist attack on an aspect of the Crimean Tatars' pre-nationalist, religious identity, *hijra*, that had long been institutionalized in Crimean Muslim society. In an article entitled "My Dear" Ozenbashli wrote:

> Oh shame! You are not ashamed and search yourself for an excuse. Why is it necessary for the Tatar people to partake in *hijra*? My dear, why are you fleeing to strange lands? What you are doing is not courageous!
>
> Why do you flee from your people?
> Do you expect to meet *Hizri* [a saint of protection] on the road?
> You are begging and this leaves shame on your face.
> What you are doing is without merit!
>
> Are the people you leave behind here lacking somehow? Hey hopeless one have you been cut off from strength! Why are you silent, has your tongue been cut off? These actions are opposed to religious creed![3]

Gasprinsky's and Ozenbashli's campaigns against emigration, marked a watershed in Crimean Tatar history. From this time forward, members of the Crimean Tatar intelligentsia with an increasingly nationalistic outlook fought against the abandonment of the peninsula. Gasprinsky's simple words "To leave one's homeland one must have some sort of reason" appear to have had resonance with his audience, who began to think of the Crimea, and not the Ottoman Empire, as their people's true Motherland. Migration to Turkey increasingly came to be seen as a betrayal of the homeland (although Gasprinsky certainly had a larger pan-Turkic vision of this homeland) and of the Crimean Tatar people. The efforts by Gasprinsky, Ozenbashli and others appear to have had an effect, and the migration of 1902 never assumed the numbers of earlier migrations. It was limited to two or three thousand people at most. Although several thousands did migrate to the Ottoman Empire to avoid military duty during the Russo-Japanese War of 1904–05, the majority of these returned to the peninsula at the end of this conflict. The more limited migrations of the twentieth century had a completely different nature to those of the previous century. These modern migrations were stimulated more by family interests, individual decisions to look for work in Turkey, or to avoid collectivization and famine in the early Soviet era. The idea of migration as an unpatriotic abandonment of the homeland clearly marked a fundamental change in Crimean Tatars' perceptions of themselves and their links to their natal territory. The traditional notion of *hijra* to the *ak toprak* of the Ottoman Empire had, by the beginning of the Soviet era, lost its influence on a people that, more and more, began to view their land as an *ata toprak* (fatherland). While students continued to travel to Istanbul to receive educations, they increasingly returned home to use their training to modernize, educate and improve their own society. That there was no great emigration from the Crimea to the Romanian region of Dobruca or Anatolia during the turmoil of the Russian Revolution or World War I (during which Crimean Tatars were drafted into the Russian army, a traditional catalyst for emigration) may, in part, be explained by the fact that many segments among the Crimean Tatar people had, by this time, begun to see the Crimea as their home.

The Role of the "Young Tatars" in Narrowly Defining the Crimean Homeland

By 1905 revolutionary movements had begun to spread throughout the Tsarist Empire and this mood also manifested itself among a new generation of Crimean Tatars who were not content with the innocuous cultural reform movement of Gasprinsky. As calls for political involvement in defense of Tatar issues became widespread in the Crimea, the era of the gentlemen reformer ended and a more overtly political movement began among the Crimean Tatars. The focus of their activities switched to the second most important Tatar enclave in the Crimea, Karasu Bazar.

Karasu Bazar, like Bahcesaray, was a mixture of the old Tatar and the new Russian. This town is overlooked by the Shirinsky Cliffs (also known as *Ak Kaya*, "White Rock" in Tatar), the sacred site of *kurultay* clan gatherings of the Shirin and other powerful *bey* (chieftain) families during the khanate period. Several mosques, including the ancient Sher Dor *madrasa*, were also located in this former seat of the Shirin *beylik* (chieftainship) and to this day the winding cobblestone streets, with their faceless white washed houses, have a Tatar air to them. By the early twentieth century paved roads and electricity had made their way to Karasu Bazar and Russians, Germans, Bulgarians and Armenians had begun to settle in the vicinity.

Perhaps the most noticeable sign of modernization in Karasu Bazar, however, was its reformist Tatar mayor from 1907 to 1912, Abdureshid Mehdi. Mehdi originally heralded from the Crimean steppe (the village of Karanki in the Perekop region) and was thus familiar with the terrible plight of Muslim peasants in the Crimea. After having been elected to the mayorship of Karasu Bazar, Mehdi launched a campaign that had as it goal winning back land for the Crimean Tatar peasants.

While Gasprinsky had been circumspect in his dealings with the Russian government, Mehdi and his cohorts (many of whom were Nogai Tatars from the northern Crimean steppe) did not hide their nationalist tendencies. Mehdi espoused his ideas in a newspaper of his own known as *Vatan Hadmi* (Servant of the Nation). Among his favorite subjects in this publication was the question of land reform.

That land reform was needed in the Crimea was beyond doubt. A mere one thousand *pomeshchiks* owned more than half the land in the Crimea by the year 1877, while most Tatars had small subsistence lots at best.[22] In some districts 40 to 50 per cent of the Crimean Tatars were landless and, by the twentieth century, destitute Crimean Tatar field hands roamed the countryside working others' lands to earn enough money to buy a house, afford *kalem* ("bride's price") or simply to survive. As Mehdi eloquently described the situation, "Among our people it is estimated that there are 50,000 landless individuals who have to look for jobs, live as hired farm laborers, and work for the *pomeshchiks*. On the other hand, here, there are *vakif* lands, confiscated lands, state lands, allocated lands and *pomeshchik* lands which can save many people from misery."[23] After having been elected to the second *Duma* (parliament) in 1906, something unheard of for a Tatar peasant, Mehdi began a campaign to return the Crimean lands lost during the previous century to his Tatar countrymen.

In Mehdi's speeches we hear, for the first time, language that defines the Crimea not as a province of the Russian Empire, a segment of the greater *Dar al-Islam* or adjunct of a larger Turkic homeland known as Turkistan, but as the national patrimony of the Crimean Tatar nation. In a speech given in 1910, for example, Mehdi uses allegories of blood mixed with soil that evoke the language of classic German nationalism. As Mehdi put it, "In our ignorance, committing mistake after mistake, we gave away our valuable lands—every handful of which is stained with the blood of our ancestors—to the hands of the enemy, while we ourselves live separated from it in misery and poverty. All who think about this sorrowful, abject position involuntarily shed tears."[24] In another speech, Mehdi went so far as to make a bold call for return of the vast *vakif* estates confiscated from his people by the Russian government and *pomeshchiks*:

> We have already written that, at the time of the Crimea's subjugation by Russia 125 years ago there had been some 300,000 des. [desiatins] of *vakif* lands. And now at the hands of the Spiritual Board and the Vakif Commission only 87,000

des. of *vakif* lands have been left. That is to say, 200,000 des. lands were usurped by several persons, and most of them seized by the state, which has been most artful in such matters, and these sacred lands, left us by our ancestors, were renamed state lands. It is our most important duty to work for the return of these lands, which are the inalienable property of the Crimean Muslims.[25]

In one of Mehdi's many impassioned orations (which won him the respect of a fellow revolutionary, Vladimir Lenin, who praised Mehdi for his "fiery revolutionary speeches") he poignantly spoke of the Crimean Tatars' position at the time of the post-Crimean War great migrations to the Ottoman Empire. Mehdi eloquently stated "fifty years ago, just after the Crimean Campaign, our Crimean Tatars faced such an economic collapse that they could hardly stand the imposts. Fifty years have passed and the Tatars are still in the same position, and they have begun to degenerate and become extinct. But we do not want to die out, we want a new life."[26] Although Mehdi was ultimately unsuccessful in his efforts to see land redistributed in the Crimea, he and the loosely organized young Tatar nationalists of the region, informally known as the Young Tatars (*Genc Tatarlari*), laid the foundation for the spread of nationalist identity among the common Crimean Muslim peasantry. Just as young Russian revolutionaries were "going to the people" at this time with the aim of spreading their revolutionary ideas to the common peasants, Mehdi and his followers brought their message to the Crimean Tatars. Their message was that the Crimea was the unique patrimony of the Tatars. Mehdi's calls for the distribution of land had particular resonance among the destitute Tatar villagers who began to see that these nationalist figures (who were previously dismissed by the stoic Tatar peasants as "hot heads") were willing to do more to improve their plight than their own obsequious village *mullahs*.

The Crimean police were aware of this activity and on several occasions sent exaggerated reports to St. Petersburg describing the undertakings of the growing number of "Muslim agitators" in the Crimea. One police report from the era made the preposterous accusation that the Young Tatars sought to resurrect the Crimean Khanate as a vassal of Turkey. According to this report:

> The teachers in the Simferopol high school, in addition to the reading of their subjects, secretly initiate the students of the upper classes into the history of Turkey and the former Crimean Khanate and agitate among them on the necessity for the Crimean Tatars to resurrect the former khanate, which should be placed under the authority of the Turkish sultan, since the latter was the caliph and the sole actual protector of the world's Muslims.[27]

Reports of this nature show that the Russian authorities in the Crimea misunderstood the program of the Young Tatars, which, by its very nature, was revolutionary and anti-monarchist (i.e. against the absolutist authority of "anachronistic" monarchs, be it the Tsar, Khan or the sultan-caliph). Mehdi's program was based on the formative principles of populism and nationalism, not nostalgia for the lost dynasty of the Girays. While the simple Crimean Muslim villagers may not have understood the language of Mehdi's early form of nationalism, they certainly understood the value of land. One method that Mehdi and the Young Tatars utilized for instilling an attachment to the Crimean homeland among the common Crimean Muslim peasantry was to use *hadiths* (collected sayings) of the Prophet, most of which were of dubious authenticity, to stress the Islamic basis for national patriotism. Hakan Yavuz has pointed out the use of one *hadith* in particular which connected the sayings of the Prophet with attachment to one's homeland. According to Yavuz, "The formation of political consciousness among Russian Muslims led to a re-examination of territory within Islamic teaching as the Muslim reformists in Russia tried to give political meaning to territory by utilizing an invented new *Hadis (Hadith)* that culminated in [the saying] 'the love of the fatherland is the love of the faith.'"[28]

As popular Young Tatar teachers began to replace conservative *mullahs* in mosques and *medreses* throughout the Crimea and to become elected to local positions, the Islamic clergy began to lose much of its hold over the hearts and minds of the Crimean Tatar peasantry. The Young Tatars also became increasingly bold in their nationalist orientation. By 1913 a Young Tatar, Shamil Toktargazi, was to write a poem entitled "On the Eulogy of the Crimea", which was daringly nationalist in its content:

> "Love of the Fatherland is part of the Faith" is *hadith*, Only a scoundrel would not love his Fatherland. Only the son of a Tatar is the inheritor of this Land, The Others cannot claim the Crimea.
>
> There is no Land like the Crimea in the world, There is no glory like Tatarness in the world.[29]

While Mehdi and the Young Tatars directed the majority of their efforts against the *Kadimists* (conservative Muslim clergy), they also appear to have split with Gasprinsky. He had come to be seen as too servile, apolitical and unconcerned with pressing issues in the Crimea by this new generation of political activists. The great (but controversial) Crimean Tatar writer Shamil Aliadin wrote of Mehdi "This man was a completely different kind of man from Gasprinsky. Gasprinsky began his activities in the last century. Mehdi—in ours. Our time is completely different. And Mehdi and his ideas were different."[30]

By the second decade of the twentieth century even some of Gasprinsky's followers from his newspaper *Tercuman* had come to see their nation in narrow terms and their home as the Crimea. As the Russian Empire tottered on the brink of World War I, the victory of Tatarness (*Tatalik*) over a wider sense of Turkicness (*Turkluk*) had been assured among the Crimean Tatar intelligentsia. In the process, it was the Crimean Peninsula that came to be defined as their sacred Fatherland.

Kirimli sums up the importance of the Young Tatars in constructing the Crimea as a homeland stating:

> It was the Young Tatars who manifestly introduced the territorially-bound and -defined Crimean Tatar national concept. For them the Crimea was the Fatherland of the Crimean Tatars who had inalienable historical rights upon it. The expropriation of the Crimean Tatar peasants was unacceptable not only because this was socially evil, but also because it represented an alien infringement upon the Crimean Tatar historical legacy and property.[31]

The Rise of the Vatan *(Fatherland) Society*

As mentioned previously, the territorialization/nationalization of Crimean Tatar identity did not occur in a vacuum. To a certain extent the rise of Crimean Tatar nationalism among the Crimean Tatars occurred as a reaction to the rise of national awareness among their two most influential neighbors, the Turks and the Russians. A mass-based nationalism began to spread in Russia after the 1861 liberation of the serfs, which replaced the previous loyalty to Orthodoxy and the Tsar. Similarly, in the Ottoman Empire the term "Turk" ceased to be a term of opprobrium applied to country peasants and became proudly worn by the Young Turks who stressed their patriotic loyalty to an ethnically-defined Turkish homeland. With the overthrow of Sultan Abdul Hamid in 1908/9 by the Committee for Union and Progress, it was the Young Turks in particular who were to serve as a model for Crimean Tatar nationalists who sought to overthrow the old order in their own homeland. For a young generation of Crimean Tatar students studying abroad in Istanbul, the first two decades of the twentieth century were a heady period. Old conventions were being broken down and writers, such as Yusuf Akchura and Namik Kemal before him, had begun forging a Turkish national identity. These two writers were helping to create a modern national awareness for a Muslim people that had previously, like the Russians, subsumed themselves in a religiously-defined community.

VATAN: THE CONSTRUCTION OF THE CRIMEAN FATHERLAND

The Turkish writer Namik Kemal's seminal work *Vatan yahut Silistre* (Homeland or Silistre) dealing with the Crimean War, in particular, made an impression on the Crimean Tatar students of Istanbul. They were also impressed by the clandestine Young Turk movement in Turkey. In 1909, a group of these Tatar students organized an underground political organization of their own known as the *Vatan Cemiyeti* (Fatherland Society).

Founded by two students in their early twenties, Cafer Seydahmet (who often added "Kirimer" to the end of his last name) and Numan Celebi Cihan, the *Vatan Cemiyeti* had as its stated goal "the liberation of our nation." The formation of this clandestine organization represents a new era in the development of Crimean Tatar national identity. For the first time in over a century, Crimean Tatars were organizing themselves on a political basis with the aim of liberating their homeland; the members of the Fatherland Society were proposing nothing less than independent Crimean Tatar statehood in the Crimean Peninsula.

The members of the Fatherland Society began working towards this objective on several fronts. Five-man secret cells were organized among trustworthy members of the Crimean Tatar diaspora in Istanbul and these in turn organized cells in the villages of the Crimea starting in the year 1912. By 1917, nationalist cells could be found in almost every village and town in the Crimea. From all accounts it appears that Tatars from the Turkish diaspora (many of whom were Ottoman citizens) who had returned to the peninsula played a key role in the development of a national movement at this time.

The first step in the development of a revolutionary program by the Fatherland Society consisted of printing proclamations calling for the distribution of lost *vakif* lands, an end to the oppression by Russian officials (*chinovniks*), an end to the dominance of the obsequious Islamic clergy class in the region and political freedom. These proclamations and hundreds of books dealing with revolutionary concepts were smuggled out of Turkey and distributed to teachers in Gasprinsky's New Method schools (most of whom were Tatars from the Turkish diaspora) throughout the Crimea. In scores of classrooms throughout the countryside, Tatar students began to take heed of the revolutionary words "For the rise of our Fatherland and Nation we have to sacrifice our lives and spill blood."[32]

This stated willingness to spill blood in the defense of the Crimean Tatars' claim to the peninsula as a Fatherland shows that the concept of nation and homeland had progressed even further than that program initiated by Mehdi (who died in 1912) and the loosely organized Young Tatars of the previous decade. The struggle to nationalize the Tatar masses was, however, by no means to be an easy one. As shall be seen, the bulk of the Crimean Tatar population on the eve of the Russian Revolution was still dominated by village *mullahs*. An equal barrier to the Tatar nationalists' goal of forging a unified Tatar nation in the Crimean Peninsula was the oft-overlooked historical differences between the Tats of the southern region and the Nogais of the northern plains.

Localized Sub-National Identities as an Obstacle to the Forging of a Crimean Tatar National Identity

One of the least explored aspects of Crimean Tatar nation construction in the early twentieth century was the continuing importance of the parochial identifications with micro regions within the Crimea by the heterogeneous Tatar population. All too often the Crimean Tatars are treated as a homogenous ethnic group and regional identities based on geography, language and differing origins tend to be glossed over.

It should, however, be recognized that those nationalists who sought to forge a unified nation on the eve of the Russian revolution were faced with the task of unifying a people that, in addition to their conservative Islamic identity, still tended to identify themselves with their region or sub-ethnic affiliation as Tats or Nogais. In his history of the formation of the Crimean Tatar people, Memet Sevdiyar writes "In the Crimea prior to the total deportation of the Crimean Tatar people, there were 22 dialects in this single Turkic language and, in addition to these dialects, they differed from one another in their physiognomy, color and also in their clothing. This was the result of the fact that the Crimean Tatars formed as a result of the mixing of different tribes."[33] Dialects varied from village to village as late as the twentieth century. While living in the Crimea in 1997, I was also told by older Tatars, who had lived in the peninsula prior to the deportation, that one could tell which village a Tatar heralded from by his or her distinct dialect and accent.

On some occasions it was more than a mere dialect that differentiated the region's villagers. Tat Oghuz-Tatar speakers of the southern coast, for example, often had difficulties in understanding the Nogai Kipchak-Tatar language from the other side of the Yaila mountain range. Tatars from the Yalta vicinity spoke an Oghuz version of Crimean Tatar that was considered more "cultured" than the hybrid Kipchak-Oghuz Tatar of the central Bahcesaray area or the "unrefined" Kipchak Tatar of the Nogai population of the steppes.

VATAN: THE CONSTRUCTION OF THE CRIMEAN FATHERLAND

These differences were so pronounced, even as late as the Soviet period, that several elderly Crimean Tatars I interviewed mentioned the fact that girls from the coast, who were still known as Yaliboyu Tats, were often forbidden from marrying Nogais from the interior as late as the 1930s.

The renowned Soviet era Tatar writer Shamil Aliadin mentioned these parochial differences in the Crimea of the early twentieth century in his work entitled *Teselli* (Consolation). According to this author:

> The inhabitants of the Crimea are distinguished by one characteristic. A person born, for example, in Simeiz (the southwestern tip of the Crimea) or Yalta, is a south-coaster. Someone born in Karangit is not linked to those on the south coast. This, in spite of the fact that Simeiz and Karangit stand on the same sea… As to Kok Koz (a village in the Crimean interior), where is it in relation to sea? In Kok even if one ascends the minaret you cannot see the sea…For this reason the inhabitants of the south coast are called haughty and arrogant since they emphasize the fact that they were born on the sea, as if they rose from the sea and have special privileges.[34]

These regional differences between Tats and Nogais extended from language and physiognomy to agricultural customs. In another passage, Aliadin speaks of the differences between the Nogai Tatars of the steppe and the Tat Tatars, and has a Nogai tell a Tat "The Tats own wide vineyards and splendid gardens. Probably there is nowhere else such fruits and apples as those they gather. But us Nogais, we have wheat! And meat!"[35]

While preventing unity on some levels, these sub-ethnic differences and stereotypes do not, however, appear to have been overtly antagonistic. During World War I a group of Crimean Tatar prisoners of war in Hungary, for example, sang of the beauty of Tat girls. The following is a stanza from one such song:

> Ah my dear Tat girl
> With cheeks of red
> I gave you an apple but you did not take it
> I gave you a shepherd's pipe but you did not play it.[36]

Historians agree that these differences were nonetheless an inhibitor to national unification by the Crimean Tatars. Valerii Vozgrin speaks of the Crimean Tatars' lack of national unity during the nineteenth century and concludes:

> The reasons for this are numerous and all lie on the surface. Firstly the ancient narrowness and isolation of the predominately village population. Moreover, this applied not only to the wider world, but between the mountains and foothills, the foothills and the steppe. The isolation was between one another and

separate villages. Hardly a nation, with distinct dialects, differing one from another even from the anthropological perspective, the Tatars were not able and did not want to unify in the face of mutual oppression.[37]

In his work, A.I. Kliachin maintains:

> It should be stated that in the 1920s a unified Crimean Tatar ethnos had not been completely formed. Far from being a homogenous nation, the Tatars were divided into three ethnographic groups, they were delineated by their language, culture, and anthropological characteristics into the south coast Tatar, the *Yaliboyu*, the mountain Tatars, the *Tats* or *Tatlars*, and of course the steppe Tatars, the *Nogais*.[38]

That the Crimean Tatars sustained their parochial identifications with their micro-homelands and sub-ethnic groupings into the twentieth century should not come as a surprise to those acquainted with the geographically and ethnically diverse history of the peninsula outlined in chapter one. As late as the Russian Revolution, the Crimean Tatar villages of Yaila Mountains remained isolated from one another, for the Russian government had little incentive to build roads into this area. While the Tatar villages of the coast had been connected by a coastal road in the nineteenth century, there was little movement between those living in villages built on the coastal mountains and those Tats of the interior mountains or Nogais of the plain.

Although the Volga Tatars were known for their traveling merchants and traders (Volga Tatar merchants could be found throughout Central Asia in the nineteenth century), the Crimean Tatars were by contrast not a geographically mobile people with a well-developed bourgeoisie. While many members of the *mirza* landowning class often sent their children to Istanbul for education, most Crimean Tatar peasants had never traveled far from their *kucuk vatan* (their "little homeland" i.e. their immediate district). In his nineteenth-century description of the Baidar Valley in the southwestern Crimea, Baron von Campenhausen, for example, wrote "Its inhabitants lead a happy pastoral life, and they are so indifferent with respect to the rest of the world, that many of them have never passed the mountains by which their native vale is surrounded."[39] In addition to their difficulties in battling the Crimean Tatars' traditional, conservative Islamic basis for communal identification, the nationalist intelligentsia of the early twentieth century was thus faced with the task of unifying three distinct peasant peoples that still did not think of themselves as a unified nation or their homeland as extending beyond their immediate vicinity. While there were factors operating in the Fatherland Society's favor, such the Tat and Nogai Muslims' cultural opposition to the Russian "Other", the task of imparting an understanding of a wider sense of homeland and nation among the simple peasants was to be no simple undertaking.

That the Crimean Tatar nationalist elite would be able to unite their divided people on the basis of their shared linguistic, ethnic, and historical commonalties was not a foregone conclusion. In addition to the difficulties in unifying the traditionally divided Tats and Nogais, the leaders of the Fatherland Society were faced with the tremendous task of politicizing an apolitical, passive peasant population that had no tradition of assertiveness or political participation. As Vozgrin notes, "Alas, we must recognize the complete absence of political activity among the Tatars of this period. Opposition was noticeable, and not unusual, but it was passive and expressed itself exclusively in emigration out of the empire."[40]

On the eve of the Russian Revolution, the leadership of the Young Tatars and Fatherland Society were, however, aided in their struggle to unify and nationalize their countrymen by several factors. Firstly, the Crimea was a compactly defined "island" homeland and easy to identify with in the common imagination. Secondly, and most importantly, the Crimean Tatars had the collective memory of historical statehood to turn to in their search to legitimize their own aspirations for nationhood. As with other ethnic groups in Europe, members of the Crimean intelligentsia had a growing awareness of their people's proud history, and the Crimean Khanate provided them with a wealth of nationalist symbols and icons. After exploring this history, members of the Crimean Tatar nationalist leadership in Istanbul, for instance, rediscovered the *Tarak Tamgha* crest of the Giray dynasty and placed this emblem on a blue flag (blue being the sacred color of the pagan Turkic tribes), making the Crimean Tatars among the first (if not the first) Muslim nations in the world to devise a national flag.

In addition, the nationalists constantly stressed the notion of the unity of the various Crimean Tatar peoples in an attempt to gloss over divisions based on sub-ethnic and regional allegiances among them. By the time World War I broke out in 1914, the Crimean Tatars were certainly among the most nationally developed Muslim ethnic groups in the Russian Empire as a result of these efforts. By contrast, Alexandre Bennigsen writes, "The feeling of belonging to a Kazakh or Turkmen nation was experienced only by a restricted modernist intelligentsia. So, before 1917 among the Muslim public there was not, and there could not be, a consciousness of belonging to a modern well-delineated nation."[41]

In the Crimea, by contrast, the Fatherland Society had established nationalist cells in practically every village by the onset of the war. Furthermore, traditionalist Islam had been largely discredited in many people's minds, and a larger sense of *Kirim Tatarlik* (Crimean Tatarness) based on secular principles had begun to be disseminated from the nationalist intelligentsia to the masses of Tats and Nogais.

One must not, however, see the Crimean Tatars of 1914 as a fully developed nation. Islam and regional loyalties were still the main bases for communal identification for the majority of the peasantry. The national platform of the well-organized Fatherland Society was largely an elite phenomenon. Galina Yemelianova's description of the Volga Tatars, who were just as developed in nationalist terms as the Crimean Tatars at this time, could very well have applied to the latter: "At the turn of the nineteenth century the large majority of Tatars, especially in rural areas, maintained a traditional way of life and continued to perceive themselves in local and religious terms."[42] This situation also applied to the Central Asian Muslims who were far less developed than the Volga and Crimean Tatars.

Ironically, it was the Crimean Tatars' experience during the Soviet period that was to see the final development of a mass-based, unified national identity that subsumed local identities and the earlier communal attachment to the larger Islamic community. While conservative *mullahs* and, later, idealistic young nationalists had played the dominant role in shaping Crimean Tatar identity prior to the Soviet period, it would be commissars and Communist bureaucrats shaped by the works of Marx and Engels that would propel the Crimean Tatar masses into the final stages of national development. It was the Soviet state that completed the development of a secular national identity (in a Sovietized form) and the construction of the Crimea as a homeland, increasingly defined by the Russian term *rodina* (homeland). The center of Crimean Tatar development during the succeeding two decades of Soviet rule was to be Simferopol, the capital of the newly established Crimean Autonomous Soviet Socialist Republic (ASSR). With its factories, university, museums, and regional Communist Party buildings, this Soviet administrative center on the Salgir River became the focus of a transformation that would see the Muslim Crimean Tatar subgroups complete their long journey of national identity construction and emerge as a secular nation.

5

SOVIET HOMELAND

THE NATIONALIZATION OF THE CRIMEAN TATAR IDENTITY IN THE USSR

One of the least explored chapters in Crimean history has been the role of the Soviet state in territorializing and shaping the modern national identity of the Crimean Tatars. While the contemporary Tatars are quick to laud the role of their own national heroes, such as Ismail Gasprinsky, Adbureshid Mehdi, Numan Celebi Cihan and Cafer Seydahmet, in developing the nation, few recognize the crucial role that the Soviet state played in constructing the territorialized, national identity of the community. Far from attempting to eradicate this national identity, in the first two decades of Communist rule, the Soviet regime actually promoted Crimean Tatar national development.

Soon after gaining final control over the Crimean Peninsula in 1920, the new Soviet government created a Crimean Autonomous Soviet Socialist Republic (ASSR)—the second highest territorial ranking in the Soviet federal system after the Soviet Socialist Republic (SSR)—and promoted the development of Crimean Tatar national identity in this republic right up until the outbreak of World War II.

The effects of this state-sponsored identity construction can still be seen in the Tatars' maximalist, late Soviet-era demands for the re-establishment of a territorial autonomy in the Crimea that recognizes their unique claim to this land. In 1991 they were unsuccessful in their bid to have the Crimean Republic reestablished as an autonomous unit with 1920s Soviet-style, ethnically-based prerogatives for its indigenous population. Instead, in a preemptive move, the local Russian population voted to establish an autonomous territorial republic within the Ukraine that made no special allowances for the Tatars' unique claim to this land as the native population of the Crimea.

There is considerable disagreement between Crimean Russian nationalists and Crimean Tatars as to the exact nature of the original Crimean Autonomous Soviet Socialist Republic established by Soviet leader Vladimir Lenin (the republic was later downgraded and transformed into an *oblast*-district within the Russian Federation after the 1944 deportation of the Tatars to Central Asia). The debate revolves around the issue of whether the Crimean ASSR of 1921–1945 was established as an *ethno-national* autonomous unit, in recognition of the Crimean Tatars' unique claim to the area, or whether it was established as a multi-national *territorial* autonomy. In this respect the Crimea is one of the most unusual territorial constructs to come out of the Soviets' vast policy of republic construction, known as the Great Delimitation (*Razmezhevanie*), since the status of the native population in the Crimean autonomy was never clearly defined.

Those opposed to the Crimean Tatars' claims point out that the Tatars were a minority (25 per cent) of the population at the time of the founding of the Soviets' original Crimean Republic in 1921, and that this precluded any discussion of this republic being established in recognition of Crimean Tatar identity or this group's unique claim to the peninsula. The region's Russian population stress that the Crimean ASSR was founded as a multi-national, territorial republic and "never was a national autonomy;"[1] the "international" Crimean ASSR never was a Crimean *Tatar* ASSR *per se*. In this respect, the Crimean ASSR had similarities to the multi-ethnic Yugoslav republic of Bosnia, which did not recognize any specific nationality (there were three ethnic groups in Bosnia, the Serbs, Croatians and Bosniak Muslims).

The Tatars, on the other hand, claim that the Crimean Republic was, like all other Soviet autonomous republics, established in recognition of the territory's indigenous population and this group's unique claim to be its officially recognized *korennoi narod* (rooted or native people). Crimean Tatar nationalists who proclaim that the ASSR was created for the Crimean Tatars point out that "Those who say that the Crimean ASSR was territorial and not national forget that autonomy did not occur without nationality."[2] The issue of the Tatars' claim to the Crimean ASSR based on "indigenousness" (*korennoinost*) takes on particular significance in this argument. A contemporary Tatar historian, R.I. Muzafarov, writes "on the territory of the Crimea at that time there was only one indigenous people, the Crimean Tatars, all the rest,

Russians, Ukrainians, Belorussians, were only national groups who appeared as a portion of their nation."³

Although the Crimean Tatars were not the *de jure* titular nationality of the Crimean Republic (as the Volga Tatars were in the Tatar Autonomous Soviet Socialist Republic), Crimean Tatar activists claim that they were the *de facto* state-sponsored minority in a republic established in recognition of their nationality. They emphasize the fact that they were recognized by the Soviet system as the Crimean population with the most legitimate claim to the region as a national homeland-republic. The Crimean Tatar leadership is also quick to point out that the ASSR was established, in part, as a propaganda showcase designed to win over the public sympathy of the large Tatar émigré diaspora in Turkey and of the Turks themselves. Crimean Tatars stress that, with the deportation of their people in 1944, this republic lost its *rasion d'etre* (i.e. to recognize the Crimean Tatar nation) and was subsequently abolished by the Soviet authorities and converted into an *oblast* (district).

To Russian claims that the Crimean ASSR was not a Crimean *Tatar* ASSR (as demonstrated by the clear absence of any reference to the Tatars in the republic's title), the Tatars point to the existence of several autonomous territories or republics in the Soviet Union that did not officially recognize the state-sponsored nationality in their title, despite the fact that they were clearly ethnically based units. Among these they point to Nagorno Karabagh (an Armenian territorial unit in the mountains of the republic of Azerbaijan), Dagestan (a multi-ethnic republic in Russia meaning Land of Mountains) and Nakichevan (an Azerbaijani autonomy between Armenia and Turkey), none of which have references to nationality in their titles.

As to the argument that the Crimean Tatars, as a mere 25 per cent of the Crimea's 1921 population, did not merit an ethnically-based territorial unit in the peninsula, Crimean Tatar nationalists point to the fact that territorial autonomies were established for the Komis, Yakuts, Volga Tatars, Mordvins, Udmurts, and other ethnic groups who were also minorities in their autonomous units. They point out that in some cases the proportion of members of the titular minority in their eponymous republic was extremely low. For instance, the Karelians made up only 11 per cent of their territorial autonomy and the Abkhaz made up only 17 per cent of their republic of Abkhazia (in Georgia) in the late Soviet period.

It will be demonstrated here that, while the Crimean ASSR was not officially an ethnically-based republic on paper (such as the Uzbek SSR, the Checheno-Ingush ASSR etc.), it had all the hallmarks of a national republic.

For all intents and purposes, the Crimean ASSR was, from 1921–1945, established as an unofficial Crimean Tatar republic and the Crimean Tatars were the state-sponsored "native people" (*korennoi narod*) of this autonomy. It will also be shown that it was the experience of two decades of nation construction in this Soviet republic that completed the development of a mass-based, modern Crimean Tatar national identity that was begun by Gasprinsky, the Young Tatars and the Fatherland Society.

Herein lies a conundrum for many Tatar nationalists. In arguing that the Crimean ASSR was an unofficial Crimean *Tatar* ASSR they must also accept the fact that the Soviet state (the *bete noire* of Crimean Tatar nationalism) contributed to the consolidation of modern Crimean Tatar identity through its policies of nativization in an ethnicity-based territorial unit constructed for their nation.

The Formation of the Crimean Kurultay *(Congress)*

Before analyzing this remarkable process of state-sponsored nation building in the Soviet period, one must first, however, turn to the brief struggle fought by Crimean Tatar nationalists to create a Crimean state during World War I. Events that took place in this chaotic period were to forge a pantheon of national martyrs, memories of lost potential for statehood and symbols that have, since the collapse of the Soviet state in 1991, become the revered icons of modern Crimean Tatar nationalism. During World War I, the members of the Fatherland Society continued to organize underground nationalist cells throughout the Crimea, despite the danger of arrest by the Tsarist police, who considered this to be yet another example of Crimean Tatar war-time treason. This work continued even though the two leading members of the Fatherland Society, Cafer Seydahmet and Numan Celebi Cihan, were drafted into the Russian army at the outset of the war. Most Crimean Tatars who were drafted fought in two light Tatar cavalry squadrons known as the Crimean Cavalry Regiment. Not surprisingly, the drafting of Crimean Tatar nationalists into these squadrons led to the formation of nationalist cells within this highly decorated unit.

With the commencement of the Russian Revolution in February of 1917 and the ending of firm Russian police rule in the Crimea, the underground Tatar nationalist cells emerged into the open. It was at this time that the idea of the Crimea as the Crimean Tatars' sacred homeland began to be openly propagated among the wider Crimean Tatar populace. But the majority had yet to conceptualize the peninsula in nationalist terms. For many Crimean Muslim peasants, the region was simply the Tauride Province of the Russian Empire. That this was the case amongst the uneducated Crimean Muslim masses in 1917 was not the exception in the Russian Empire. Robert Kaiser writes "On the eve of World War I, with the exception of the indigenous nations of the more developed northwest (Polish, Finnish, Estonian, Latvian, Lithuanian), mass based perceptions of national homeland were only beginning to take shape."[4] This situation began to change as nationalist entrepreneurs began to take advantage of the gradual breakdown in central Russian authority throughout the Crimea in the winter of 1917 to gain influence among the Tatar villagers. In the spring of 1917, this agitation bore its first fruit as 2,000 popularly elected delegates from Tatar villages throughout the Crimea (the vast majority of whom were nationalists with ties to the Fatherland Society) convened an "All Crimean Muslim Congress" in Simferopol to determine the fate of their people. At this meeting a Crimean Muslim Central Executive Committee was chosen and it promptly elected Numan Celebi Cihan as the Crimean *Mufti* (Chief Religious Official) and Cafer Seydahmet as head of a commission in charge of *vakif* affairs (although both of these leaders were still serving in the Russian army at the time).

Among the most important measures taken by the *Kurultay* (congress) was the decision to call for Crimean cultural autonomy. In addition, Celebi Cihan demanded that the Vakif Commission, which had been established by the Russian government in 1885 to control these lands, transfer control over this vast property to his authority. This effort to regain control of the Crimean land culminated in Cihan's declaration that "All *vakif* property and capital from the taxation of this property is considered national property belonging to the Crimean Tatars." The entire Crimean Tatar people were considered by the nationalists to be the exclusive inheritors of this unique historical patrimony with roots that lay in the distant khanate's past. In spite of the *Kurultay's* demands, the Provisional Government, which assumed power in Petrograd/St. Petersburg after the overthrow of the Tsar, reconfirmed the state's control of the *vakif* lands and maintained the conservative *mullahs* on them as the state's representatives. Not surprisingly, this led to the growth of tension between the representatives of the old order (the *mullahs*) and the increasingly popular Crimean Tatar nationalists. Acting under the influence of the nationalists, Crimean Tatar peasants began seizing both *vakif* land and land belonging to wealthy *pomeshchiks* throughout the Crimea. A new spirit of assertiveness had begun to make its appearance among this passive community of

Muslim Tatar peasants as central authority waned and nationalist sentiments seeped among many segments of the population.[5]

As this mood spread, the defenders of the old order, the *mullahs* and *mirzas*, actively worked with the Provisional Government against the nationalists from their own ethnic group. In early September 1917, the reactionary clerics were still planning to oust Celebi Cihan by relying on the "religious attitude of the mass of the Tatar population."[6] In response, Celebi Cihan declared that the new foundations for Crimean Tatar society were not to be decided by the Islamic clergy, whose legitimacy he claimed had been tainted by their links to the Tsarist government. Celebi Cihan also spoke out against the *mirzas* and, by the end of the summer "The reactionaries [i.e. the *mullahs* and *mirzas*] were driven away and for the time being their open activities ceased."[7]

The moribund Islamic clergy's fate was sealed with the establishment of a Crimean Tatar nationalist party in the summer of 1917 known as the Milli Firka (the National Party). Soon thereafter the Crimean Tatar nationalists moved to assume control throughout the Tatar villages and towns of the Crimea. The torch of leadership had finally been passed from the conservative clergy to a new generation of leaders shaped by the Young Tatars and the Fatherland Society, who were avowed nationalists.

In December 1917 an election was held among the Crimean Tatars to choose candidates from throughout the Crimea for the *Kurultay*. It was dominated by members of the Milli Firka. This election was notable for the fact that universal suffrage was extended and Tatar women throughout the Crimea were given the right to vote for local representatives to the *Kurultay*. It should be noted that this was the first time women were given the right to vote in the Muslim world and preceded suffrage in many Western countries.

On December 9, 1917, the first Crimean Tatar *Kurultay* was held in the khan's palace in Bahcesaray, a site replete with national symbolism for the Crimean Tatar nation. The delegates posed for a group photograph before the *Demir Kapi* (Iron Gate, the ornate entrance to the Khan's palace on which could be found the seal of the Giray dynasty, the *Tarak Tamgha*) and the picture survives to this day. The first thing that strikes those viewing the photograph is the relative youthfulness of the *Kurultay's* two most prominent leaders, Cafer Seydahmet and Celebi Cihan, who were both in their early thirties. It was these two young leaders, shaped by the reform movement of the Young Turks and the notions of Western democracy, liberalism and nationalism, that were to be the guiding forces in the creation of the extraordinary Crimean constitution. The constitution drawn up by these two leaders was undoubtedly the most progressive of its kind in the Muslim world and declared among other things:

> The *Kurultay*, standing on the principle of equality, recognizes and affirms complete equality of women with men and commissions parliament to uphold this law.
>
> The *Kurultay* considers as a necessity in public life: freedom of identity, word, press, conscience, meeting, dwelling, union, protest, and protection of life and work as practicable principles of self determination of peoples and rights of minorities. These laws which are guaranteed by the *Kurultay* may be guaranteed only in a democratic republic recognized and proclaimed as the Crimean democratic republic.[8]

As the Crimean Tatars organized around the *Kurultay*, they were acutely aware of the fact that the local Russian population felt threatened by their activities (as was the case throughout the Russian Empire whenever the local Russian populations were confronted with non-Russian national movements). In order to assuage the Russian population's fears, the *Kurultay* announced that it was "against the Tatarization of the Crimea" and declared:

> If we convoke a Tatar national constituent assembly or "*Kurultay*" then it is only in order to explain ourselves and reveal to others the will of the Tatar nationality, however, the voice of the Tatars is still not the voice of the entire Crimea. For this to occur it is necessary to convene an all-Crimean constituent assembly, which should include the participation of all peoples inhabiting the Crimea.[9]

The *Kurultay's* position on foreign policy was, however, less flexible and shows that, while the Crimean Tatar leadership officially respected the rights of the non-Tatar Slavic majority in the Crimea (the Ukrainians and the Russians made up 50 per cent of the Crimea's population), the nationalists felt that the Tatar nation had a unique claim to the Crimea as a homeland. An article in the Tatar newspaper *Golos Kryma* (Voice of the Crimea) announced "Let it be known that the Crimean Tatars will not allow anyone to establish any sort of hegemony over the Crimean Peninsula. The Crimean Tatars will not abandon their territory without a determined defense of their rights and the attainment of freedom."[10] This statement clearly shows that the Crimean Tatars' nationalist leadership's conceptualization of the peninsula as their nation's homeland had come a long way in just four years. Certain nationalized segments of the Crimean Tatar population were willing to fight for this territory rather than abandon it as their ancestors had.

The Tatar leadership had come to demand not just cultural autonomy for the Crimea, but territorial autonomy. This escalation in demands was soon to be supported by a viable Crimean Tatar military force. With the long awaited transfer of the Crimean Tatar cavalry from the war front to the Crimea, a masterstroke achieved by Cafer Seydahmet, the *Kurultay* had a military force of approximately 3,000 soldiers (actually a mixture of cavalry and dragoons) at its disposal to enforce its authority throughout the region. In a short time, the Tatar government used this cavalry force to assume control over most of the disorganized Crimean Peninsula. By the autumn of 1917 it had become evident to all that the Tatars were better organized than the local Russian and Ukrainian populations and were the most unified force in the area.

By this time, the *Kurultay* felt strong enough to open diplomatic relations with the revolutionary Young Turk government in Istanbul and the growing ties between Turkey and the Crimean Tatar government were evinced on many levels. An Ottoman fleet, for example, visited the Crimea in May of 1917 and was warmly received by the local Tatars. In addition, the Young Turk leader Talat Pasha met with the Tatar leader Cafer Seydahmet and pledged his support for Crimean independence. At this time, newspapers in Istanbul were full of calls for an Ottoman-Crimean-German alliance.[11]

In spite of all these activities, the Crimean Tatar *Kurultay's* influence did not, however, extend to Sevastopol, site of the Black Sea Fleet headquarters. The vast majority of sailors and marines in this strategic naval base had, by 1917, thrown in their lot with the Bolshevik Party and were disinclined to acknowledge the Tatar *Kurultay's* authority. As these two centers of power began to compete for influence in the peninsula, it was obvious that a showdown was inevitable.

Realizing the strength of the Bolsheviks, the left leaning Celebi Cihan was interested in negotiating a power sharing deal with the Sevastopol Bolsheviks. In his own words Celebi Cihan warned "I am convinced that the Bolsheviks represent such a force that no weapons can suppress them."[12] Celebi Cihan's warning was, however, ignored by the right wing of the Milli Firka, headed by Cafer Seydahmet, and in any case the Bolsheviks rejected overtures from the *Kurultay*.

In January 1918, a division of approximately 3,000 Bolshevik marines and sailors armed with machine guns and two cannon marched on the headquarters of the Tatar *Kurultay* in Simferopol. Their intention was to eliminate this ethnically-based challenge to Bolshevik (and local Russian) power in the Crimean Peninsula. The Crimean Tatar government found itself outgunned and retreated, only to be caught by the Bolsheviks outside Simferopol at the Suren train station. Prior to engaging the Bolsheviks, Cafer Seydahmet is reported to have given the following speech to his Tatar troops:

> Comrades, today the Crimean soldiers are the first to swear an oath to truly and faithfully serve their homeland, their nation and to obey its founding laws. When the vast Russian empire falls into anarchy, when out of 170 million Russians not even 50 people are guaranteed safety from danger, when robbery, murder and crime occurs everywhere and Russia is flowing with blood, when the personal rights and culture of Russian citizens are crushed underfoot, the Crimean Muslims in the Crimea uphold and defend the general peace and quiet and will not crush the Crimea underfoot. Therefore, today the Crimeans will not only be defending their own interests but the interests of all Crimeans.[13]

Although the Crimean Tatar cavalry had considerable experience earned on the battlefields in the West, the Bolsheviks' superior firepower enabled them to disperse the *Kurultay's* forces. Many members of the Crimean Tatar force, such as Numan Celebi Cihan, were captured by the Bolsheviks after this defeat. The majority of the Tatar force retreated to the Yaila Mountains or, like Cafer Seydahmet, fled south across the Black Sea to Turkey.

Having captured the president of the *Kurultay*, Celebi Cihan (who remained in Simferopol hoping to negotiate with the Bolsheviks), the Sevastopol Bolsheviks exhibited appalling political myopia and had Cihan, who had been willing to work with them, killed and his body thrown into the Black Sea. While this action was probably carried out without the blessing of the Bolshevik central leadership, it certainly did not strengthen Bolsheviks' relations with the local Tatar population. On the contrary, by killing Cihan the Sevastopol Bolsheviks created the first *milli sehit* (national martyr) to the Crimean Tatar cause and his death led to a radicalization of the Crimean Tatar populace.

Celebi Cihan's sacrifice is still remembered today by Crimean Tatars throughout the Crimea and in the diaspora. Cihan's nationalist ode "I Pledge" (*Ant Etkenmen*) has become both their national anthem and a commemoration of Cihan's sacrifice for his people. Cihan's verses are full of nationalist allusions and state:

> I pledge to heal the wounds of my nation, Why should my unfortunate brothers rot away?
> I pledge to bring light to that darkened country, How may two brothers not see one another?
> I pledge to give my word to die for knowledge.
> Knowing, seeing, to wipe away the teardrops of my nation.

During the Central Asian exile, the singing of Cihan's "I Pledge" became a means of expressing national identity when all other outlets were forbidden.

With the return of the Crimean Tatars to the peninsula, this anthem was openly sung in the historic second *Kurultay* held in Simferopol in 1991 by newly returned exiles from Central Asia. Celebi Cihan's legacy is still felt today on many levels in the Crimea and among the Crimean Tatar diaspora. A well known portrait of Celebi Cihan, with his Nogai features and youthful appearance, for example, hung above *Kurultay* President Mustafa Dzhemilev during the second *Kurultay* and can be found on the walls of the *Kirim Turkleri Amerikan Birligi* (Association of the Crimean Turk Americans) in New York. Cihan's face also appears in a stylized form on Crimean Tatar journals, on the walls of the Crimean Tatars' parallel government headquarters in Simferopol, and on banners hanging in Crimean Tatar associations in Turkey. I also found a simple monument built in honor of this *buyuk sehit* (great martyr) on the grounds of the restored Cuma Cami mosque in Evpatoriia, western Crimea. This marker was built by one of Celebi Cihan's descendants (who is now caretaker of sixteenth-century Turkish architect Sinan Pasha's famous Ottoman style mosque). The inscription on the monument reads in Tatar "Our pledged national martyr, Numan Celebi Cihan was slain in Sevastopol, The Black Sea is my grave, the white waves my shroud."

The Struggle for Power in the Crimea, 1918–1920

Having killed the leader of the Crimean Tatar national movement, the Bolsheviks proceeded to ravage the Crimean countryside and engaged in "mass slaughter" in Bahcesaray and Simferopol.[14] By the spring of 1918, the Sevastopol Bolsheviks had, however, begun to fall apart as the German offensive against the crumbling Russian Empire cut them off from Russia proper. As the victorious German invaders approached the Crimea, the leaders of the Sevastopol Bolshevik party fled first to the southern city of Yalta, then to nearby Alushta. There, they were captured by Crimean Tatars, who controlled much of the coast and Yaila mountain range. After the earlier execution of their president, the Crimean Tatar nationalist guerrillas appear to have had little mercy for the Bolsheviks and, in April of 1918, the captured Crimean Bolshevik leadership was executed in Yalta.[15]

This willingness to resort to bloodshed on the part of the Crimean Tatars represents a transformation of the passive Tatar peasant into what has been described in the Balkan context as an "ethno-warrior". As in the Balkans, the nationalization of both the Russian and Tatar communities in the Crimea destroyed much of the goodwill that had long existed between the peasants of both groups.

As the invading German army approached the peninsula during the closing days of World War I, Cafer Seydahmet left his place of asylum in Turkey and met with German officials to organize a Muslim cavalry unit in Romanian Dobruca (a coastal area where many Tatars had settled over the centuries) with the aim of assisting the Germans.[16] In the summer of 1918, this Tatar force, headed by a Russified Lithuanian Tatar, General Suleiman Sulkiewicz (who had earlier led the Russian Muslim Corps), joined with the Milli Firka Tatar nationalist forces still operating in the Crimea and assisted the German army in defeating the Bolsheviks in the peninsula.

In the aftermath of the German victory in the Crimea, Seydahmet and the newly regrouped *Kurultay* had great hopes for some form of Crimean Tatar autonomy under the Germans. Interestingly, the *Kurultay* leadership also hoped for the return to the Crimea of their lost *"kardeshler"* (brothers) who were found scattered throughout the Balkan and Turkish diasporas. In a letter to the German High Command, dated July 21, 1918, the Crimean Tatar nationalist leadership, for the first time, spoke of returning this diaspora to the Crimean homeland:

> To the German Supreme Command
>
> The Crimean Tatar people who, owing to the fall of the Crimean Khanate 135 years ago, fell under Russian yoke, have been fortunate to have the possibility to report their political aspirations to the attention of the German Government ... From the statistical collection of the *Zemstvo* of the former Tauride province for 1915 one sees that up to the year 1790, 300,000 Tatars abandoned the Crimea as a result of injustices and, in the period from 1860–1862, another 181,177 Tatars left. As a result it turned out that 687 villages were completely abandoned in the Crimea.
>
> One section of the oppressed people, who suffered thousands of hardships and oppressions, sought refuge in Dobruca and Bulgaria, but the main part settled in Turkey...
>
> If the entreaties of the emigrants were to be heeded and they were guaranteed a return to the Crimea, then one would assume the Crimean Tatars would make up 75–80% of the Crimean population. Those Tatars who migrated to Turkey and Dobruca cannot forget their historical connection with the Crimea and day and night, in their literature as in their songs, they pour forth grief over being reunited with the Crimea. In spite of all the cruel acts of oppression, the size of the Crimean Tatars could not be shaken. Equally, no acts of oppression could make them forget that respect held by the supremacy of their ancestors, before whom Moscow once bowed. The castles of Oskiuz Kapa, from the era of Tatar dominion, ruined mosques, closed educational institutions and, like a pitiful shadow of past glorious might, the destroyed religious-legal institutions, all instilled in them a glorious belief in liberation and energized them.[17]

The German administration of the Crimea, headed by General Aleksander Sulkiewicz, appears to have acted on this request for help in repatriating "lost brothers in the Balkans" and Turkey, and an open invitation to all Tatars living abroad to return to the Crimea was proclaimed in 1918.[18] The repatriation plan called for the offering of citizenship in the Crimea to all Crimean Tatars from the diaspora. The German occupation of the peninsula was, however, too short lived (the Germans only occupied the Crimea for five months) to see the implementation of the *Kurultay's* ambitious program of repatriation. After the German evacuation of the region there followed a confusing period in which local Russians, the Bolsheviks and White Armies (seeking to reconstitute to the Russian Empire) fought for control of the peninsula. As the White Armies were routed by the Bolsheviks throughout Russia, the Crimea became the last bastion for anti-Communist White forces in the Russian Empire. The White leader, General Anton Denikin, hoped to make the Crimea an "island bastion of anti-Communism" (a Russian version of nationalist Chinese "Taiwan" in every respect), but the Whites, who arrived with tens of thousands of Russian refugees, had no tolerance for the political movement of the indigenous Tatar population of the Crimea (many right-wing Crimean Tatar nationalists fled to Turkey at this time). After considerable anti-Tatar repression at the hands of the Whites, the majority of the Milli Firka Tatar nationalists followed the left side of the party and went underground to fight with their former enemies, the Bolsheviks, against the White regime.

Many Crimean Tatars formed guerilla units to fight against the Whites who were engaged in attacks on Tatar villages. These so-called "green bands", proliferated in the Yaila Mountains. According to one account, "For the first time since the annexation, the most peaceful and inoffensive population of the Crimea, the Tatars, took up arms, not under the influence of any sort of patriotism but completely spontaneously and on their own."[19] One cannot, however, doubt that the spread of nationalism among the Tatar and Russian populations of the Crimea had the effect of leading to increased inter-ethnic violence.

The most influential leftist leader of the Milli Firka fighting against the Whites during this period was a Crimean Tatar socialist named Veli Ibrahimov (of whom much will be written below). As the Bolsheviks appeared closer to victory, a desperate White general, Baron Pyotr Wrangel (successor to General Denikin), promised Veli Ibrahimov's soldiers that, if they assisted his forces, he would discuss self-rule for the Crimean Tatars.[20] By this time they had, however, already thrown in their lot with the winning Bolshevik side and Wrangel's defenses soon thereafter collapsed.

SOVIET HOMELAND

The Prelude to the Formation of the Crimean ASSR

In October of 1920, the Bolsheviks finally succeeded in driving the Whites from the Crimea (tens of thousands were evacuated by sea to Turkey and the Balkans) and Soviet power was again established in the war-torn peninsula. A new era had arrived for the Crimean Tatars who, having assisted the victorious Bolsheviks against the Whites, expected some recognition of their national aspirations in return. There were grounds in particular for expecting some acknowledgment of Crimean Tatar nationality from the Bolshevik leader, Vladimir Lenin. Prior to the Civil War, Lenin had actually singled out the Crimean Tatars in his 1917 "Proclamation to all the Muslims of Russia and the Orient" which declared:

> Muslims of Russia, Tatars of the Volga and the Crimea, Kirgiz and Sarts of Siberia and Turkestan, Turks and Tatars of Transcaucasia, Chechens and mountaineers of the Caucasus and all of you whose mosques have been destroyed, whose beliefs and customs have been trampled underfoot by the tsars and the oppressors of Russia. Your beliefs and usage, and national and cultural institutions are henceforth free and inviolable. Organize your national life in complete freedom. You have the right. Know that your rights, like those of all the peoples of Russia are under the powerful safeguard of the revolution and its organs, the Soviets of workers, soldiers, and peasants. Lend your support to this revolution and its government.[21]

Despite these lofty sounding words, the Bolsheviks initially appeared to be uninterested in collaborating with the Crimean Tatar nationalist leadership and quickly moved to outlaw the Milli Firka as a "counterrevolutionary party". In addition, the local Communist Party made no effort to redistribute land to the Crimean Tatar peasants and instead established large state farms (*sovkhozes*). Richard Pipes claims that "the heaviest losers" in the new system were the Crimean Tatars, who formed the bulk of the landless peasant population in the Crimea.[22] In addition, a famine swept through the peninsula in 1921 with devastating results for the Tatars, who as well as landless were largely impoverished.

If the situation in the Crimea at this time was not bleak enough, the Bolsheviks placed the Hungarian Communist, Bela Kun, in charge of the Crimean *Cheka* (Bolshevik secret police) and his administration was given the task of weeding out all "White Guardists", "reactionaries", "bourgeoisie", "Tatar nationalists" etc. Kun appears to have relished his task and as many as 60,000 Crimeans belonging to the above-mentioned classifications may have been killed in his deadly purges of the Crimean countryside and cities.

In response to these activities, the Crimean Tatars again spontaneously took to the Yaila Mountains and launched a guerrilla campaign against the Bolshevik authorities. When word of the anarchy in the Crimea reached Moscow, Vladimir Lenin sent the highest ranking Muslim in the Bolshevik hierarchy, the Volga Tatar Mir Said Sultan Galiev (Galiev was Stalin's advisor on Muslim areas in the *Narkomnats*—the Commissariat for Nationality Affairs) to the region on a fact-finding mission. Galiev's report called on the Soviet government to create an Autonomous Soviet Socialist Republic in the Crimea, halt the harmful land reform then in progress and attract the disenfranchised Tatars into the Communist Party. In response to this report, in October 1921 the Crimean Autonomous Soviet Socialist Republic (ASSR) was formed under the jurisdiction of the Russian Federated Republic. This event was to drastically alter the collective sense of identity of the Crimean Tatars and finish the job of nationalization begun by The Young Tatars.

The Position of the Crimean Tatars in the Crimean ASSR

One of the most interesting aspects of the Crimean ASSR was the dominant role that the Tatars were to play in this newly organized autonomous territorial unit. Although the Crimean Tatars, whose number had declined to 150,000 by 1923, formed a mere 25 per cent of the Crimea's population (as opposed to the Russians and Ukrainians, who together formed approximately 50 per cent, i.e. 306,000), they were soon to fill many of the top leadership positions. The leftist Milli Firka leader, Veli Ibrahimov (now a Bolshevik), for example, was given the highest posts in the Crimean ASSR administration, as chairman of the Crimean Central Committee and chairman of the Crimean Council of People's Commissars. Throughout the Crimean Republic, Crimean Tatars were placed in charge of factories, *kolkhozes* (collective farms), *sovkhozes* (state farms), town administrations and republican leadership positions.

In an interview with the author in 1998, Crimean Tatar diaspora leader Memet Sevdiyar (who was himself brought into the Crimean administration in the 1930s during this process) elaborated that Moscow's *volte face* was so sudden and complete that many inexperienced, illiterate Crimean Tatar peasants found themselves in leadership positions in industry, local town administrations and even in the Republican hierarchy.[23]

As in Central Asia, the Crimean Muslim population was largely agricultural at this time and there was virtually no Tatar proletariat. Most jobs in the industrial centers of Kerch, Simferopol and Sevastopol had previously been filled by Russians, Germans and Ukrainians. Many of the simple Crimean Tatar peasants given leadership slots were forced to rely on more qualified Russian "big brothers" to help them in their new positions. The influx of Crimean Tatars into the Crimea's industrial and governmental administrative positions was so pronounced that, when Russian workers in Sevastopol could not fill their production quotas, they would justify their failure with the excuse "How can one hope to fulfill the industrial finance plan when Tatars have been put to work on the lathes?"[24]

The local Russian-dominated Communist Party appears to have been adamantly opposed to the creation of the Crimean ASSR, which soon promoted Crimean Tatars at the Russians' expense, but it was overruled by Moscow. During my stay in the Crimea in 1997, I was told that those Crimean Tatars suddenly propelled from their villages into management positions were pejoratively called *"cigboreks"* (the Crimean Tatars' distinctive fried meat pastries) by many of their Russian "comrades". That there was tension between the local Russian population and the Tatars at this time was of course largely due to the state policy of promoting the needs and culture of the latter at the expense of the larger, and previously dominant Slavic population.

This process of promotion of Tatars was not unique to the Crimean ASSR and was in fact part of a state-wide national policy being implemented throughout the Union of Soviet Socialist Republics and other autonomous units known as *korenizatsiia*. *Korenizatsiia* was a Soviet term based on the Russian word *koren* (root), and literally means "rooting". In the Soviet context, *korenizatsiia* meant indigenization and positive discrimination for ethnic groups who were designated as the *korennoi narod* (rooted or native people) of a Soviet republic or smaller administrative territory.

The policy of *korenizatsiia* was implemented throughout the entire Soviet Union in the 1920s and led to the creation of local leadership cadres developed from native ethnic groups for autonomous districts, autonomous republics and the highest-ranking administrative territorial unit, the Soviet Socialist Republic (SSR). In implementing this program, quotas were established for recruiting local ethnic populations into industry, the Communist Party, local leadership positions etc., and this led to a mass process of nativization in government, the judiciary, trade unions, newly established educational institutions and industry throughout the newly formed Soviet state.

To understand this policy, one must understand the Communist leadership's views on the nationality issue in the USSR. Previously, the multiethnic Russian Empire of the Tsars had, of course, made no allowances for the ethnic identity of the myriad peoples who were considered *inorodtsy* (internal alien races). Similarly, Marxist Socialism considered nationality to be an anachronistic form of social organization that would eventually disappear as the class affiliation of the proletariat rendered nationality meaningless. As the workers of the world were to unite and meld, Karl Marx argued that this borderless proletarian class would no longer be divided by national homelands or nationality.

Vladimir Lenin, however, had been given ample evidence of the growing importance of nationality to the multitude of ethno-national groups inhabiting the lands of the former Russian Empire during the Russian Civil War. Throughout the borderlands of the fallen empire, national movements for independence had arisen, from Khokand in the Uzbek-dominated Fergana Valley, to Finland. In light of these manifestations of national aspiration among the non-Russian populations of the Russian Empire/USSR, Lenin appears to have recognized the importance of nationalism and its links to territory. He fought against his fellow Communists in order to create a federal system of territorial autonomies that would recognize ethnicity. Lenin felt that an attempt to create a homogenous proletarian state united on the basis of the Russian language (the obvious choice for a *lingua Sovietica*) would make the revolution inaccessible to the various non-Russian ethnic groups and nationalities of the new state and would antagonize their national leaderships.

Lenin eventually won the day, even against Stalin, the Commissar of Nationalities (whose Caucasian origins may have made him more acutely aware of the problems that might arise from promoting ethnic identity in the new state), and the Soviet leadership engaged in a process that was to be one of the most extravagant, state-sponsored, territorial recognitions of ethnicity and nationality in history. In an attempt to reach the shamanist Evenk reindeer herder, Buddhist Kalmyk shepherd, Ingush Muslim mountaineer, Georgian peasant and Uzbek cotton farmer, a nationwide bureaucracy was established to develop the languages of even the smallest and undeveloped of "nations" in the USSR. These new state-sponsored languages, many of which received an alphabet for the first time (such as Tajik, Kyrgyz, Turkmen, Kalmyk, Ingush, and Buryat), would be used as vehicles for introducing the proletarian ideology of the Communist Party to the remotest corner of the USSR. Lenin felt that "By 'fostering national cultures' and creating national autonomies, national schools, national languages and national cadres, the Bolsheviks would overcome national distrust and reach national audiences."[25]

All of these policies of national identity construction (*natsional'noe stroitelstvo* in Soviet parlance) were to be territorially based. A Soviet citizen who left his or her ethno-territorial unit lost the prerogatives that would automatically come from living in his titular SSR, ASSR, Autonomous District (*oblast*) or Autonomous Territory (*okrug*). This was to have the effect of territorializing identity in these regional constructs throughout the USSR and discouraging migration. Anatoly Khazanov writes "Not only did Soviet legislation make ethnic affiliation ascriptive. In addition, it directly connected nationality with territory, linked ethnic status with the degree of ethno-territorial autonomy, and made cultural autonomy dependent on the level of corresponding autonomous formation."[36] A 1923 description of this "Bantuzation" of the former Russian Empire proclaimed:

> The majestic ancient mosques of Samarkand…the white minarets of Azerbaijan; a colorful Armenian tower; a strikingly Oriental building from Kirghizia; a solid Tatar house covered with grillwork; some picturesque chinoiserie from the far east; and further on the *yurts* and *chums* from Bashkiria, Mongol-Buriatia, Kalmykia, Oiratia, Iakutia, the Khakass, the Ostiak and Samoed; all of it surrounded by the artificially created mountains and villages of Dagestan, the Caucasian Highland Republic and Chechnya…They have *their own* flag; signs in *their own* language; maps of *their own* expanses and borders; diagrams *of their own* riches. Nationality, individuality and uniqueness are forcefully emphasized everywhere.[26]

Westerners are quick to impugn the Bolshevik leadership's motives for creating this vast hierarchy of ethnically-based territorial units in the USSR. Most pass it off as a nefarious attempt at *divide et impera* (especially in the Central Asian context) or as a propaganda device meant to attract sympathy from abroad. There does, however, appear to have been a genuine attempt by the Soviet leadership to use territoriality-based positive discrimination programs to modernize some of the most socially, economically and culturally underdeveloped ethnic groups of the USSR. The aim was to introduce them to the benefits of the revolution. Why else grant a small, relatively unknown ethnic group in Siberia, the Yakuts, political, judicial, and educational prerogatives over a vast territorial unit of their own (with considerable natural resources) if not to include this people in the Soviet process? No program better exemplifies the Bolsheviks' real desire to spread modernization to non-Russian ethnies and nations in the Soviet Union and extend to them the perceived benefits of the revolution than the policy of *korenizatsiia*. *Korenizatsiia* was, in addition, the answer to a threat that Lenin feared—"Great Russian chauvinism"—for it established quotas and preferential treatment for all *korennye narody* (rooted-native peoples) in their own ethno-territorial autonomies, to the exclusion of Russians. In the Crimean ASSR there was no mistaking Lenin's intentions. The Crimean Tatars, as the *korennoi narod* of the Crimea, were to receive the full benefits of "nativization". The policy of *korenizatsiia*, developed by Lenin, and grudgingly supported by Stalin until the late 1920s, contributed to the territorialization and consolidation of Crimean Tatar nationality by supporting the development of the Crimean Tatar language, increasing the national intelligentsia and formally institutionalizing ethnicity in the Crimean state apparatus.

Korenizatsiia *in the Crimean ASSR*

The average Crimean Tatar living in the Crimean ASSR in the 1920s was exposed to *korenizatsiia* on many levels. While collectivization may have wreaked havoc on large landowners in the Crimea, landless Crimean Tatars, as recipients of *korenizatsiia*, often stood to benefit from this process. A Soviet propaganda account from 1934, for example, trumpets the success of the Soviet state in defending the rights of Crimean Tatar peasants in comparison to the Tsarist regime as follows:

> The Simeiz [a village in the south] Tatars who originally owned the lands here and who were driven out by the tsarist government during the nineteenth century, were forced to surrender all their vineyards to a powerful landed proprietor by the name of Martsov, who paid for these fertile tracts only a fraction of their value, while the Tatars had to move their villages to the stony hillsides.
>
> The October Revolution redressed the wrongs of the Tatar peasants and restored them the vineyards of which they had been deprived by Martsov. Now these Simeiz vineyards belong to a *kolkhoz* [collective farm] and there is no longer a single individual farmer in the village of Simeiz, all 82 farms, of which 29 were Tatar, have united into one large collective farm.[27]

Universal education was also introduced in the Crimea and all Crimean Tatars were taught in their native language through a score of new textbooks written in Crimean Tatar (with Arabic characters initially and later in Cyrillic alphabet). While only 17 per cent of Crimean Tatar girls were enrolled in schools in 1917, the Soviets could proudly proclaim that the number had risen to 44.9 per cent by 1928 and this percentage was to increase dramatically in the following decade.[28] Those Crimean Tatars who graduated from school could go on to attend the Tauride University in the ASSR capital of Simferopol (this town was now officially known also by its ancient Tatar name as Ak Mecit, or White Mosque). There they could study Crimean Tatar history, language and culture in the newly established Oriental Institute. Anthropologists and linguists who were trained at the institution went throughout the Crimean countryside systematically collecting Tatar poems, legends, and stories, which were reproduced in illustrated volumes. Crimean Tatar ethnographic museums were also established in Evpatoriia (for the Nogais) and Yalta (for the coastal Tats). In addition, the Soviet government supported considerable archeological research in the peninsula that explored the ruins of Eski Kirim (the old regional capital of the Golden Horde) and the mountain fortress of the Crimean Goths at Mangup Kale. In school and university, Tatar students were taught that their roots (*koreny*) could be traced back to the primordial Scythian, Greek, Italian, Kipchak and Mongol inhabitants of the Crimea who forged their own bloodlines (especially the Tats). Prior to this, the Tatars had very little reason to identify with the Greek and other classical monuments in the Crimea, which were claimed by the peninsula's Orthodox population.

All of this Crimean Tatar cultural development had a Socialist subtext, of course. The Tatars' *mirza* nobility class, for example, was depicted as "bourgeois exploiters of the Tatar toiling class", the Ottomans were "imperialists bent on enslaving the Crimea's peasantry", and the mullahs were "social parasites who played on the simple Muslims' superstitions". The ultimate aim was to subtly inculcate the Crimean Tatars to the ideas of the Revolution through their own state sponsored language. Many former Young Tatars, and members of the Milli Firka nationalist party who had fought for modernization, education, women's rights, and an end to the power of the mullahs, genuinely identified with the ideals being propagated by the Soviet system via the vehicle of their own language. In addition to rooting the Crimean Tatar culture to the Crimean ASSR, the Crimean Tatar language was promoted as a state language of the Republic along with Russian. Soviet linguists, such as V.V. Radlov and the famed Crimean Tatar Turkologist, Bekir Cobanzade, created a common Crimean Tatar grammar and language based on the central mountain dialect, which was a hybrid Nogai (Kipchak), Tat (Oghuz) language known as the *Orta Yolak* (Middle Road). While the Young Tatars had begun this linguistic unification movement, it was the Soviets who produced scores of grammar books, readers, children's school books and texts in a common Crimean Tatar for students in technical universities, the government bureaucracy, farming collectives, and scholarly programs. In the process, they made considerable progress towards homogenizing the Crimean Tatar language and people.

For the first time, hundreds of books were also made available to Crimean Tatars in their native language and journals and newspapers in Tatar flourished. A Crimean Tatar had the choice of journals and papers such as *Eni*

Dunya (The New World), *Yas Kuvvet* (Young Strength), *Illeri* (In Front), *Koz Aydin* (Greetings), *Proliter Medeniyeti* (Proletarian Culture), *Kadinlik Sotsializm Elinda* (Women on the Road to Socialism), *Yas Lenindzhiler* (Young Leninists), *Kizil Krym* (The Red Crimea) and *Ilk Adim* (First Step).

Crimean Tatar was used in schools, libraries, theaters, museums and reading rooms throughout the peninsula. Newly established journals, newspapers, and books in the language contributed to the spread of mass literacy among the previously poorly educated Tatars by the 1930s. Alexander Solzhenitsyn wrote of this indigenization process as it was applied in the Crimea: "In the twenties, all those minority languages were encouraged; it was endlessly dinned into the Crimea that it was Tatar, Tatar, and nothing but Tatar; it even had the Arabic alphabet, and the signs were in Tatar."[29] A Soviet account describes *korenizatsiia* in the Crimea as follows:

> 343 primary schools and 12 secondary schools, where teaching was done in the Tatar language, were opened. Special Tatar technical schools (pedagogical, medical, village agriculture, artistic production, and others) were founded. Tatars went to study in factories and colleges. The Crimean Tatars were granted more privileges than other nationalities living in the Crimea. Their language, along with Russian, became the state language. The allocation of cultural work for the Tatar population was proportionally higher.[30]

A recent work similarly describes the course of *korenizatsiia* in the Crimea and its impact on the peninsula's *korennoi narod* as follows:

> The Crimean Tatars were actively included in all spheres of activity in the Crimean ASSR, their representatives grew in the organs of the Soviet apparatus; in 1926 in the Crimean Central Committee they [the Tatars] had 26 representatives, in the town soviets 280, in the village soviets 1,439 and from these 159 were representatives in the administration of the village soviets. It was at this time, in 1926, the course of *korenizatsiia* emerged and called for mandatory translation of the bureaucracy into the Crimean Tatar language and the preparation of cadres for the soviet party organs and also specialists.[31]

No one who visited the Crimean ASSR in the 1920s could fail to notice the distinctly *Tatar* nature of this autonomy. Paul Kolstoe writes of the Crimean ASSR as it existed from 1921 to the 1944 deportation of the Crimean Tatars: "at that time the autonomy was usually regarded as existing by virtue of the Crimean Tatars, even though they made up no more than a quarter of the population."[32] Proof of this can be seen in the fact that, despite their comparatively small numbers within the autonomy, the Crimean Tatar representation in Soviet and Party organs in the Crimean ASSR ranged from 30 to 60 per cent during the *korenizatsiia* period.[33]

All of these examples of national identity promotion in the unofficially Crimean Tatar ASSR were, of course, strictly controlled. Many of them were cultural. While the Soviet government supported native Crimean Tatar dance troupes (which produced "Sovietized" versions of traditional village dances), archeological expeditions into the pre-Mongol roots of the Tatars in the peninsula, and the development of vernacular Crimean Tatar into a state language, it tolerated no unsanctioned political manifestations of nationalism. All aspects of Crimean Tatar identity construction in the Crimean ASSR were to strictly follow the maxim "socialist in content, national in form". This government program of co-opting nationalism and channeling it off into harmless cultural directions has been described as a "licensing" of nationality. It was a tame, Soviet version of nationality that was permitted in the Crimean ASSR and various other ethnic republics and autonomous territories of the USSR.[34]

In the long term, the Soviet leadership expected the importance of cultural nationality to gradually diminish as ethnic/national groups throughout the Soviet Union were exposed to the ideas of the proletarian revolution in schools, party meetings, newspapers, and history textbooks. There were, in fact, two processes of identity construction underway simultaneously in the USSR during the 1920s. While "ephemeral" national identities were being constructed as a means of moving closer to the ultimate goal of ethnic blending (*slianiye*) between the various nations of the Soviet "Great Friendship of Nations", the Soviets were also constructing a more "permanent" transnational *homo sovieticus*.

The new Soviet man was to be "international" in outlook, a proletarian first and foremost, and only secondly a Soviet citizen of Uzbek, Russian, Kalmyk etc. background. Most importantly, the fully developed Soviet citizen was to identify with the Soviet *Rodina* (Homeland) first, and his micro-homeland second. As "the world's first workers' state" the greater Soviet homeland was to be the ultimate focus of loyalty for the workers and peasants of the various constructed autonomous territorial units of the USSR.

It should also be stated that the modern *homo sovieticus* was to be an atheist, for there was no place in the Soviet Union for religion, "the opiate of the masses". In the Crimea, as elsewhere in the Soviet Union, the religious facet of national identity was ruthlessly attacked between 1931 and 1936. Hundreds of mosques were closed; by 1938 there was not a single working mosque in the Crimea, according to Edige Kirimal.[35] In the newly established Crimean ASSR mullahs were condemned as "parasites" and deported to Siberia in the 1930s. Those who were outwardly religious were excluded from the Communist Party and local administrative positions even as the young were actively recruited into the "Godless Society" (by 1932 there were 42,000 *Allahsizler*—"Godless Zealots" in the Crimea).³⁶

In many ways, the Bolsheviks carried on the struggle against "feudal relics" (the conservative clergy) fought by the earlier Young Tatars and Milli Firka Tatar nationalists to its culmination, albeit with a ruthlessness that even the leftist Milli Firka party members would have shied away from. By administrative caveat Moscow also changed the Crimean Tatar alphabet from Arabic to Latin and then to Cyrillic in an effort to eradicate the Tatars' traditional alphabet with it religious implications and links to the Muslim *umma* beyond the borders of the USSR. With a simple decree, the Crimean Tatars were thus cut off from their religious past and from all works published in Arabic over the centuries. In essence, throughout the 1920s and 1930s, the Soviet regime was undermining their traditional Islamic basis of identity and replacing it with a secular identity based on Marxist materialism and nationalism.

Unintentionally, the Soviet regime also led to an increasing identification with the Crimea as a homeland-republic by the territory's state sponsored "native people", the Crimean Tatars. The identification with the Crimean ASSR as an emotional and bureaucratic homeland was certainly the result of policies enacted by the Crimean ASSR's nationalist leadership headed by the Tatar Veli Ibrahimov. As shall be seen, former Milli Firka members, such as Ibrahimov, who had since 1921 been co-opted into the Crimean ASSR government by the Soviet regime as part of its policy of *korenizatsiia*, took advantage of this program to enact many of the policies earlier formulated by the Milli Firka nationalists.

The Veli Ibrahimov Years

The so-called *Veliibrahimovshchina*, the years in which the wily Tatar nationalist Veli Ibrahimov was in power in the Crimea as the chairman of the Crimean Central Committee and Crimean Council of People's Commissars, is considered a halcyon period by today's Crimean Tatar nationalists. While Robert Kaiser points out that "National territory was for Stalin merely an empty container within which nations were created or destroyed through development or disappearance of their objective cultural features", the Crimean territory was certainly more than an "empty container" for Veli Ibrahimov and other ex-Milli Firka nationalists.³⁷ Although Ibrahimov may have genuinely been an internationalist and a Communist, he was certainly a crypto-nationalist as well. He used his position to promote many of the objectives of the

Milli Firka and indeed to directly recruit members of the earlier Crimean Tatar nationalist party into the Crimean ASSR administration. For seven years Ibrahimov was able to quietly promote Tatarization in the Crimea, always with the stated aim of Sovietizing the working Crimean Tatar peasant class. Under Lenin's watchful but tolerant eye, Ibrahimov was also able to use the state machinery at his disposal to actively work towards the goal of instilling in his more narrowly-defined countrymen, the Crimean Tatars, a sense of identification with the Crimea as a Fatherland. The Soviets had given Ibrahimov and his ex-Milli Firka colleagues access to state organs and institutions, such as mass media, and these were used to nationalize the Crimean Tatar masses as well as to Sovietize them. The Crimean Tatar national-Communists used this new power and medium to forge a mass-based sense of Crimean Tatar identity in ways the Young Tatars and Fatherland Society before them could not have dreamed of during the late Russian Imperial period.

This example of a local national Communist cadre using republic institutions to construct a distinctly Soviet national identity was not unusual in the Soviet Union of the 1920s. Philip Groder has written:

> The indigenous cadre was given an institutionalized monopoly on the public expression of ethnic identity, that is, it defined the ethnic markers that distinguish nationality. These markers were then central to communicating the socialist message in national cultural forms and propagandizing the populations being brought into the modern sector. For many Soviet citizens undergoing social mobilization the first sustained contact with the great traditions of their own ethnic group was in the form of this national-Soviet hybrid.[38]

In addition to his policies designed to disseminate a sense of Crimean Tatar national identity among his people, Ibrahimov also distributed land to Tatar peasants, long a desideratum of Crimean Tatar nationalists. Edige Kirimal points out that Ibrahimov also made plans for the "gradual repatriation of Crimean Turks from abroad."[39] Alan Fisher claims that Ibrahimov planned to offer amnesty to all Crimean Tatars who had emigrated to the Ottoman Empire in the nineteenth century and to encourage their participation in the development of the Crimea's economy.[40] This plan to return the Crimean Tatars from the diaspora was first mentioned at the end of an article published in *Krasnyi Krym* (The Red Crimea) in 1921 which is also interesting for its description of plans for *korenizatsiia* in the Crimea:

> The main nations inhabiting the Crimea are the Tatars, Russians and, in part, the Germans. All the remaining nations form insignificant minorities and groups around one of the three national groups having the nearest language...Of

all these nations, prior to the revolution, the Tatar were oppressed doubly as a hard working population and as internal aliens (*inorodtsy*). Therefore they remained backward, uncultured, and unyielding to the acceptance of a new life, which requires a certain economic and cultural level. What is necessary to give the Crimean Tatar masses the possibility of catching up with the rest of Soviet Russia? Transfer the center of important work to the native sphere. Allot land to the Tatar peasant. Factually introduce the native language to the Soviet establishment. Involve the local population in the administration of the native territory. Form cadres of Soviet workers from among the Tatars, return to the Crimea those Tatars forced by Tsarism to emigrate. These and other measures will create solid support among the Tatar population for Soviet authority.[41]

Significantly, land reform programs instituted during this period of "positive discrimination" towards the Crimea's indigenous population called for the establishment of "reservations" for the return of Crimean Tatars "expelled by Tsarism".[42] This plan to return emigrés to the Crimea may have had the Soviet center's tacit support. One has but to look to the Soviet state-sponsored return of Armenians from Turkey to the Armenian SSR for another example of just such a policy.[43]

The Soviet government-sponsored repatriation of Armenians from Turkey was a subplot to its larger schemes involving the Republic of Turkey, and this may have also been the case in the Crimea. There are reasons for believing that the Crimean ASSR was established, in part, as a result of foreign policy directives aimed at Turkey. At the time of the Crimean ASSR's founding, for example, this autonomous republic was described by the Soviets as "yet one more brilliantly flashing beacon destined to attract all the best yearnings and aspirations of the multi-million East now under the slave yoke of the international imperialists."[44]

This would not be the first time that the Soviets had created a national autonomy based on foreign policy exigencies. The Circassians of the northwestern Caucasus who numbered only 200,000 in 1917, for example, were given four autonomous ethnic territories in the USSR in an obvious effort to influence the large Circassian diaspora of millions living in Turkey, Jordan, Syria and Palestine/Israel.[45] Sultan Galiev, the Volga Tatar Communist who called for the establishment of the Crimean ASSR, was certainly aware of the "five million" Crimean Tatar émigrés said to be living in Turkey. In addition, with its long history of ties to Turkey, the Crimea could serve as a springboard for spreading the Communist revolution to the Muslim Middle East. Alexandre Bennigsen claims that Sultan Galiev urged that Communism should be spread abroad, and said that the Soviet republic of the Crimea "ought to become the window of Communism opening towards the East, and first of all towards Turkey."[46]

At the time this may not have been as far fetched a scheme as it might seem today. In the 1920s the Turkish Socialist Party, the Socialist Party of the Workers and Peasants of Turkey, and the International Association of Workers and the Turkish Communist Party all appeared in the newly established Republic of Turkey just after Ataturk's war of liberation. In this period, when the Bolsheviks had real expectations of spreading the Communist revolution to Western Europe and beyond, the granting of autonomous status to the Crimea may have been done, in part, as a showcase for Turkish domestic consumption. By showing the Turks the benefits fellow Turkic Muslims received in the USSR, the Soviet regime hoped to contribute to the spread of Communism in Turkey. In addition, Sultan Galiev would have known that approximately one third of the Turkish Communist Party consisted of Crimean Tatars.[47]

Neither Sultan Galiev's dream of spreading Communism to the Muslim world nor Veli Ibrahimov's grandiose plan to return Crimean Tatars from the diaspora to the Crimea were, however, destined to be fulfilled. By the late 1920s Vladimir Lenin was dead, the liberal New Economic Policy (NEP) period was ending, and the Kremlin had a new leader who (correctly!) saw the burgeoning national identities being promoted throughout the USSR's republics and autonomies via *korenizatsiia* as a centrifugal threat to Soviet authority and plans for creating a homogenous Soviet Man. Lenin's successor, Josef Stalin, was to launch a bloody campaign in the late 1920s and early 1930s that would decimate the national Communist cadres of the various republics and smaller territories throughout the USSR and bring a halt to the "blossoming of nations" in this vast land.

The Fall of Veli Ibrahimov

The catalyst for the fall of Veli Ibrahimov stemmed from another one of the Crimean party boss's plans that was later criticized by Stalin as an example of "bourgeois nationalism", namely his plan to re-Tatarize the Crimean steppe. Prior to this period, the majority of Crimean Tatar state and collective farms was in the Crimean mountains and foothills of the south.[48] According to a census of 1926, there were more than twenty-six villages on the southern coast that had Crimean Tatar populations of more than 1,000.[49] The Crimean Tatar population in the largely Russian, Ukrainian and German steppe, by contrast, was small, while districts in the south (such as the Yalta district, which was 72 per cent Tatar at the end of the nineteenth century) had a surplus Crimean Tatar population.[50]

Between 1925 and 1927, Ibrahimov had established two dozen villages for 20,000 Crimean Tatars estimated to be returning from the Dobruca region of Bulgaria and Romania (a prime area of migration over the last century) on the Crimean steppeland that had been largely abandoned by the Nogais during the 1860 emigration.

In addition, Ibrahimov planned to move Crimean Tatars from the crowded Yaliboyu coast and Yaila Mountains to settle in the open plains of the northern Crimea in an effort to regain this area for his people. As this plan was being implemented, Ibrahimov was informed that Moscow intended to settle several thousand European Jews from Belorussia on the Yaliboyu coast, and even more on the Crimean steppe. According to one estimate, approximately 400,000 Jews were slated to be settled in the Crimea and this would have certainly created a whole new set of ethnic tensions in the peninsula.[51] The local Crimean Tatars, Russians, and Ukrainians were, of course, quite opposed to these plans to create a Jewish national homeland in the Crimean ASSR.

After being informed of Stalin's plans, Ibrahimov sent a protest to Moscow and subsequently began to set up administrative roadblocks to prevent the mass settlement of Jews in the Crimea (for which he was later branded an "anti-Semite"). According to a recent account, the "Veli Ibrahimovists" attempted to conceal the amount of empty land available in the Crimean steppe from the central authorities and Ibrahimov established a "a special land fund for Crimean Tatar emigrants from Turkey and those to be resettled from within (the Crimea)."[52] In addition, Ibrahimov began the transfer of as many as 8,000 Crimean Tatar peasants from Karasu Bazar, Bahcesaray and Simferopol-Ak Mecit to the steppe region in an effort to preempt Moscow's plans for the steppe.

When news of his activities reached Moscow, the leader was accused of supporting Crimean Tatar *kulaks* (wealthy peasants), and *mirzas* (an elite class that had been wiped out prior to this time), to which he is reported to have replied "Among the Tatars there are no rich or poor, there is but one nation."[53] It soon became apparent to Stalin that Ibrahimov and his indigenous Tatar leadership cadre were involved in a program that could best be described as "nationalist in content and socialist in form."

Ibrahimov's nationalist program and his stand in defense of it could not have come at a worse time. Having recently consolidated power, Josef Stalin was just beginning his statewide campaign against "nationalist deviations" (which had begun with a clamp down on Ibrahimov's powerful Volga Tatar sponsor Sultan Galiev), and Ibrahimov was arrested and subsequently executed in May of 1928.

Ibrahimov thus had the dubious honor of being one of the first nationalist Communist leaders purged in a nationwide campaign that would virtually wipe out the native cadres throughout the USSR who had collaborated with the Bolsheviks in the 1920s. It had become obvious to Stalin that the native leaders of the Soviet Union's various territorial "homelands" were now worse than superfluous: their policies of nativization were a threat to the unity of the Soviet state. Having established firm control over the various nationalities via these very native intermediaries, Stalin cynically disposed of this element by the tens of thousands in a bloodletting that was to leave the republics and autonomies of the USSR in stunned submission for decades to come.

In the aftermath of Ibrahimov's execution, as many as 3,500 of the newly developed Crimean Tatar leadership and intelligentsia were executed or exiled. Among these were some of the brightest former Milli Firka members, Young Tatars and *Jadids*, such as Gasprinsky's companion Seyit Abdullah Ozenbasli, executed in 1924. The great Crimean Tatar Turkologist Bekir Cobanzade was also executed in 1937. This gifted scholar's poems of the Crimean homeland may have been too narrowly nationalistic for the times. One poem of interest addressed the perennial problem of Crimean Tatar emigration and captures some of Cobanzade's passion. In a work from 1917, Cobanzade wrote:

> Ah, my neighbors emigrate,
> As they drink their last cup of coffee,
> I would like to be there so I could say "Stay"!
> So I could say "There is nothing like your homeland."

Many of the purged writers, scholars and political leaders had willingly joined the Communist Party to fight against obscurantism within their own society, only to be betrayed by the very system they looked towards to improve their people's lives. The purge of this intelligentsia was a terrible blow to the Crimean Tatar nation. Subsequently, a new class of less educated Tatars who were less willing to confront Moscow on nationalist issues made their way into the Crimean ASSR administration.

The purging of the nationalist intelligentsia was followed shortly thereafter by another tragedy. In the 1930s tens of thousands of Crimean Tatars were deported to Siberia as part of Stalin's brutal collectivization campaign. This had the effect of turning many segments of Crimean Tatar society against Soviet rule on the eve of World War II. A Russian witness to the deportation of thousands of Tatars in the 1930s (in many ways a rehearsal for the later mass deportation of 1944) wrote:

Whole villages of Crimean peasants were liquidated. Thousands of people were herded behind the barbed wire of deportation camps. People who had grown up in a mild, southern climate and who had never before left their native mountains and sea coast were transplanted to the taiga and the tundra and began to die off even during the first stages. This was not the application of some sort of mass measures, but the physical destruction, the merciless and senseless destruction of a whole people.⁵⁴

The Continued "Rooting" of the Crimean Tatars in the Crimean ASSR

In the aftermath of the purge of the "Veliibrahmiovists", the executed leader was accused of having had contacts with Crimean Tatars from the diaspora with the aim of establishing Turkish influence in the Crimea. In addition, Ibrahimov's plans to Tatarize the Crimean steppe were canceled in part due to the fact that the Soviet authorities felt that the Yaliboyu and Yaila Tatars were unsuited to the conditions of this open plain. In this regard, the new Crimean ASSR administration, headed once again by a Crimean Tatar Communist, Mehmet Kubay (a clear indicator that *korenizatsiia* had not completely ended in the Crimea), may have been correct. For its part, the Soviet regime also decided to cancel its plans to settle the Crimean plain with European Jews (in 1934 a Jewish autonomy was created in the Soviet Far East, known as Birobidzhan) and it was largely Ukrainians and Russians who settled this steppe in the following decades.

In the years that followed, the situation of the Crimean Tatars deteriorated as many of the aspects of *korenizatsiia* gradually disappeared in the 1930s. There were, for example, the above mentioned purges of Crimean society in which some 30,000–40,000 Crimean *"kulaks"*, intellectuals, and party officials were deported, and private property was collectivized from 1931–34, causing tremendous hardship and famine. But the idea that the Crimean Tatars were the "rooted" *korennoi narod* in "their" republic did not cease to be subtly propagated by the Crimean bureaucratic machinery.

While Veli Ibrahimov, who has largely gone unlauded by modern day Crimean Tatar nationalists, had overseen the final nationalization and territorialization of his ethnic community, his ideas continued to be inadvertently reinforced by subsequent Soviet policies in the 1930s. The Crimean Tatars, for example, were identified in their *propisky* (internal passports) by their nationality (there was no "Soviet" option to match the "Yugoslav" choice of nationality assumed by many Bosnian Muslims, for example, in Communist Yugoslavia). They also continued to have ethnic privileges (albeit in a curtailed form) in the Crimean ASSR based on their unofficial status as the native population of this autonomy. In school, they learned the history of their narrowly-defined republic-homeland, and the Crimean Tatar language and identity were promoted in the region via, for example, dance troupes, literature, and Tatar language media.

Even the most uneducated Crimean Tatar *kolkhoznik* (collective farm worker) living in the most isolated farm in the Yaila hinterland would have been aware of the fact that the Crimean ASSR was his homeland and that the Crimean Tatars were an ethnically-defined people with special prerogatives on this territory. Those who left the borders of this micro-*rodina* effectively lost their special status. By the late 1920s, Yuri Slezkine writes, "The administrative units created just a few years before in order to accommodate pre-existing nationalities were now the most important defining feature of those nationalities."[55] Rieks Smeets further points out that "Recent history confirms that the Soviet Union with its specific approach to minorities functioned rather as an incubator of nationalism than as a melting pot for nations."[56]

The Crimean ASSR as it functioned from 1921 to 1944 certainly acted as a promoter and incubator for Crimean Tatar nationalism. While it can be safely argued that the ASSR was not officially established as a Crimean *Tatar* autonomy, all the policies of *korenizatsiia* benefited this group the most. The Tatars, as the Crimea's state-sponsored "rooted people", certainly identified the peninsula as their official homeland more than the local Russian and Ukrainian population. This was the result of intentional government policy and was carried out in the Crimean ASSR right up until the advent of World War II.

It should also be mentioned that the Crimea's unique geography as an "island" further facilitated this compact territory's construction as a homeland in the Tatars' common imagination. The sprawling republic of Kazakhstan or the gerrymandered republic of Uzbekistan (to name just a couple of examples), by contrast, were more artificial, non-historical territorial constructs and less effective as national symbols.

These policies all had the effect of territorializing Crimean Tatar communal identity, and administratively and psychologically "rooting" this people in their state-sponsored territory. Shirin Akiner describes the territorializing effects of Soviet nationality policies as they applied to ethno-national groups in the Soviet Union:

> The histories of the titular national groups were framed as histories of their respective republics, thus emphasizing the symbiotic bond between the land and the people. Maps, geography textbooks and photographic albums further

strengthened this link, fostering a sense of personal identification with the contours of the republic, and at the same time, marking off this territory from that of other, neighboring republics.[57]

For the most part, the Crimean Tatars of today, who make their claims to the territory of the peninsula in "Sovietese" (they still use the term *korennoi narod* to legitimize their superior claims to this disputed land), overlook the role of the USSR in completing the forging of their modern national identity and administratively rooting it to its secularly-defined homeland. They do, however, recognize the fact that Islam as a competing base for communal identity among their people was destroyed only during the Soviet period. During the subsequent decades, a whole generation of Crimean Tatars was raised in the officially atheist Soviet Crimea constructing its links to territory on the basis of a uniquely Soviet and secular version of nationalism.

This new territorialized, secular identity of Soviet citizens of Crimean Tatar nationality was not to be established on the religious laws of the Qur'an, or solely on the basis of traditional romantic nationalism of the West, but was primarily based on Marxist-Leninism and the policy of *korenizatsiia*. The process that began with Gasprinsky's attacks on emigration from a larger Turkic homeland was completed in the 1930s as a whole generation of Crimean Tatars came to see the Crimean ASSR as their people's Socialist *vatan* or *rodina* (most spoke Russian by this point). A Tatar who was born in the Tsarist Crimea during the Great Migration of 1861 to the Ottoman *ak toprak* would have, in a life span, lived to see the complete redefinition of his ethno-religious community's links to its native soil. The Soviet period thus saw the culmination of the development of a territorialized nationalist identity among this people that has retained its communal hold on the Crimean Tatar masses to this day.

The communal memory of the Crimean ASSR and the Tatars' unique position in this autonomous republic was to remain with them during the long years of exile in the Soviet republics of other peoples, such as the Uzbeks, and is key to an understanding the Tatars' half-decade long struggle to return to their Crimean *vatan*. This memory was also to strongly influence the Crimean Tatars' demands for voting quotas and special acknowledgment of their unique status as the peninsula's indigenous population following their return to the region after 1989.

Stalin and the Crimean ASSR

There was, however, a certain arbitrariness associated with this state sponsored, territorial-nation development in the Soviet Union. Ethnic groups, such as the Nogai Tatars of the Kuban and Uighurs who were *not* granted autonomous ethno-territories, did not develop territoriality in the same way as those that did. Most importantly, those who did receive autonomies were not always guaranteed that this status would be permanent. Borders and the ranking of territories fluctuated in the USSR depending on internal and external political exigencies. The Crimean ASSR as a showpiece to Communists in Turkey, for example, certainly lost its value as a "beacon" for Turkish Communists after Ataturk outlawed the Turkish Communist Party in the newly established Turkish Republic. In the Soviet federal system, where citizens received state sponsored benefits based on their territorial-national status, the arbitrary demotion of a nation's territorial unit from an SSR to a lesser ranked ASSR, for example, directly impacted the titular nationality. This demotion process could be taken a step further. Put bluntly, "if the legitimacy of an ethnic community depended on the government's grant of territory, then the withdrawal of that grant would automatically 'denationalize' that community."[58] Stalin defined a nation as "a historically constituted, stable community of people, formed on the basis of common language, *territory* [emphasis mine], economic life and psychological make-up manifested in a common culture."[59] In an ominous clause, however, Stalin qualified this definition by stating that if even one of these characteristics was absent, then "the nation ceases to be a nation."

On May 18, 1944, mechanized divisions of the NKVD (The People's Commissariat of Internal Affairs, the progenitor to the KGB) surrounded the Crimean Tatar villages and suburbs of the Crimea and loaded this entire national group onto cattle trains bound for the vast steppe and desert republics of Soviet Central Asia. Overnight the Yaila Mountains, the Yaliboyu coast and the parts of the Crimean steppe still inhabited by Tatars were brutally cleansed of their populations. In one night, half a century of homeland and national identity construction begun by a young idealist who dreamed of modernizing his dying people by means of a humble printing press in Bahcesaray was eradicated. With the loss of their territory, a prerequisite for a group to be recognized as a nation according to Stalin's definition of the concept, the Crimean Tatars had quite simply been "denationalized" and no longer officially existed in the "Great Friendship of Nations". No longer a state-sponsored *korennoi narod*, this "rootless" non-nation was scattered throughout the vast republics of Central Asia and, to a lesser extent, Siberia. Using the vast Orwellian resources at his disposal Stalin had, in perhaps a moment of administrative caprice, wiped out the remnants of some of the oldest inhabitants of the Black Sea shores and consigned this people to death and assimilation.

Dispersed far from their peninsular homeland on the Black Sea, those Crimean Tatars who survived the horrors of deportation were to begin to rebuild their lives in a strange land populated by Uzbek oasis dwellers, Kazakh shepherds, and Tajik farmers. The level of cultural development in this Soviet hinterland made up of the dry expanses of the Kizil Kum desert, the wide steppes of Kazakhstan and the unforgiving Pamir Mountains of Tajikistan was far below that found in the Europeanized Crimean Peninsula.

The Crimean Tatars' new homes were to be found in primitive mud huts, barracks and dugouts surrounding the simple *kishlaks* (villages) and factory towns of Central Asia. The stunned survivors of "The *Deportatsiia*" would have to adapt to life as low-paid factory workers, coal miners, day laborers and menial workers in cities and villages strewn, for the most part, throughout eastern Uzbekistan. Towns like the dreary industrial village of Circik at the foot of the brown Chaktal mountains, the poor village of Yangi Yul in the suburbs of the Uzbekistan SSR's capital Tashkent, the ancient caravan city of Samarkand (which was gradually being enveloped by factories) plus a variety of towns previously unknown to the Crimean Tatars, such as Margilan, Namengan, Fergana, Andijan, Angren and Gulistan, were to be their homes.

The devastated Crimean Tatar community was to spend half a century in this land during the so-called *ikinci surgun* ("second exile", the first being the nineteenth-century emigrations to the Ottoman Empire). One cannot understand the contemporary, post-Soviet identity of the Crimean Tatars and their struggle to reclaim their rights without first comprehending the ways in which this traumatic event determined and shaped the Crimean Tatars' entire understanding of themselves and their homeland since 1944.

6

SURGUN

THE CRIMEAN TATAR EXILE IN CENTRAL ASIA

The defining event in twentieth-century Crimean Tatar history is the brutal deportation of this entire people to Central Asia in the closing days of World War II. More than any other event, the removal of this small nation from a land it had come to define as its *natsional'naia rodina* (national homeland) under the first two decades of Soviet rule has shaped the Crimean Tatars' contemporary national identity. For two generations the Tatars worked in the factories, mines and industrial centers of a Central Asian landscape that was in many ways different from their peninsular homeland on the Black Sea. This experience of deportation and living in the Central Asia during the *ikinci surgun* ("second exile") continues to shape the modern Crimean Tatars' language, customs, labor skills, gender relations, political activities and views of themselves and their community.

No chapter in Crimean Tatar history is as hotly contested as that which charts the events that led to the mass deportation. Soviet accounts from the late 1940s are clear in their indictment of the Crimean Tatar people as a nation of traitors to the Soviet *rodina* and leave no room for doubt concerning the reasons for their expulsion. After their deportation (along with that of several other small Soviet nations, including the Chechens and Ingush) an article appeared in the Soviet newspaper *Izvestiia* which announced:

> During the Great Patriotic War when the people of the USSR were heroically defending the honor and independence of the Fatherland in the struggle against the German-Fascist invaders, many Chechens and Crimean Tatars, at

the instigation of German agents joined volunteer units organized by the Germans and together with German troops engaged in armed struggle against units of the Red Army... meanwhile the main mass of the population of the Chechen Ingush and Crimean ASSRs took no counteraction against these betrayers of the Fatherland.[1]

The opinion that the Crimean Tatars had betrayed the Soviet homeland during World War II was widespread throughout the Soviet period and has not died to this day. While visiting a memorial to the deportation recently built by the Tatar returnees in the center of Simferopol, a Crimean Tatar Red Army veteran pointed out to me the recently painted swastikas and anti-Tatar graffiti on this modest edifice to his people's suffering. Crimean Tatar cemeteries in the peninsula are also routinely defaced with Nazi graffiti. Long after the Soviet Union has ended and most of Europe has come to terms with the events of Second World War, the Crimean Tatars of the twenty-first century continue to be saddled with the stigma of *izmeniky rodiny* (traitors to the homeland) by their detractors.

Not surprisingly, Crimean Tatar nationalists refute Soviet claims that their people betrayed the USSR during World War II. The Tatars see in the deportation a more sinister plot to complete the process of creating a "Crimea without Crimean Tatars" that began with the "expulsion" of their ancestors in the great migrations of the eighteenth and nineteenth centuries. The Crimean Tatar nationalist leader Edige Kirimal, who was vitally involved in events in the region during World War II (as a self-proclaimed Crimean Turk), claimed:

> Soviet propaganda tries to justify before world opinion the liquidation of the autonomous Crimean Republic and the deportation of the Turkish population from the peninsula by qualifying this measure as a punishment deserved for "universal betrayal of the Soviet government". Nevertheless, vast evidence proves that the charge of "universal betrayal" only served as a pretext for earning out a long-prepared plan devised by Moscow to clear the peninsula completely of the Turkish population...In view of the foregoing, we are bound to state that the deportation of the whole Turkish population from the Crimea was actually the final step in the extermination of the Crimean Turks by Moscow, started in 1921/22 by deliberately provoked famine and by various measures for that purpose during the period between 1928 and 1941. The real cause of this crime, unheard of in history, was the Russian wish to transform the peninsula into a stronghold and one of the strategic bases for the aggressive aims of Soviet Russia.[2]

In light of such diametrically opposed interpretations of war-time events in the Crimea, a brief analysis of the Crimean Tatars' role during the Nazi invasion of the USSR during World War II is a prerequisite for understanding the causes for the traumatic forced removal of this people from their homeland and their continued stigmatization to this day.

Crimean Tatar Activities During the German Invasion of the Crimean ASSR

The German *blitzkrieg* on the Soviet Union's western marches, which aimed to exterminate Communism and topple the world's first "workers' state", caught Soviet leader Josef Stalin by complete surprise. Hitler's fast moving *Panzer* tank divisions and *Luftwaffe* airforce appear to have rolled back the poorly led Red Army divisions with ease in the early summer of 1941. Throughout that summer, the Red Army desperately mobilized millions of Soviet citizens from all nationalities to halt the progress of the seemingly invincible *Wehrmacht*. Soviet sources claim that in the process approximately 20,000 able bodied Crimean Tatars were mobilized (from a total national population at that time consisting of approximately 218,000, i.e. almost 10 per cent of the total Crimean Tatar population) and sent to the front against the German forces.[3] In the initial days of the war, Soviet losses were exceptionally high and, as the German army cut through Belorussia and the Ukraine towards the Crimean Peninsula, entire Soviet armies were encircled by the fast moving German forces and captured. The defeat of the Red Army has been described as a "great round up" and on two occasions Soviet armies with as many as 600,000 men in them were surrounded and captured. During this process, Soviet sources point out that "Many of these [20,000 drafted] Crimean Tatars gave their lives in the struggle against the Hitlerite invaders on both Crimean soil and on other fronts."[4]

On October 21, 1941, the German 11th army broke through the superior Soviet defenses at the narrow Perekop Isthmus linking the Crimea to the Ukrainian mainland and forced its way into the peninsula. The Soviet 55th army retreated in headlong flight towards the fortress city of Sevastopol in the southwest and towards Kerch in the southeast. According to German accounts, thousands of Soviet prisoners of war fell into enemy hands during the Soviet retreat across the Crimean steppe. As the Red Army evacuated Kerch and dug in for a heroic defense at Sevastopol, the Romanian Mountain Corps (the Romanians were German allies in the war) and the German 11th army occupied the bulk of the Crimean Peninsula.

According to Crimean Tatar historian Necip Adulhamitoglu, thousands of Tatars serving in the Red Army were captured by the Germans at this time as whole Russian armies (most notably General Andrey Vlasov's army) surrendered to the seemingly invincible enemy forces. Many of the Crimean Tatars captured were taken to prisoner of war camps where the mortality rate was exceptionally high.

Although the Nazis had initially called for the murder of all "Asiatic inferiors" (Hitler considered "Mongols" and Tatars to be *Untermenschen*—subhumans who were even lower on the race scale than the despised Slavs), in addition to that of the Jews and Communists, Hitler's generals in the field began to revise this hasty policy when the Red Army began to put up a more determined resistance before Moscow, Stalingrad and Leningrad. In a sharp reversal of Hitler's genocidal racial policies, the pragmatic German high command "realists" began recruiting from among the Soviet prisoners in 1942. In this fashion the German army created several distinct support armies from the groups of Soviet prisoners of war. Most of those in these armies were ethnic Russians.

As news of the Crimean Tatar prisoners' fate reached members of the large Crimean Tatar émigré diaspora in Turkey (Turkey was technically neutral at this time but was being courted by Germany as an ally), leaders of this community used Turkey's history of good relationships with the Germans to arrange a visit to members of their nationality being held in German prison camps in Poland and the Crimea. A message sent from Turkey to Germany (and discovered in Berlin in the final days of the war by the Soviets) introduced the Dobrucan Tatar nationalist Mustecip Fazil Ulkusal and his companion Edige Kirimal to the German high command and announced that:

> Two men—the lawyer Mustecip Fazil and Edige Kirimal—will be arriving to you. They have a project to offer the Germans that will be of help in the Crimea and, at the same time, it will be beneficial to the Crimean Turks...Both of these men are completely trustworthy people. I request that you send them to the Crimea and use them there in German-Turkish interests.[5]

These two "Crimean Turk" nationalist leaders succeeded in obtaining the release of their Crimean Tatar countrymen from the German prisoner of war camps and enrolled them in an independent Crimean support legion for the Nazi *Wehrmacht*. According to Crimean Tatar, Soviet and German sources, this legion eventually consisted of eight battalions with a total of 20,000 soldiers.[6] A historian who has analyzed wartime collaboration between Soviet citizens in POW camps and the Germans claimed that "The captors simply handed out German uniforms and only the foolhardy refused."[7] Kirimal supports this claim and states "Officially they were volunteers, but they had almost no other choice because the majority were recruited from among prisoners of war facing starvation or death from disease in German camps in Simferopol and Nikolayev."[8] Many of the Crimean Tatar "collaborators" were utilized in the Crimea by the German army, which favored this nationality over the Slavs in the peninsula. As in other areas occupied by the *Wehrmacht*, where local non-Slavic populations had suffered from the horrors of collectivization, de-kulakization, purges and other excesses of Stalinism, many Crimean Tatars initially saw the Germans as liberators and remembered their positive treatment at Germans' hands during World War I. In light of this feeling, Crimean Tatar nationalists from the Crimea and the Turkish and Romanian diasporas convinced the Nazi government to allow the formation of "Muslim Committees" in the peninsula that would allow the Crimean Tatars some form of autonomy. According to Alexander Nekrich "The establishment of the Muslim committees gave a boost not so much to collaboration with the occupation forces as to Tatar nationalism. Just as the Nazis wished to use the Tatar nationalists for their purposes, the nationalists in turn hoped to utilize the situation to advance their own purely Tatar interests, as they saw them."[9]

The formation of Muslim Committees in the peninsula headed by a Crimean Tatar nationalist who had fled to Turkey at the end of World War I, Ahmed Ozenbashli, led to rising tensions between the Russian population and the Tatars seeking autonomy under the Germans. As the Crimean Tatars were formed into *Schutzmannschaftsbataillonen* (police battalions) or *selbschutze* (self defense) brigades, often headed by exiles from Turkey or Romania, they were used by the German army to protect Tatar villages from partisan (Soviet guerilla) attacks. On occasion they were also deployed to track down Soviet partisans in the Yaila Mountains.

For the most part, however, the Tatar village defense units acted only to defend their villages from the partisans and rarely engaged in offensive operations against them. While the German forces may have had high expectations for the village defense units, they usually sided with whomever was strongest in the area and could not be automatically counted on by either the Germans or the partisans. Their prime concern appears to have been preventing partisans and German units from attacking Crimean Tatar villages.

Many Russian partisans in the Crimea began raiding Tatar villages in reprisal for the perceived collaboration of Crimean Tatars in certain districts with the Germans. A deep cleavage was subsequently formed between the two populations. Russian partisan commanders were known to shoot Tatars who attempted to join their bands and messages were repeatedly sent to Moscow from Russian partisan leaders in the Crimea referring to the Crimean Tatars' "treachery".[10]

There was not, however, any more unity among the Crimean Tatar community at this time than there was among the Slavic population and it should be mentioned that, after the Russians, the largest number of local guerrillas fighting among the Soviet partisans in the Crimea against the Germans were actually Crimean Tatars, not the more numerous Ukrainians. In 1944, approximately one fifth of the partisans in the Crimea were Crimean Tatars.[11] Several Crimean Tatar partisan commanders earned fame for their activities and the following account is typical of this group's activities:

> The Commissar of the Eastern formation was named captain Refat Mustafaev [prior to the war he was secretary of the Crimean regional party]. Here is one episode of the military actions of his formation. At the end of the 1943 the divisions of the second and third brigades destroyed the fascist garrison in Stary Krym (Eski Kirim) destroying on that occasion two tanks and 16 vehicles with gasoline and ammunition. The partisans occupied the building of the commander of the city police and threw grenades into the restaurant where the Hitlerites banqueted. One of the group seized the Gestapo jail and freed 46 Soviet patriots.[12]

As the war progressed, more and more Crimean Tatars actually joined the underground to attack German units that had begun seizing crops and supplies from the local population. The Tatar-inhabited Yaila Mountains, with their multitude of karstic caves for hiding weapons and winding roads for staging ambushes, were a prime region for launching guerrilla attacks against the occupying force. As the Crimean Tatars joined the Soviet partisans, it is not surprising that their villages suffered heavily from German reprisals. The following account is typical:

> Dozens of Crimean Tatars were shot in Alushta on the banks of the Demerci, in the foothills of the Kastel, in dozens in the villages of Ulu-Sala, Kizil Tash, Degirmen Koy, Tav-Bodrak, Saly and many others. In July 1988 the country learned from information from Tass [the Soviet News Agency] that in the partisan regions in the mountainous part of the Crimea all villages were burnt and a "dead zone" was created. Yes it actually happened. More than 70 villages were destroyed. In them dwelt more than 25% of the Tatar population of the Crimea. In these villages, in remote woodlands, in the mountains lived only Tatars.[13]

Most importantly, the German occupiers lost all Crimean Tatar support when it forcefully shipped thousands of Tatars west to Germany to work as *Ostarbeiters* ("Eastern Workers") in the plants and factories of the Third Reich. Like tens of thousands of other forced laborers conscripted to work in German industry, healthy Crimean Tatars were rounded up by the Crimean *Gestapo* and transshipped to Germany, which was described as a "vast slave workshop" in the last years of World War II.[14] At the war's end Crimean Tatars were scattered throughout Germany, with 2,000 being located at a camp in Mittenwald and others in Augsburg and Neu-Ulm. Many of these forced laborers could not return to the Soviet Union where they faced death or imprisonment as "collaborators". They were given the choice of migrating to the USA or Turkey or staying in Germany after the war.

The death toll in the Nazi factories was high and, to this very day, the Crimean Tatar leadership in the American diaspora, formerly headed by Fikret Yurter in New York, is working to receive compensation from the German government for this brutal policy. In a letter sent to United Nations High Commissioner for Refugees, Sadako Ogata in November of 1998, Fikret Yurter stated his people's claim for recompense from the German government claiming:

> As a start we feel that the German Republic has a very real moral and financial obligation to the Crimean Tatars. During the German-Nazi occupation of Crimea in World War II, more than 115 Crimean Tatar villages were burned to the ground and thousands of Crimean Tatars unjustly killed by Nazis. More than 15,000 Crimean Tatars were taken to Germany and Austria for forced labor (so called *Ostarbeiters*) and to concentration camps where most of them perished.[15]

Soviet documents corroborate Yurter's claim and show that tens of thousands of Soviet citizens were indeed forcefully taken from the Crimea by the Nazis during the German occupation of the Soviet Union.[24]

The Decision to Deport the Crimean Tatars

As the tide of war turned following the German defeats at Stalingrad, Leningrad and Moscow, a large German army was trapped by the advancing Red Army in the Crimean Peninsula. This force was destroyed only after a bloody battle at Sevastopol, in which thousands of Red Army soldiers lost their lives. After experiencing such horrific losses at Sevastopol, the victorious Soviet army was known to be in an unforgiving mood. The Crimean Tatars, as an accused nation of "collaborators", were quickly targeted for reprisals.

This was in spite of the fact that the majority of Crimean Tatar *hiwis* (German for literally "helpers"), their families, and all those associated with Edige Kirimal's Muslim Committees had been evacuated from the Crimea by the retreating *Wehrmacht* and Romanian army to Germany and Hungary (where they joined the Eastern Turkic Division) or the Romanian Dobruca. Soviet sources claim that 20,000 Crimean Tatars were evacuated with the retreating German army in 1944 (this was perforce a rough estimate) and this corresponds with the number of those estimated to have been involved in collaborationist activities.[16] It should also be stated that many Soviet officials recognized that the guilty segments of the Crimean Tatar population had retreated with the Germans and rejected claims that they had betrayed the Soviet Union *en masse*. The following Soviet report is typical of this more informed attitude:

> The secretary of the Crimean *obkom* (district committee) of BKP (Communist Party), V. S. Bultaov, pointed out that the main mass of Tatars remained loyal to the Soviet authorities and after the arrival of the occupiers they supported the partisans, whole villages offered support to the partisans, and many of these were burnt by the Germans for supporting the partisans.[17]

With the retreat of the German army, however, these voices were increasingly drowned out by those calling for the punishment of the Crimean Tatars. No mention was made of the Tatars' widespread participation in the anti-Nazi partisan groups or the burning of Tatar villages by the Germans. As the reports from Crimean Russians came in, none doubted that Stalin would seek to punish those segments of the population deemed guilty of betraying the Soviet Motherland, but few could guess at the sheer randomness, brutality and all encompassing nature of Stalin's subsequent punitive actions.

As the war drew to an end, it became obvious that many nations in the Soviet Union had provided collaborators from amongst their midst for the Nazi army, most notably the Russians and Ukrainians. Even the Karaims, a small Jewish group in the Crimea, joined Nazi SS units during the war (the fact that a Jewish group served in the SS would obviously indicate that there was duress used in recruiting Soviet citizens into the German war machine).[18] The existence of Muslim Committees in the Crimea organized from Berlin by Edige Kirimal and other members of the Turkish and Dobrucan diaspora, however, appeared to be particularly damning in the Soviet government's eyes.

Nekrich furthermore claims "It was Kirimal, together with other emigres who went to Germany and then to fascist-occupied Crimea, who put the term 'Crimean Turks' into circulation, a term that did much harm to the Crimean Tatars in the fateful year of 1944."[19] By using this term, the Crimean Tatar émigrés led by Edige Kirimal, who collaborated with the Nazis by establishing the Muslim Committees, tainted the others and linked them to Russia's traditional enemy of Turkey, as well as the Germans.

In these circumstances, a pall of suspicion fell on the community, despite the fact that tens of thousands members of this small nation had fought in the ranks of the Soviet Army and partisans against the Germans and many more were still fighting in the Red Army's ranks as it stormed towards Berlin. A Crimean Tatar source captured the mood of his people at the time, writing:

> People were happy that the Germans had been expelled, that all would be as it had been. That the war would end soon, and those on the front would return, that life would be put in order. But nevertheless, a sense of disquiet crept into our hearts. At the entrance to the Khan's Palace-Museum, before a large crowd of villagers they led a group of Crimean Tatars. As they explained to all who were gathered, these were people's traitors.[20]

Thousands of Crimean Tatars were subsequently arrested as the Red Army regained control of the Crimean countryside. According to Edige Kirimal, "in Simferopol the trees lining the streets were used as gallows, so great was the number of executions."[21] On May 10, 1944, the chief of the NKVD (People's Commissariat of Internal Affairs, the predecessor of the KGB), Lavrentii Beria, sent one of his many letters to Josef Stalin which was subsequently published when the USSR collapsed. Ominously, this letter stated:

> Considering the traitorous activities of the Crimean Tatars against the Soviet people, and as a result of the undesirability of the further habitation of the Crimean Tatars on the borders of the Soviet Union, the NKVD of the USSR brings to your attention a project decided upon by the State Committee of Defense on the resettlement of all Tatars from the territory of the Crimea.
>
> We consider it useful to settle the Crimean Tatars in the category of special-settlers (*spetsposelenets*) in the districts of the Uzbek SSR for the utilization in work such as village labor, on *kolkhozes* and *sovkhozes* (state farms) and in industry and transport. The question on the resettlement of the Tatars in the Uzbek SSR has the agreement of the secretary of the CP (Communist Party) of Uzbekistan, comrade Iusupov.[22]

With this simple telegram, the Crimean Tatars' fate was sealed. But there is considerable controversy over the real motives for deporting this small remaining nation of less than 200,000 people when as many as 20,000 soldiers from this people fought for the USSR during the war. The real reason for the deportation, as previously noted, could probably be found in Stalin's plans to invade Turkey. In particular, as the Red Army moved into a collapsing Germany and Eastern Europe, Stalin contemplated the annexation of the Turkish *vilayets* (provinces) of Kars and Ardahan on Turkey's northeastern border with the USSR.[23] At that time the Soviets commenced a broad propaganda campaign designed to lead to an Armenian uprising in this region of Turkey.

As Stalin prepared for this operation against Turkey he, as a Georgian, must have been keenly aware of the existence of several Muslim, traditionally pro-

Turkish, ethnic groups located on the invasion route through the Caucasus. Most importantly, small distrusted ethnic groups, such as the Karachai, Balkars, Chechens, Ingush and the Meshketian Turks, occupied the two main highways running southward to Turkey (the Georgian military highway and the coastal highway) or were settled on the Turkish frontier itself. In addition, the "Crimean Turks" occupied the USSR's main naval bastion facing Turkey across the Black Sea.

As preparations for a confrontation with Turkey were made in the USSR, all these suspect Muslim groups had blanket charges of treason leveled against them, except for the Meshketian Turks (also known as Ahiska), who were never officially charged with any crime. The mountainous homeland of this small conglomerate ethnic group, made up of Turkic Karapapakhs, Muslim Armenians (Khemshils), Turkicized Kurds and the Meshketian Turks proper, located far to the south, on the Turkish border in the Georgian SSR, had never been close to the scene of combat with the German invaders. Yet they too were deported *in toto*. The fact that this innocent ethnie was chosen for group deportation lends the strongest credence to the claim that the deportation of the Crimean and Caucasian peoples had more to do with Soviet foreign policy exigencies than any real crimes of "universal mass treason" committed by these groups.

The Deportation

As early as 1943, Stalin had already launched a series of surprise operations which aimed to do nothing less than eradicate several entire national groups: men, women and children that were arbitrarily deemed to have been guilty of "mass collaboration" with the enemy. While the targeted nationalities have argued endlessly since this time about the injustice of punishing whole nations, including innocent, un-armed civilians, for treason (especially when most of these ethnic groups had more soldiers fighting in the Red Army than with the invaders), the charges of mass national treason were in all probability simply a pretext for ethnic cleansing (Stalin actually used the term *ochistit*', 'to cleanse', in his orders) the Soviet Union's borderlands of non-Slavic, predominantly Islamic, populations. Regardless of the motives, the results were to be a terrifying example of a totalitarian regime's capacity to use its tremendous resources to engage in total cleansing with a speed and all-encompassing nature seen only in the Third Reich. In the first move of what Soviet historian Alexander Nekrich has called "Operation Deportation", Josef Stalin deported the Volga German population from its republic to the steppes of Kazakhstan in 1941. Following the Nazi retreat, the NKVD then commenced a "cleaning up" of the Soviet southern borders that began in November of 1943 with the deportation of a small group of Muslim people from the northern Caucasus mountains, the Karachais. This was followed by the punitive deportation of the Buddhist Mongol Kalmyks in December 1943, the Chechens and related Muslim mountaineers, the Ingush, in February 1944 (even though the Nazis had never invaded their joint repubic), the Muslim Balkars later in 1944, and in May of 1944 the Crimean Tatars came to know the horror of the sanitized term *deportatsiia*.

On the night of May 18, 1944, less than a week after the bloody German retreat from the Crimea, the *Kara Gun* (Dark Day), commemorated by Crimean Tatars throughout the Central Asian, Balkan and Turkish diasporas, commenced. NKVD mechanized infantry units surrounded all the Tatar villages and suburbs and herded the startled inhabitants to several designated transshipment points. The traumatized Tatars were given less than an hour to gather a few belongings. They were then transported at gun-point (on American lend lease Studebakers sent from Iran) to major rail hubs in the Crimea.

Crimean Tatar survivors of the deportation claim that many people assumed they were to be executed *en masse* in much the same way the Nazi *Einsatzgruppen* (mobile killing units) had murdered the Crimea's Jewish population during the occupation.[24] Crimean Tatar activist, Reshat Dzhemilev, who died soon after returning to the Crimea in the 1990s, wrote that "The cruel treatment by armed soldiers convinced the Crimean Tatars that they were being taken out to be shot at the anti-tank ditches just as the fascists had shot all the Jews. Some of the Tatars even began bidding each other farewell."[25] Russian author Alexander Solzhenitsyn provides a vivid description of the deportation process as it occurred in the Crimea with his characteristic bitter irony:

> The whole Crimean Peninsula (newly liberated in April, 1944) echoed with the hum of engines, and hundreds of motorized columns crawled snakelike, on and on along roads straight and crooked. The trees were just in full bloom. Tatar women were lugging boxes of spring onions from hothouses to bed them out in the gardens. The tobacco planting was just beginning. And that's where it ended. Tobacco vanished from the Crimea for many years to come.
>
> The motorized columns did not go right up to the settlements, but stayed at the road junctions while detachments of special troops encircled villages. Their orders were to allow the inhabitants an hour and a half to get ready, but political officers cut this down, sometimes to as little as forty minutes, to get it over with more quickly and be on time at the assembly point—and so that richer pickings

would be lying around for the detachment of the task force left behind in the village. Hardened villages like Ozenbash, near Lake Biyuk, had to be burned to the ground. The motorized columns took the Tatars to the stations, and there they went on waiting in their trains for days on end, wailing and singing mournful songs of farewell.[26]

In a manner that was indeed reminiscent of Hitler's treatment of the Jews, 11,000 able-bodied Crimean Tatar men were forcefully separated from their families at the train stations and herded on to cattle cars for utilization in coal mines in the vicinity of Moscow and Tula. The men who found themselves in the forced labor brigades were not released until 1947–48.

The women, children, elderly and large number of Tatar war invalids were packed onto sealed and guarded cars, which made their way thousands of kilometers east in the following two weeks. Interviewees who survived the horror of the deportation reported to the author that the only modification to the train carts for humans was the introduction of a pipe, which served as a latrine in the corner of some carts. Many of the wagons, described by the deportees as freight (*tovarny*) or cattle (*tel'icah'ie*) cars, still bore blood and feces left behind by those who were earlier deported from the Caucasus.

In his account of the war, the writer Cengiz Dagci provides the following account of the return of young Crimean Tatar partisan fighter to his home village in the south Crimean mountains. He arrived to find that the inhabitants of his village had just been deported, leaving only his friend Alim behind.

"Tell me Alim, what's happening in Chukurdja?"

Alim stared at him in silence like a dumb man.

"Who is here in Chukurdja Alim?"

"What about Bilal Agha?"

Alim turned his eyes to the ground and began to speak in an anguished voice. "Two days ago the Russians came to the village. They hanged Grandpa Djavit and Kaytiz on the tree by the mosque. They shot fifteen people including Hassan Agha, lining them up against the mosque wall. They killed some other people too, but this I didn't see. Then they gathered the people in the village square. I stood near Bilal Agha. He whispered in my ear 'You run away Alim. Run away to the mountains, look for Selim, find him and tell him what you've seen. Tell him to stay in the hills. You too stay there, don't come back to our village. Because the village isn't ours now.'"[27]

Survivors of the subsequent deportation remember the weeks spent in the sweltering, cramped train wagons with special horror. The deportees, who had already experienced the horrors of the Nazi occupation and the war, speak of whole wagons arriving at their destinations with their inhabitants dead. A Tatar survivor of the deportation described the mortality rate as follows:

> The doors of the wagons were usually opened in stations where the train stopped for a few minutes. The panting people gulped for fresh air, and they gave way to the sick who were unable to the exit to breath it. But along the length of the wagon one officer in a blue hat strolled with soldiers and glancing into the wagons asked the same question "Any bodies? Any bodies" If this was the case, they pulled them out of the wagon; they were mainly children and the old. There and then, three meters from the rail embankment (the bodies) were thrown into the hollows with dirt and refuse.[28]

The trains carrying the bulk of the population trundled across the hot plains of the Northern Caucasus and Kazakhstan and, after a two week journey, made their way to Tashkent, the capital of the dry, desert republic of Uzbekistan. Between 187,000 and 191,000 Crimean Tatars were deported from the Crimean autonomous republic in that May of 1944. Of these, N. F. Bugai claims, 151,604 were sent to the Uzbek SSR and 8,597 to the Udmurt and Mari Autonomous *oblasts* (Ural mountain region, part of the Russian Federated Republic) where they were employed in the lumber industry.[29] Another 10,000 were settled in the Molotov *oblast* (District).[49] Approximately 7,900 died during the actual deportation process, according to Michael Rywkin.[30]

Crimean Tatar Relations with Central Asian Populations

There was considerable ambiguity in the West concerning the fate of the deported nations in the years following World War II. Little news of these missing peoples made its way out of the Soviet Union in the 1940s and 1950s, and Sovietologists were forced to hypothesize when guessing as to their ultimate fate. In his work on Turkic languages written as late as 1965, Nicholas Poppe, for example, wrote "No details with regard to the exact whereabouts or numbers of the Crimean Tatars are available."[31] Most Western accounts simply made vague claims that the deported nations had been exiled to somewhere in "Siberia", and very little effort was made to trace them. It was only much later, in the 1960s, that news of the fate of the Crimean Tatars and other deported peoples made its way to those in the West and a picture of the Central Asian exile emerged. It is only since the collapse of the Soviet Union in 1991, however, that the full story of their fate has been told. From newly released Soviet records it appears that Tashkent served as the main dispersion center for the majority of the Crimean Tatars who were sent to Uzbekistan (other deported groups, such as the Chechens and Ingush, were sent to Alma Ata, the capital of the Kazakh SSR). From Tashkent the deportees were then dispersed throughout eastern Uzbekistan, from the Fergana Valley in the northeast to the deserts of the barren Kashga Darya *oblast* in the south. According to records sent to Beria in June 1944, the Crimean Tatars were settled in Uzbekistan in the following *oblasts:* Tashkent—56,632, Samarkand—31,540, Andijan—19,630, Fergana—16,039, Namangan—13,804, Kashga Darya—10,171, Bukhara—3,983.[32] Another 2,426 ended up in Kazakhstan and 2,472 were eventually transported to Tajikistan

The Crimean Tatar men who were still fighting for the Soviet homeland on the front (and had thus avoided deportation) were demobilized after the fall of Berlin and joined by the Tatar males deported from the Crimea in labor brigades in Siberia and the Urals region. Many Soviet military commanders, however, hid the identity of the Crimean Tatar soldiers with whom they had served during the war to protect their trusted comrades from the NKVD. Those who were not so fortunate were forced to engage in labor in the harsh conditions of the Siberian lumber, coal and gas camps where the mortality rate from the bitter climate and stressful work meant that thousands never again saw their families or their homes.

From my own interviews with survivors of the deportation held in the Crimea and Uzbekistan, it appears that most deportees who were deposited in Kazakhstan were treated well by the indigenous populations. Those who were exiled in the Siberian Mari Republic found that many of the local inhabitants were themselves deported *kulaks* and political prisoners from the 1920s and 1930s, and that they were quick to offer assistance. Most accounts, however, stressed the hostility of the Uzbeks towards the deportees in the first year or two in Uzbekistan. The NKVD had been active in the region prior to the deportations, spreading anti-Tatar propaganda against this "nation of traitors" and it seems to have been particularly effective among the simple Uzbek *kolkhozniks* who had a xenophobic distrust of outsiders. According to the testimony of one deportee, in some instances the Uzbeks stoned the already stricken Tatars when they arrived in the comparatively backward countryside. The Crimean Tatar physicist and dissident, Rollan Kadiyev claimed "I personally recall how we were met by the local inhabitants, who had been poisoned by Stalin's propaganda. One of the rocks hit me. I was still only a boy."[33]

The Crimean Tatar dissident, Reshat Dzhemilev, wrote "People were dying in droves every day, from hunger, exhaustion, and the unaccustomed climate, but no one would help them bury their dead." According to Dzhemilev, "People died from the sharp changes in the climate and the unbearable work, from dystrophy and other illnesses, from cold and malnutrition in the absence of medical care, from nostalgia and from grief over the lost members of their family."[34] All Crimean Tatar families have stories of lost family members that recall the horrible conditions their people encountered in their first two years in Central Asia. The following account given by one deportee is sadly typical:

> My niece, Menube Seyhislamova, with ten children, was deported with us. Her husband, who had been in the Soviet Army from the first day of the war had been killed. And the family of this fallen soldier perished of hunger in exile in Uzbekistan. Only one little girl, Pera, remained alive, but she became a cripple as a result of the horror she had experienced and of hunger.
>
> Our men folk were at the front and there was no one to bury the dead. Corpses would lie for several days among the living. Adshigulsim Adzhimambetova's husband had been captured by the Fascists. Three children, a little girl and two boys, remained with her. This family was also starving just as we were. No one gave either material or moral help. As a result, first of all, the little girl died of hunger, then in one day, both the boys. Their mother could not move from starvation. Then the owner of the house threw the two children's bodies onto the street, onto the side of the irrigation canal. Then some children, the Crimean Tatars, dug little graves and buried the poor little boys.
>
> Can one really tell it all? I have such a weight on my heart that it is difficult to remember it all. Tell me why did they allow such horrors to happen?[35]

Survivors of the deportation claim that the local Uzbeks did eventually come to aid of the outsiders who had been dumped in their midst after the first year or two. In interviews I conducted in Tashkent with elderly deportees, they emphasised the fact that the Uzbeks accepted the Crimean Tatars when the latter made a point of stressing their shared Islamic beliefs and traditions. The exiled Crimean Tatars made a point of emphasizing the Muslim aspects of their culture and identity to open a dialogue with the local Uzbeks who had maintained much of the traditional, conservative religious traditions lost by the less religious, Europeanized Crimean Tatar population. Islam, in effect, provided a common language of idioms, symbols and shared cultural norms that bridged the differences between these two peoples.

Several older interviewees also claimed that the local Uzbeks were taken aback when they discovered that the vast majority of the "traitors to the homeland" dumped in their midst were the elderly, women and children, with many wounded Red Army officers and veterans in their midst. Many Uzbek villagers were, according to these sources, ashamed to discover that they had been so initially harsh to women and children who hardly looked like hardened Nazi collaborators.

Soviet statistics back up the Crimean Tatars' claims that the majority of those transported on the terrible journey to Uzbekistan were indeed women and children. Of the 151,529 deposited in Uzbekistan an astounding 68,287 were children, 55, 684 women and a mere 27, 558 men according to a letter sent to Beria.[36] A full 82 per cent of the "Nazi collaborators" brutally deported in 1944 to Uzbekistan then were actually women and children. The majority of the men included in this number were, in all probability, war invalids from the Red Army or the elderly. The abundance of children came as a pleasant surprise for those involved in the deportation for they could squeeze more deportees in a wagon due to their smaller size.

In paintings depicting "The Deportation" that now hang in art exhibitions presented by the Crimean Tatars in the post-Soviet Crimea and Uzbekistan, the author noticed a common theme. Invariably the artists portrayed the horror stricken victims of the *"echelons"* (cattle transport carts) as weeping women, children and the elderly. Young men never appear in these works. To this day, the Tatars reserve particular revulsion towards the Soviet regime for its treatment of this non-combatant segment of their population who were left defenseless while thousands of their husbands, brothers and fathers were fighting on the front against the German invaders in the ranks of the Red Army.

The desperate situation of the Crimean Tatar elderly, women and children in Central Asia improved significantly when the war ended and many (although not all) Tatar soldiers were allowed to search out their families in the various places of exile between 1945 and 1948. The Crimean Tatars have a distinct genre of stories that speak of the anguish of their soldiers who were discharged from the Red Army, only to return to a Crimea that had been emptied of their families, and entire people. Those who did make their way with great difficulty across the war torn Soviet Union to their families in their special settlement camps in distant Central Asia were automatically declared *spetspereselenets* ("special settlers"), along with their relatives, and confined to the special settlement regime. Soviet sources recorded the arrival of approximately 9,000 demobilized Crimean Tatar soldiers to the *spetsposelenets* (special settlement) camps after the war. Most interestingly, Soviet sources mention that 524 of these veterans who automatically became "traitors to the homeland" were in actuality Soviet officers and 1,392 were sergeants in the Red Army.[37]

With the arrival of many of their fathers, sons, and brothers in 1946, this largely defenseless population had thousands of hardened war veterans to protect them from the abuse of MVD (Ministry of Internal Affairs) *"kommandants"* and help them rebuild their lives in their places of exile. Several older Crimean Tatar interviewees recalled the rare feelings of joy their community felt when the men came back in waves from the front to be reunited with their families. One recalled:

> In the first months in Uzbekistan after arrival more than 40,000 Crimean Tatars perished. A primary role in this was played by the circumstance that the local population received the exiles as their personal enemies. Anti-Tatar propaganda was spread among the peoples of Central Asia and the Crimean Tatars were pictured as traitors who had betrayed Central Asian men who were fighting for the Soviet *Rodina* on the front. A short time passed, then the local population began to understand. Dozens of disabled soldiers without arms or legs, with medals clinking on their chests returned from the front and searched for their mothers, wives, and children but they were no longer in this world…And then the Uzbeks understood that a monstrous injustice had taken place and they began to share their last scrap of *lepishka* (scone), their last handful of *kishmish* (raisins) or nuts.[38]

The establishment of a rapport with the indigenous Uzbek population certainly eased the resettlement process for the deported Crimean Tatars. According to first hand accounts, some Crimean Tatar widows initially married Uzbek men who were Hanafi Sunni Muslims like themselves (the war and labor camps had decimated the Tatar male population) and in some cases orphans were adopted by the local Uzbeks. If one believes Soviet mythology, this tradition of adopting war orphans was an Uzbek national characteristic. One Uzbek of the period, Sham Akhmudov, was reputed to have adopted fifteen war orphans and a massive statue to this socialist hero still dominates the square in front of Tashkent's Palace of the Friendship of Peoples.

The Special Settlement Regime

Establishing good relations with the indigenous Central Asian populations was not, however, the deportees' only concern. Upon arrival in Central Asia, the Crimean Tatars, who were considered to be traitors to the homeland by the state and its officials, were forced to live under a punitive regime, in the so-called *spetsposelenie* settlements, (special settlement camps). These informal camps, which were surrounded by barbed wire, and were run by the *otdel spetsposelenii* (special settlement department) of the MVD, are remembered with particular repugnance by the Tatars who lived in them. The heads of Crimean Tatar households were required to report to the *spetskommandants* every three days for a *spetsial'nyi uchet* (special accounting report on their family deaths, births, work progress etc.). Those exiles who illegally left their assigned region were arrested and sentenced to five years of hard labor. In these camps Crimean Tatars report that the "The commandants were God and Tsar." In interviews I held in Uzbekistan, Crimean Tatars told of being woken before dawn for twelve-hour workdays in the fields and factories, of members of their community who were sentenced to the labor camps for leaving their restricted areas to visit family members in other camps, and of the cruelty of the hated camp *kommandants*. Living conditions in the settlements were abysmal. Most deportees lived in barracks constructed next to factories, in dugouts, or simple huts hastily built of unbaked dried mud bricks during the *spetsposelenie* years.

As "enemies of the people", the Crimean Tatars had no rights as Soviet citizens during this period and their aspirations were reduced to one basic objective: communal survival. One Tatar whose mother died in the settlement camps remembers her last words, "continue the race" (*prodolzhit rod*), and this appears to have been a national mission for the group.[39]

This simple task was made all the more difficult by the Crimean Tatars' difficulties in adjusting to their new surroundings. The natural environment of Uzbekistan, with its blistering dry summers, droughts and desert oasis conditions (except in the high Fergana Valley) differed markedly from that of their coastal Black Sea home. The majority had previously lived in the valleys and foothills of the peninsula's Yaila Mountains or on the Yaliboyu coast and were unaccustomed to the conditions they found in the arid lands of Uzbekistan. Uzbek medical facilities were filled with Crimean Tatars who began to die in large numbers due to their lack of immunity to local diseases, such as malaria, dysentery, dystrophy, yellow fever and other intestinal illnesses, which were not found in the Crimean Peninsula, where the water was purer. The elderly, women and children died in the greatest numbers.

In addition, the majority of the deportees were from the Crimean countryside. According to NKVD sources, a mere 18,983 of the exiles were deported from towns in the Crimea.[40] Few Crimean Tatar farmers could acquire fields in the land-starved Uzbek oases and overpopulated Fergana Valley. Most of these village peasants were forced to find work in mines or factories (the only jobs available due to the Uzbeks' loathing of such work) located for the most part in large cities such as Tashkent.

One source records that during the first few years in Uzbekistan "It was characteristic that the *spetspereselenets* from the Crimean Tatars were frequently assigned to the most trying and heaviest construction enterprises."[41] Crimean Tatars who were settled in the Tashkent vicinity in such towns as Chircik, Angren, Gulistan and Yangi Yul, or in the Fergana Valley towns of

SURGUN: THE CRIMEAN TATAR EXILE IN CENTRAL ASIA

Marghilan, Andijan, Namangan, and Fergana, were forced to labor as menial workers in the many factories that had been evacuated to this region from the western Soviet Union during the German invasion. In an order made in May 1944, Stalin commanded Uzbek officials to place the "special settlers" from the Crimea in *sovkhozes*, *kolkhozes* and factory settlements for "utilization" in village agriculture and industry. According to one source "The Crimean Tatars, to a considerable degree, satisfied the need for the speedy development of industry in the republics of Central Asia."[42] In their important work on the Crimean Tatars, M. Guboglo and S. Chervonnaia write:

> In the places of "special settlement" the Crimean Tatars were subjected to a special regime, the aim of which was the destruction of the traditional modes of production, which had been forged over the centuries by systems of life security among the Crimean Tatars. Prior to the war, in the Crimea, they were primarily involved in village production and were especially famous for their skill in gardening, in wine producing, and tobacco growing. In their new regions of inhabitation they were settled in barracks, communal housing, hurriedly constructed temporary shelters, and annexes located by factories. The Crimean Tatars, regardless of their previous occupation, were transferred to heavy labor in various spheres of industry. The roots of national distinction were cut to the root.[43]

The cutting of the Crimean Tatars' "roots" in the soil of the Crimea was to be permanent and few of the Tatars' centuries old agricultural skills were to survive this disruption. In the post-Soviet Crimea, the repatriated Tatars suffer from this sundering of their agrarian ties to the peninsula.

Not all of the exiles, however, worked in factories. In the southern Uzbek region of Kashka Darya and Bukhara another form of forced labor prevailed. Tatar farmers who had worked for centuries maintaining the specialized mountain irrigation canals of their forefathers in the Crimean mountains, were now forced to work twelve-hour days under the hot sun in Uzbekistan's "cotton *gulag*". Moscow had turned much of the deserts of Central Asia into a vast, artificially irrigated cotton field and, with the arrival of the Crimean Tatar deportees, a class of *helots* had been provided to develop this region. Many Crimean Tatars suffered subsequent health problems from working in the pesticide-coated cotton fields or as menial laborers in the unhealthy conditions of Uzbekistan's factories.

Release from the Special Settlements

The Crimean Tatars suffered in this alien land for twelve long years under the *kommandant* regime before they were finally released from the special settlements. With the death of Josef Stalin in 1953, the Soviet Union experienced a political thaw, which had a direct impact on the punished peoples that had been deported to Central Asia. In an effort to rectify some of Stalin's greater injustices, new Soviet leader, Nikita Khrushchev, lifted the special settlement regime in 1956 and allowed the Crimean Tatar survivors to begin the process of reintegrating themselves into Soviet society. In addition to exculpating the Crimean Tatars and other deported nations of the spurious charges of "mass treason" leveled against them by Stalin, Khrushchev went so far as to allow several of the exonerated nations to return to their reconstituted home republics in the following year. These included the Kalmyks, Karachai, Balkars and the bellicose Chechen and Ingush highlanders who had begun an uncontrollable surge to their Caucasian homelands after Stalin's death. In regard to the Chechens, Khrushchev's decree may have actually been a reaction to events from below, for this restless nationality had never accepted its exile in Central Asia graciously. Three national groups were, however, omitted from Khrushchev's amnesty decree allowing for the repatriation of the various ethnic groups deported from the Caucasus region: the Volga Germans, Meshketian Turks and the Crimean Tatars. For reasons that were undoubtedly related to the strategic and economic importance of their former homeland republics, these three groups were completely ignored by Khrushchev and condemned to remain in Central Asia. Their forced exile was to be permanent.

The Crimean Tatars, Meshketian Turks, and Volga Germans were allowed to leave their camps but were subject to arrest if they attempted to resettle in their former republic-territories. All three groups were forced to witness the joyous repatriation of the other deported nations and to begin the process of rebuilding their own lives in the homeland-Soviet republics of the Uzbeks, Kazakhs, Kyrgyz and Tajiks.

Aleksander Nekrich has claimed that "If the Crimean Tatars had done as the Caucasians then did, had flooded back to the Crimea by the thousands, it is likely that they too would have won the restoration of their autonomous republic in the framework of the Ukrainian SSR."[44] This statement, however, overlooks the fact that the Crimean Tatars were not a numerous people like the Chechens, nor did they have the martial tradition of the highlanders. In addition, the Crimean Peninsula was harder to access (the narrow Perekop entrance was easily controlled), and the distance to the Crimea, which had been filled with Slavs in their absence, was greater. The Crimean Tatars were a minority in their own homeland. It became obvious to the exiles that they could not force their way back to their distant *vatan*.

SURGUN: THE CRIMEAN TATAR EXILE IN CENTRAL ASIA

Assessing the Damage of the Deportation

It was at this time that the Crimean Tatars began the task of rebuilding their shattered society and assessing the damage to their nation. Among the first tasks was the uniting of splintered families and discovering which neighbors, friends or family members had been lost in this communal disaster. Tatar activists and members of the pre-deportation Crimean ASSR government, which had been placed in power during the *korenizatsiia* period (and had been deported despite its loyalty), traveled through the settlements and conducted a census. Their aim was to ascertain the magnitude of the damage to their nation in numeric terms.

As the results were correlated by the activists, the enormity of the tragedy became apparent. The Crimean Tatar census committees came to the conclusion that 46 per cent of their nation had been killed in the deportation and settlement process. This statistic is treated with caution by outside observers, and Ann Sheehy and Bohdan Nahylo dispute this number in their work.[45] Soviet sources based on the bi-weekly reports made by Crimean Tatars in the special settlements claim that the Crimean Tatar population in Uzbekistan dwindled from 151,604 to 119,460 by the year 1946 (i.e. a loss of approximately 30,000, roughly 20 per cent of the exiled population in Uzbekistan).[46] By 1948, between 40,000 and 44,000 Crimean Tatars had died in Uzbekistan. Their numbers were hardly replaced by the birth of 6,564 Tatars in this period.[47] The Crimean Tatars I interviewed claimed that the death rate was higher among their people exiled in Siberia, where the winters were extremely cold, than in Central Asia, but there are no accurate statistics from this region. The total percentage of those killed in the deportation and resettlement in the first five years was thus probably closer to 30 per cent of the deported population, than 46 per cent as the Tatars claim.

By the 1950s, the Crimean Tatar death rate had fallen dramatically and this community once again appeared stable, but the losses incurred during the war, deportation and resettlement took a considerable toll. At a minimum, this small nation lost 80,000 people out of a pre-war population of 218,000 due to evacuation by the Nazis, forced labor in Germany, war-time losses in combat and raids by partisans and German forces, and deportation and resettlement. In sociological and demographic terms the communal trauma resulting from the loss of such a high proportion (more than one in three) of this community on the Crimean Tatar people cannot be overestimated. The entire nation was traumatized by this event and it is this trauma more than anything else that shapes their communal history. To compound matters, this tremendous injustice was covered up both domestically and abroad by propaganda, which stressed the "voluntary" nature of the Crimean Tatars' transfer to Central Asia.

The Tatars were not unique in experiencing heavy losses during this "voluntary resettlement". In his work on genocide in the Soviet Union, R J. Rummel estimates that of the 1,600,000 members of the Soviet nations deported during the war, almost one in three (approximately 530,000) died, vividly demonstrating that the war time deportation of Soviet nationalities was one of the best kept secret examples of genocide in the twentieth century.[48]

For the surviving Crimean Tatars, Guboglo and Chervonnaia claim, "It is apparent that the authorities planned on [them] being assimilated by the population of the Central Asian republics."[49] Most scholars familiar with the Tatars' plight predicted that this scattered people, who had been deprived of their identity and officially-sanctioned republic homeland would, in a generation, be assimilated in the Central Asian ethnic cauldron like many ethnic groups before them. The process of assimilation would, in theory, be facilitated by the fact that the customs, Islamic cultural identity and shared Turkic language (excluding the Tajiks) of the surrounding indigenous Turko-Muslim population of Central Asia were closely related to those of the Crimean Tatars.

In socio-political terms, the Crimean Tatar nation had been all but destroyed by the deportation and was in danger of complete social disintegration as a distinct ethnie. By stripping them of their territorial basis for recognition, the Crimean ASSR, the Kremlin had erased this non-nation of "traitors" from the USSR's ethnic map. Schooling for the Crimean Tatars was now to be in Russian, their national literature had been destroyed, they had no prerogatives based on nationality and they were no longer recognized as a distinct people. It soon became apparent that the unique Crimean Tatar national identity forged by the Young Tatars, the *Vatan* Society, the Milli Firka and "Veli Ibrahimovists" had been slated for total eradication by the Stalinist regime. By 1945 the entire Crimean Tatar people were in diaspora and found themselves dispersed throughout displacement camps in Italy, Germany and Austria, in exile in Central Asia and Siberia or living in the Romanian-Bulgarian Dobruca or Turkey. With the complete dispersal of this people, their distinct identity appeared to be in danger in all of these various diasporas.

Scattered across thousands of miles, throughout four Soviet Central Asian republics and Siberia, with none of the institutions of *korenizatsiia*, few expected the Crimean Tatars to maintain their recently forged secular national identity in the post-war years. Fewer still expected them to sustain any sense of cohesion or links to the Crimea for over a generation.

The all-powerful bureaucracy of the Soviet government was now devoted to "de-rooting" this *korennoi narod* from its republic and the Crimean Tatars' prospects for returning were virtually non-existent. Lemercier Quelquejay's gloomy pronouncement in the 1960s was that they "are doomed to be assimilated by the peoples among whom they are now living. Thus a people with a long, glorious and tragic past will disappear from history."[50]

As if the forced dispersion of this group throughout the USSR was not sufficient to achieve the "de-nationalization" of the Crimean Tatars, the Soviet government enacted a policy of "de-Tatarization" in their former homeland, designed to obliterate all traces of the Crimean Tatars' centuries-long inhabitation of the peninsula. In many ways this destruction of the their heritage in the region paralleled the destruction of hundreds of years of Muslim culture in Bosnia by Serbian and Croatian forces in areas cleansed of their Muslim populations in the 1990s. Only, as will be shown, the state sponsored de-Tatarization of the Crimea and dismantling off *korenizatsiia* in the peninsula was far more systematic.

The De-Tatarization of the Crimean Homeland

Following the demotion of the Crimean Autonomous Soviet Socialist Republic into a regular *oblast* in 1945, the Soviet government used its vast resources to eradicate any memory of its existence. Crimean Tatar language textbooks published in the 1920s were burned, all manifestations of *korenizatsiia* in the Crimea were removed and many aspects of the Crimean Tatars' long history in the peninsula destroyed. The local Crimean authorities actively severed many of the Tatars' historical and cultural "roots" to the region. In the Crimean Tatars' villages, for example, many traces of Tatar culture (such as simple village mosques, fountains and Muslim cemeteries) were destroyed. While most of the large mosques of the Crimea, such as the Cuma Cami in Evpatoriia, the Khan Cami in Bahcesaray, the Kebir Cami in Simferopol, and the Uzbek Khan mosque in Eski Kirim, were left alone (or utilized as atheist museums or warehouses), small village mosques of less historical importance, local *medreses* and ancient marble fountains were decimated.

Crimean Tatar village or topographic names (often with pre-Mongol origins) were changed overnight by administrative caveat. Thus the Ak Mecit (White Mosque) district became the Chernomorskii (Black Sea) district, Alushta became Kutusovskii (in honor of a Russian general wounded by the Turks in the vicinity), Bahcesaray became Pushkinskii (in reference to this

Russian writer's famous visit here), Balaklava became Nakhimovskii (a Russian general who served in the Crimean War) Karasu Bazar (Black Water Market) became Belogorsk (White City) and the district around it became Partisankii, Buytik Onlar became Gvardskii (Guard), Kolay became Vasilievskii (in honor of Soviet general of World War II) and so on.

This cultural and administrative Russification of the Crimean Tatars' homeland was paralleled by government-sponsored settlement of Russians from the Voronezh, Briansk, Tambovsk, Kursk and Rostov regions and Ukrainians from Kievsk, Chernigovsk, Poltavsk, and Kamenets-Podolsk regions in the Crimea. With the departure of the industrious Crimean Tatars from the southern Crimea, the abandoned *kolkhozes* and *sovkhozes* of this region were in dire need of labor hands and the Soviet government actively transferred tens of thousands of Slavs to meet the lack of work hands. In many ways the effects of the departure of over 200,000 Crimean Tatar peasants from the Crimea who were skilled in viniculture, tobacco farming, grain growing and step terracing had the same devastating effect on this unique region that the departure of approximately 200,000 Crimean Muslims had almost a century earlier after the Crimean War. According to V. Broshevan and P. Tygliiants "After the deportation from the Crimea of the 'punished' peoples a catastrophic situation arose on the peninsula. In addition to the damage wrecked on the economy by the war, the republic now lost many work hands, specialists."[51] An eyewitness to the desolation left behind in the empty Crimea countryside of the south reported that:

> In the region of Ulu Uzen in the Alushta region in the mountains there were tens of thousands of herds of small cattle remaining after the expulsion of the Tatars. The cattle were not guarded by anyone and there were instances when certain soldiers drove off huge herds of 100–200 head explaining that this herd had no owner. In the village of Ulu Uzen, on the premises of a mosque, all the possessions left by the Tatars were gathered. As a result of the lack of guards this state property was constantly plundered.[52]

As this disaster unfolded, hundreds of thousands of simple Slavic *kolkhozniks* from southern Russia were resettled in the farms, houses and villages of the deported Tatars. According to most estimates a full 90 per cent of the Slavic population of the Crimea actually arrived in the peninsula after the deportation of the Tatars.[53] In many instances the newly arriving Slavs subdivided the long, stone houses of the Crimean Tatars built to house several generations and turned them into several smaller units. These can still be found in divided, stone apartments throughout the Crimea. Many of the new

SURGUN: THE CRIMEAN TATAR EXILE IN CENTRAL ASIA

Slavic settlers found household items such as chairs, beds, farming tools and utensils left behind by the Crimean Tatars awaiting them. Crimean Tatar exiles who managed to furtively return to visit to their old homes and villages in the 1960s have left many stories of the sorrow that confronted them upon arriving in the off-limits Crimea to find strangers living in their ancestral cottages. The following poem by one such secret returnee entitled "Ballad of the Ancestral Home" (*Ballada ob Otchem Dome*) captures some of this anguish:

> I am a Crimean Tatar. I am the son of these sunny mountains, To which I have stolen today like a thief. A squeamish functionary, having lowered his fish-like eyes, issued me a residence permit...for 24 hours.
>
> I greet Ayu Dag [Bear Mountain] and the dove gray misty Yaila! I have not been to my sad homeland for so long! Here is the mud walled house in which I was born and lived. The fig tree my grandfather planted has grown so much!
>
> Our vineyard and tiny stone garden, are, as before, filled with the festive ringing of cicadas. The bumpy muscles of vine, like my grandfather's hands, Are hard, resilient, and darkened by rain and dew.
>
> The muscat is ripening! But I will not harvest it.
> I am stealing along the back yard of my father's house like a thief...
> Here is the white well and the frail, singing source....
> Some jaunty retired officer is busying himself in the garden.
>
> He is digging a cellar [or maybe a latrine].
> Oh, what has he done, he has overturned the stone in the corner! The age old gravestone under the quince tree full of chinks, Where all my ancestors are lying...their heads pointing eastwards!
>
> He thinks the sacred bones are those of a goat and breaks them with a spade...
> Allah forgive the unbeliever!.
> We look at each other in the eyes for such a long time and with such difficulty...
> He calls for somebody, letting his dog with its long mane loose.
>
> Do not do it colonel! I will not take your fruit...
> You can run my mud walled house for now...
> Tomorrow I will go back to faraway Chimkent [S. Kazakhstan].
> I am only an observer, a keeper of ancestral legends.
>
> I am an unwanted ghost, a fleeting shade on the wall,
> Although bitter ashes churn and smolder in me...
> I am conscience and a riot, and someone's deep shame...
> I am a Crimean Tatar, I am a son of these sunny mountains.[54]

Elderly Crimean Tatars who have returned to the Crimea since 1989 have similar tales of visiting their white-washed former homes and seeing chests, tables, wall hangings, farming implements and other treasured heirlooms from their youth still in place in Russian-inhabited homes. It is increasingly rare, however, that the previous inhabitants of these houses are granted access. Most Slavs living in these distinctive stone cottages are made to feel uneasy by the return of former owners and refuse the distrusted Crimean Tatar repatriates entry.

This attitude of distrust towards the Crimean Tatars was of course promoted from the 1940s right up to the 1990s by popular works such as P.N. Nadinskii's *Essays on the History of the Crimea (Ocherkii po Istorii Kryma)*. It was endlessly taught in the post-deportation Crimea that the primitive Tatar-Mongols who had previously "occupied" the peninsula were traitors to the Soviet homeland, and undeveloped Mongol nomads with no links to the land. In 1948 a conference was held in the Crimea in which such topics as the "Bolshevik Party in the Struggle Against the Tatar Bourgeois Nationalists" were discussed and everywhere crumbling village mosques were destroyed, villages, hills and streams given Russian names, Tatar street names were removed, and the memory of the departed Tatar-traitors eradicated. Stories of the Crimean Tatars' "betrayal" were spread and exaggerated and, in the process, the Russian and Ukrainian settlers (many of whom were themselves forcefully settled in the peninsula) legitimized their occupation of the coastal and, to a lesser extent, mountain villages of the Crimea's traditionally Tatar south.

In subsequent years, word of the Crimean Tatars' "mass betrayal" spread even beyond the borders of the USSR. Several thousand emigrants who made their way from displacement camps in Europe to the USA (mainly to New York and New Jersey) after the war, for example, were reluctant to identify themselves as Crimean Tatars in this new land for almost thirty years for fear of being labeled "Nazis".

While this emigrant group's fears may appear to have been exaggerated, it is interesting to note that perhaps the greatest exaggerated indictment of the Crimean Tatars as Nazi collaborators in fact comes from the USA. In a 1993 article on ethnic cleansing published in the highly respected journal *Foreign Affairs*, Andrew Bell Fialkoff makes a preposterous accusation against the Crimean "Tartars" (who were of course a minority in the largely Slavic Crimea during the war) that surpasses even Stalin's blanket accusations of mass betrayal as an excuse for deporting the Crimean Tatar people. According to Bell Fialkoff:

> During the war Crimean Tartars formally requested permission from Romania, the occupying power, to exterminate all Russians remaining in the peninsula.

SURGUN: THE CRIMEAN TATAR EXILE IN CENTRAL ASIA

When the request was denied, the Tartar Council organized a mass slaughter on its own, killing between 70,000 and 120,000 Russians. Consequently the Tartars too were transferred en masse by the Soviets after the war.[55]

If an American scholar in the late twentieth century is willing to propagate such dangerously preposterous accusations about a "Tartar" minority killing as many as 120,000 Russians from the majority population, how much easier was it for the simple Russian and Ukrainian peasants in the 1940s to believe government propaganda concerning the reasons for the deportation of the Crimea's Tatar population?

On June 30, 1945, Stalin had the Crimean ASSR downgraded to the status of a regular *oblast* (district) within the Russian Republic and, for all intents and purposes, the Crimea, cleansed of its previous inhabitants, was now in every sense an integral part of the Slavic world. In 1954 Stalin's successor, Nikita Khrushchev, transferred the Crimean *oblast* from Russia to the Ukraine in a (at the time) purely symbolic gesture celebrating the 300th anniversary of the Cossack Ukraine's unification with Russia in 1654. Khrushchev may have had the ulterior motive of winning over the Ukrainian Communist leadership in his struggle for the Kremlin following Stalin's death.

By the late 1950s, the sun baked, semi-tropical shore of the protected southern Crimea had been developed into the USSR's premiere vacation resort. What had previously been sleepy Tatar coastal hamlets were replaced by bustling sanitoria and *khirorts* (resorts). Young Pioneer and Komsomol (Communist Youth League) camps, and hotels which catered to millions of Soviet citizens who vacationed in a proletarian playground few could guess had been inhabited by Yaliboyu Tatar farmers for centuries. Soviet guidebooks for the Crimea mentioned the "Tatar Mongol" inhabitants of the Crimea in passing, as if this people were barbaric Scythians or Huns of a bygone era, not a living Soviet people languishing in exile in the depths of the USSR.

The following account from a 1961 guide to the Crimea is typical of works from the era, which stressed the Crimea's natural beauty, while overlooking its indigenous inhabitants' history on the land:

> The Crimean landscapes are remarkably unique. The resort cities form amphitheaters at the foot of mountains, on the shores of tranquil, cozy bays. The evergreen parks, the quaint summits with glistening snowcaps, the white-stone sanitarium buildings, the blue of the sea expanses, create a splendid harmony of colors.[56]

To most Soviet citizens, the Crimea was an All-Union Resort. With the exception of the Bahcesaray Palace People's Museum, an oft visited tourist site dedicated to Pushkin's "Fountain of Tears" (a well-known nineteenth-century poem about a Polish female captive in the Khan's harem which enforced the notion of the Crimean Tatars as barbarians), there was little in the Crimea to remind one of the flourishing *korenizatsiia* period or six hundred years of Muslim presence in the Crimea. Alexandre Bennigsen provided a post-script for this lost Muslim Tatar nation during this time, writing: "There are no Tatars left in the Crimea and the territory which played a considerable role in the history of the *Dar ul-Islam* is lost forever to that world."[57]

The Crimean Tatars did not, of course, lose their unique national identity in Central Asia despite all of these events and, generation after generation, this small nation kept its emotional link to the Crimean Peninsula alive. The Crimean Tatars of Central Asia, from 1944 to the present, are in every respect a classic diasporic group in their refusal to assimilate in their surrounding environment and their conscious effort to actively link themselves to another place that continued to be constructed as a "homeland". This typical diasporic group phenomenon (which has been completely overlooked by the majority of works dealing with the durability and tenacity of diasporic identities) was certainly responsible for sustaining this small community's sense of cohesion, identity, language, traditions and culture in the face of almost a half century of displacement and state-sponsored ethnocide.

With the weakening of the Soviet center's power in the late Gorbachev era, the Crimean Tatars began a return migration to an imagined homeland that had every bit the lure to this new, nationalized generation that the religiously-defined Ottoman *ak toprak* (holy "white soil") had to their ancestors a century earlier. The Crimean Tatars' amazing ability to rebuild their society after the horrors of state-sponsored nation destruction and their capacity to organize a mass repatriation to the Crimea since 1989 provide one of the most enduring testimonies to the durability of modern, territorialized national identities.

While the collapse of the Communism in Soviet Eurasia has led to many unforeseen occurrences in this diverse region, few events would have been deemed as improbable during the Soviet period as the return of several generations of exiled Crimean Tatars from Central Asia to their Slavicized homeland in the West. Even fewer could have imagined this group reconstituting itself as a nation in the Crimea and once again holding *kurultays* in this playground for the Communist elite. An analysis of the Crimean Tatars' struggle to return during the Soviet period and the post-Soviet repatriation movement will trace the final development of their modern national identity and shed light on the difficulties this long-suffering people have come to face in the post-Soviet context.

7

RETURN

THE CRIMEAN TATAR MIGRATIONS FROM CENTRAL ASIA TO THE CRIMEAN PENINSULA

One can imagine the psychological impact that the mass return of a quarter of a million Tatar Muslim exiles to the Crimean Peninsula had on this region's Slavic population in the early 1990s. For over forty-five years the Crimea had provided a stable environment for Muscovites on which to build their beloved *dachas* (summer houses) in the warm Black Sea sun. It had become a welcoming destination for retirees from the Soviet navy and a safe Slavic haven for Russians who had begun to feel insecure in the early 1990s in the *blizhnee zarubezh'e* ("near abroad", i.e. former Soviet republics) due to rising national tension and anti-outsider nativism in the Soviet republics from Dushanbe to Vilnius.

As the Tatars began to arrive in the region in the early 1990s by the tens of thousands, they commenced several actions that worried the local Slavic population. These activities included well-organized seizures of marginal lands; the building of squatter camps; and clashes with the local authorities. It may very well have seemed to the Crimea's conservative, predominately pro-Communist Russian population that the troubles of distant Armenia, Azerbaijan, Tajikistan, Uzbekistan, Moldova and Georgia had finally arrived on their doorstep in the form of the long-banished Muslim descendants of Genghis Khan's Mongol hordes. As in the West, the Russians of the Crimea were quick to attribute any Muslim group's collective action to Islamic fundamentalism and many Crimean Russians feared for the peninsula's stability with the potential arrival of half a million "Muslim fanatics".

Even a cursory glance at the Crimean Tatars' history during the twentieth century would have shown, however, that the return movement of the early 1990s was hardly motivated by what local Crimean Russians often described as a *"jihad"*. While it is true that the Crimean Tatars had been deposited by Stalin in a land that was more Islamic in its ways and mores than the Crimea, this experience had little effect in Islamicizing the exiles.

As will be shown, it was actually a very secular nationalist movement based on a territorialized communal identity that led to the unexpected migration of a quarter of a million Crimean Tatars to the Crimean Peninsula in the aftermath of the Soviet collapse. It was this unique identity, based on the diasporic notion of a lost Fatherland, that enabled the Tatars to maintain their sense of community during almost fifty years of exile. It was this constructed identity based on an attachment to the Crimea that ultimately made their repatriation there possible, not a fundamentalist Islamic tradition.

Sustaining Group Identity in Exile

An analysis of the ways in which the Crimean Tatar people sustained their national identity in the most unpropitious of circumstances presents an interesting case study in the durability of the political phenomenon of mass-based ethno-nationalism. Such an analysis can also provide considerable insight into the ways in which diasporic national movements can unify and politically mobilize even small, fragmented ethnic groups.

In seeking to answer the question of how this exiled micro-nation preserved its national identity in the Central Asian context, many of the answers I initially received pointed to the tremendous role of family in keeping a sense of "Crimean Tatarness" alive. Robert Kaiser has pointed out that "A population's national self-consciousness must be reconstructed with each generation" and among the Crimean Tatars it was the parents and grandparents who acted as the repositories of the customs and memories of the old homeland and perpetuated a Crimean Tatar identity in their new land.[1] The women in particular taught the new generations growing up in Central Asia how to make *ciborek, sarma, kubitye, yantyk, burma* and other examples of Tatar "national" cuisine. It was they who kept traditional songs from the Crimea alive and instilled in succeeding generations a sense of identification with the Crimean Tatar people, and a related sense of separateness from the surrounding peoples.

In addition, the older generations kept the memory of "The Deportation" alive in the minds of new generations born in exile that had not experienced it themselves. In this fashion they perpetuated the communal memory of this great injustice to the Crimean Tatar people. Just as the post-Holocaust Jewish community kept the memory of the unparalleled atrocity of the *Shoah* alive as a primary symbolic marker of their communal identity, all Crimean Tatars could cite the 46 per cent deportation mortality statistic and retell stories of the deportation as if they had themselves experienced it.

There are of course many parallel examples of this sort of trans-generational transmission of a "chosen trauma". This widely studied sense of communal grievance played the same role in the eventual political mobilization of the Crimean Tatars that the communal history of group expulsion played in politicizing Tutsi expellees from Rwanda living in Uganda, Burundi, and the Congo (Zaire) from the 1950s to the 1990s. The Palestinian refugees' sense of profound injustice, which came about as a result of their expulsion from their homeland in 1948 following *al-Naqba* (The Disaster), had a similar effect. In these cases, the communal memory of this chosen trauma has served to mobilize and politicize a previously latent national identity. This strong sense of injustice also prevented the Crimean Tatars in Central Asia, like the Palestine refugees in Gaza, the West Bank and Lebanon or Tutsis living in African diaspora, from accepting their exile condition as permanent.

Ritualized narratives that expressed communal grievances and kept alive the memory of the injustices committed against the people were passed on from generation to generation among the Crimean Tatars of Central Asia. In this fashion memories of the *Deportatsiia* and the lost homeland, once again described as the *yeshil ada* (green island), were kept alive in the minds of children and grandchildren of the deportees.

The narratives of the deportation from the "island" usually begin with an idealistic portrayal of the Crimean ASSR and home village or micro region prior to the deportations. The Crimean countryside is glorified and the political rights of the Tatars in "their" republic recalled. The narratives describe the horror of removal from the "Eden" of the peninsula and seek to bring to life the true nature of the tragedy. All families have experienced personal losses, which are commemorated. A grandmother who died of a heart attack on the trains, an uncle who was shot for moving too slowly to the deportation trains, an aunt who died of malaria in the special settlements. The narratives provide graphic details of the hostile "welcome" of the indigenous population of Uzbekistan upon arrival. They then speak of the shame these Uzbek populations later felt when they realized that they had fallen for unjustified, anti-Tatar propaganda.

The ritualized deportation narratives stressed the loyalty the Crimean Tatars continued to feel towards the Soviet government in spite of the unfair treatment they received in the special settlement camps and afterwards. In proclaiming this loyalty, the archetypal hero of the deportation narrative was a young Crimean Tatar soldier in the Red Army who was wounded while heroically defending the Soviet Motherland. After demobilization from the front, the decorated soldier searches for his young wife and children and finally finds their unmarked graves in a village inhabited by native Uzbeks. In the exile narratives, the local villagers are ashamed to convey this defender of the Soviet homeland to the graves of his loved ones whom they might have saved. The local population, however, compensates for their previous mistreatment of the deported Tatars by sharing their bread with the exiles and reaffirming the two peoples' shared sense of Islamic identity. The story ends with a reaffirmation of the Crimean Tatars' determination to return to the land, which was unjustly taken from them, and a vow to reclaim their ancestral homes and graveyards in the "Green Isle".

Lilia Bujurova, perhaps the most famous Crimean Tatar writer and poet to emerge from the exile period, had her poems about the Crimean homeland published throughout the former Soviet Union during the *glasnost* period. She deals with this subject in several of her works. She captures her experience growing up in Central Asia and hearing stories of The Deportation and her lost homeland in the following poem, titled "Speak" (*Govori*).

> Speak father speak,
> Speak until the dusk!
>
> Speak of the cruel war,
> Speak of the terrible day,
> In my veins let the tragedy flow,
> How salty is the seawater,
> Don't spare me, don't leave anything out,
> Go again out of your native home,
> Again lose your relatives on the wagons
> Again count who remains among the living!
>
> I want to know about everything,
> So that I can tell it to your grandchildren,
> Your pain cries to me,
> I will bring every moment to life in them!
> It will also become a homeland for them
> The word "Homeland" and the word "Crimea"!
> Speak father speak,
> Speak father until the dusk![2]

RETURN

Most Crimean Tatars remember growing up in Central Asia with stories of the Crimean *vatan* and many recall having developed images and mental "maps" of a homeland most had never seen. All Crimean Tatar children heard stories of the Salgir River, legends of Chadir Dag Mountain, tales of the Bahcesaray's beauty and idealized narratives of such terraced Yaliboyu coastal villages, such as Yalta, Uskut, Tarak Tash, Alushta, and Dere Koy. A typical source, for example, recalls "Everyone dreamed of his village in the Crimea, his birthplace and no one wanted to believe that the homeland had been lost for ever."[3] Not surprisingly, a similar phenomenon has been noticed among the children of displaced Palestinians. A visitor to Palestinian refugee camps has written, "when I had talked with other Palestinians in other camps in Jordan and Lebanon. I began to realize the depth of their sentiment for their former homes and lands. Children who had been born in camps talked of 'home' as though they knew every inch of ground, every tree and bush."[4]

A typical Tatar repatriate to the Crimea from Central Asia described the trans-generational "rooting" of Crimean Tatar identity in the region as follows "Around the family table, every day we talked about coming back here. We were raised on the idea of motherland."[5] Another claimed "among the Crimean Tatars not a single action, great or small, took place during visits to houses among friends and acquaintances, during the entire deportation period, without recollections of the Crimea, of the land on which our parents, grandfathers and great grandfathers lived and worked."[6] A Tatar who was two years old during the deportation claimed "Every Crimean Tatar child had it drummed into his head that he had a homeland," while another explained the importance of the Crimea in nationalistic terms, saying "Most children say 'mama' or 'papa' as their first word. Our children said '*Kirim*', the word for Crimea."[7] There is no doubt that the family played the primary role in preserving an imaginary territorial link to this *vatan* during the long years of exile when assimilation would have proven the easiest option for a people still known as "traitors to the homeland".

There were, in addition to the trans-generational narratives, also several external factors that helped the Crimean Tatars keep their distinct national identity alive during the half century of Central Asian exile. Perhaps one of the most interesting causes of the lack of assimilation among the Crimean Tatars in Central Asia stems from the overlooked differences between this group and the indigenous Central Asian populations. Due to their comparatively long history of exposure to Russians and Western nationalism, the Crimean Tatars were among the most Europeanized and nationally developed

Muslim groups in the Soviet Union. While many Uzbek and Tajik men, for example, continued throughout the Soviet period to don Muslim skull caps, wear *khalats* (the traditional robes of Central Asia), shave their heads, and grow beards (traditional outward forms of expressing Muslim identity), the Russified Crimean Tatars dressed much as the Russians did. In many subtle ways they behaved more similarly to the Russians than the conservative Uzbeks and Tajiks.

In my interviews with Crimean Tatars who survived the deportation, most stressed what they saw as the relative backwardness of the Uzbeks and other Central Asians. To many exiles, the deportation to Central Asia was more than a deportation from one continent to another; it was a journey back in time. Gavin Hambly described Soviet Central Asia as "the most backward of all Muslim regions in the empire" and, to the Crimean Tatars who were settled among the suspicious Uzbek villagers, this was truly an alien, undeveloped land.[8] While veils, *kalems* (bride prices), polygamy, traditional Muslim attire and many other aspects of Muslim life had long ago fallen into disuse among the Europeanized Crimean Tatars, the old traditions of conservative Central Asian Islam continued in the *kishlaks* of Uzbekistan (especially in the conservative Fergana Valley) throughout the Soviet period. In her description of the social conditions found in Uzbekistan during the 1960s, for example, Elizabeth Bacon wrote:

> Such Uzbek regions as Samarkand, Surkhan Darya, and Khiva appear to be as conservative as Tajikistan. In these regions polygamy is widespread, women cover their faces in the presence of men, and husbands often refuse to allow their wives to be treated by a male doctor. Even in Tashkent some *paranjas* (veils) are seen on the streets, while in Fergana, according to reports, active Party members often go into seclusion after marriage.[9]

By comparison, the veil had fallen into disuse among Crimean Tatar women by the late nineteenth century and had never been prevalent among the coastal Tats and Nogais. Women also played a considerable role in the reform and national movement of the Crimean Tatars, and it should be remembered that women had been granted the right to vote by the Crimean *Kurultay* as early as 1917. These seemingly trivial societal differences between the Crimean Tatars and their new Central Asian neighbors (whose culture reflected many of the ancient traditions of their land in much the same way the Crimean Tatars' did) certainly contributed to their lack of assimilation once the exiles had been released from the special settlement regime. Similarly, while the hospitality of the Central Asians is legendary, they and the Crimean Tatars also tend towards endogamy. This further contributed to the maintenance of separate national identities. After the initial years of the deportation there was very little intermarriage between Uzbeks, Tajiks, Kazakhs and Kyrgyz on the one hand, and Crimean Tatars on the other hand. This appears to have been a result of mutual traditions. With an endogamy rate of 91 per cent, the Crimean Tatars were among the most endogamous nations in the Soviet Union. As many threatened peoples do, the Crimean Tatars appear to have had a desire to preserve their community and prevent their sons and daughters from losing their identity through intermarriage with the indigenous peoples of Central Asia. For their part, the Tajiks and Uzbeks of the *mahallas* (traditional neighborhoods) and villages of Central Asia also frowned upon marriage with outsiders.

Another phenomenon that contributed to the maintenance of Crimean Tatar identity in Central Asia included the regime's discrimination against this group. Had the Crimean Tatar people been given full political rights and recognition of their ethnicity, they might not have been so vigilant in actively defending their endangered national identity. Walker Connor points out that, as in many areas of the world, state sponsored attempts to suppress or eradicate national identities usually have the opposite effect. They result in a defensive heightening of a people's sense of national awareness. While it was possible to assimilate ethnic groups *prior* to the advent of the political phenomenon of nationalism, Connor claims "No examples of significant assimilation are offered which have taken place since the advent of the age of nationalism."[10]

Although the Soviet government granted the exiled Crimean Tatars token cultural opportunities and outlets for expression after their release from the camps in 1957 (for example, it allowed the publishing of a Crimean Tatar language paper known as *Lenin Bayragi*—Lenin's Banner—and a journal known as *Yildiz*—The Star) this could hardly satisfy this exiled people's aspirations for full ethno-national expression of the sort found during the *korenizatsiia* period of the 1920s and 1930s. These limited mediums made available to the Crimean Tatars in exile did, however, provide this diaspora people with an additional vehicle for preventing assimilation in Central Asia. The end sections of *Lenin Bayragi*, for example, had columns of Crimean Tatar words and their translation in Russian to help an increasingly Russified generation of young Crimean Tatar exiles (who received no schooling in the Crimean Tatar language) preserve their language.

THE CRIMEAN TATARS

The Political Mobilization of Crimean Tatar Ethnicity in Central Asia

Having sustained their ethno-national identity in Uzbekistan and elsewhere (many Crimean Tatars in Siberia migrated to Uzbekistan to be with friends and relatives after 1957) in the first two decades of exile, it was not surprising that the Crimean Tatars took advantage of the gradual post-Stalin thaw in the USSR to begin agitation for a return to the Crimea in the mid-1960s. The 1957 decree allowing the Chechens, Ingush, Karachai, Balkars and Kalmyks to return to their reconstituted republics, but forbidding the Crimean Tatars from doing the same, had disillusioned a whole generation who had earlier believed in working within the framework of the Soviet system to achieve their goal of repatriation. The feelings of shock and disappointment among the Crimean Tatars were profound. In response, a generation that had grown up believing in the reversible nature of their exile began to devise a new strategy to fulfill their goal of returning to the Crimea.

As their identity continued to be suppressed, the Crimean Tatars' growing frustration was summed up by one exile who claimed "Who are we now, nobodies living nowhere."[11] The Crimean Tatars' shared sense of injustice and their growing frustration with the Kremlin gradually fostered the rise of a mass "Return to the Homeland" movement among this dispersed people. In a remarkable display of organizational and national unity, Crimean Tatar activists began to form action committees in all the places of their exile that worked to mobilize their people politically, keep their culture alive and forge greater national solidarity. All of these activities had the long-term aim of pressuring the Kremlin into allowing for the full repatriation of the Crimean Tatar people.

Far from witnessing the breakdown of the Crimean Tatar ethnos, the 1960s thus witnessed the rise of a greater sense of cohesion and national activism among the deportees as their shared sense of grievance provided a platform for political mobilization. In Uzbekistan, in particular, initiative groups were formed at the grass roots level, which were organized to pressure both local authorities and the Kremlin into politically rehabilitating the Crimean Tatars and allowing for their return to the Crimea. In this fashion, the Crimean Tatar nationalists issued the first ethnicity-based, frontal challenge to the Soviet regime since World War II. Operating from 1957 to 1989, the Crimean Tatar repatriation movement was also to be the longest running dissident challenge to the Kremlin in Soviet history and was to be matched only by the Jewish emigration movement in its longevity. This movement was, however, to take a heavy toll on the Tatars, with hundreds of activists and dissidents arrested and given lengthy jail terms in the *Gulag* during the 1960s, 1970s and 1980s.

Although the Crimean Tatars had, by the 1960s, tenaciously overcome the previous political and socio-economic obstacles confronting their people in their places of exile (in most instances, the hardworking Crimean Tatars had by this time surpassed their Central Asian hosts in educational and economic terms), many continued to agitate for a return to a lost territory still defined as a homeland. Contemporary accounts point out that an increasingly broad base of the Crimean Tatar exile population had become involved in the struggle to return by the 1960s. In one mass petition to the Twenty Third Party Congress, for instance, more than 120,000 Crimean Tatars—virtually the whole adult population—took the decided risk of signing a document requesting the rehabilitation and repatriation of their nation. Communist authorities in the normally quiescent Central Asian republic of Uzbekistan began to fear the ripple effect that the Crimean Tatars' unprecedented challenge to the regime would have on the surrounding Uzbek population.

Finally, on July 21, 1967, a committee of Crimean Tatar representatives, headed by the prominent dissident Ayshe Seytmuartova and several others, from a group of 400 who had been lobbying in Moscow itself, was granted permission to meet in the Kremlin with several high ranking Soviet officials, including KGB chairman Yuri Andropov.[12] In one of the most improbable events in modern Soviet history, the representatives of this small "non-nation" confronted the most powerful officials in the Soviet state. In the meeting they demanded redress for the wrongs done to their people over the previous twenty-three years. After a surprisingly accommodating session, the Crimean Tatar representatives returned to their communities in Central Asia believing that their people would soon be rehabilitated and the issue of their return to the Crimea would be addressed. After two tense months, the Presidium of the USSR Supreme Soviet finally released a decree in September 1967 formally absolving the Crimean Tatars of the accusations of mass betrayal during World War II and granting them greater rights in the USSR.

As important as this exoneration was, the second part of the decree revealed the Kremlin's true stance on the most important of the Crimean Tatars' national demands—the right to return to the Crimean Peninsula. The carefully worded decree claimed that "citizens of Tatar nationality who had formerly been living in the Crimea *have taken root* [emphasis mine] in the territory of the Uzbek and other Union Republics" and there "they enjoy all the rights of Soviet citizens."[13] With the stroke of a pen the Crimean Tatars' dream of returning to their homeland had been once again crushed and instead they were said to have spontaneously "taken root" (*ukorenilis'*) in

Uzbekistan. In addition, the very existence of the distinct *Crimean* Tatar nationality had been refuted by the wording of the decree, which referred not to the "Crimean Tatars", but to the "Tatars who had formerly been living in the Crimea."

From this time forward the Crimean Tatars of Central Asia were, for all official purposes (i.e. passports, censuses etc.), considered to be a sub-section of the Volga Tatars.[21] The real meaning of this decree was clear for all to see for, as Alan Fisher pointed out: "a people without a nationality has no homeland to which to return."[14] After twenty years of mass-based nationalization during the *korenizatsiia* period, which saw the construction of the Crimean Tatars as the "primordial, rooted people" in the Crimean Peninsula, the Soviet government had apparently reversed itself. It had now hit upon the idea of "de-rooting" this scattered nation and simply transplanting its roots in Central Asia by administrative caveat.

Had the Kremlin given careful consideration to the importance of the Crimean homeland as the foundation for the Crimean Tatars' diasporic identity they would have, however, foreseen that this decree would not placate this increasingly assertive people. In these circumstances it is not surprising that the Crimean Tatar national movement developed into a uniquely territorialized pressure group with repatriation as its main goal. Other issues on the nationalist agenda were considered of secondary importance to the main task of regaining the peninsula. It was felt by the increasingly organized leadership that issues such as the maintenance of Crimean Tatar language, culture and identity could be solved only within a restored Crimean ASSR.

The idea of regaining the lost homeland continued to provide the main foundation for the maintenance of a separate national identity for the exiles. They actively resisted assimilation into the surrounding Central Asian milieu and refused to accept the Uzbek SSR (or any other people's Soviet republic) as their home. Azade-Ayse Rorlich succinctly summed up the importance of the Crimea to them, claiming "The struggle for their homeland is at the center of their struggle to endure as a nation. It unfolds the twin banners of political activism and cultural assertiveness."[15] This attitude among the Crimean Tatars owed some of its origin to the deeply ingrained belief in all Soviet citizens that national groups "belonged to" or were "rooted in" their titular republic or autonomy and could not legitimately express their identity in another nationality's republic.

1. The 16th Century 'Iron Gate' entrance to the Khan's Palace complex in Bahcesaray, Crimea (photo by Robert Brooks)

2. Crimean Tatar cavalry fording a stream

3. Entrance to the Khan's palace at Bahcesaray

4. The Iron Gate ceremonial entrance to the Khan's Palace complex, Bahcesaray

5. Tatar musicians playing at a wedding

6. A Crimean Tatar wagon known as an ʻaraba

7. Crimean Tatars at prayer in Karasu Bazar, 19th century

8. Tatars smoking traditional pipes in a cafe

9. The west Crimean port of Evpatoriia, known in Tatar as Gozleve

10. Tatars at a traditional outdoor cafe

11. The Divan-Council room and Harem in the Khan Complex, Bahcesaray

1. Royal entrance to Khansaray complex.
2. Main palace complex.
3. Harem.
4. Falcon Tower.
5. Khan Cami (Khan Mosque).
6. Royal Turbes (Mausoleums).
7. Stables.

12. Map of the Crimean Khan Saray complex

13. The Crimean Tatar nationalist leadership (including Numan Celebi Cihan and Cafar Seydahmet) standing before the Iron Gate in the Khan Saray complex during the Russian Revolution'

14. Crimean Tatar youth perform traditional dance in the Khan Saray Palace

15. The Khan Cami (Mosque) in the Khan Saray complex

16. The 16th Century Cuma Cami (Friday Mosque) built in Evapatoriia (Gozleve in Tatar) by the famous Ottoman architect for Sultan Suleiman the Magnificent, Sinan Pasha

17. The Shirinsky Cliffs overlooking the town of Karasu Bazar (Belogorsk) where the Crimean Tatar nobility traditionally elected the new khan

18. The south Crimean mountains, traditional homeland of the Tat Tatars

19. The harbor of Kaffa with the Medieval Genoese fortress in the foreground

20. Traditional tiled roof Crimean Tatar house, Simferopol (the Crimean capital)

21. Traditional tiled roof Crimean Tatar house, Simferopol

22. Photo of Crimean Tatars doing traditional dance in the terraced Tat mountains a few days before they were deported on May 18, 1944

23. Rare photo of the Crimean Tatars being deported to Central Asia by Stalin in 1944

24. The horrors of the deportation as depicted by Crimean Tatar artist Rustem Eminov (courtesy of Fikret Yurter)

25. "Facia" (Tragedy). The deportation as depicted by Crimean Tatar artist Seit Xalil Osmanov (courtesy of Mubeyyin Batu Altan)

6. "Malaria." Depiction of the harsh conditions awaiting Crimean Tatars in their places of exile in Central Asia by Tatar artist Seit Xalil Osmanov (courtesy of Mubeyyin Batu Altan)

27. Crimean Tatar anti-Soviet dissident and former head of the Crimean Tatar Mejlis (Parliament), Mustafa Dzhemilev "Kirimogolu" (Son of the Crimea) who played a key role in leading his people back to their homeland from Soviet-imposed exile

28. Crimean Tatar activist Reshat Dzhemilev who was arrested for his dissident activities in the 1970s

29. October 1992, Simferopol. Crimean Tatar protestors storm the Crimean Parliament building demanding the release of their compatriots arrested during the destruction of a Tatar settlement on the coast called Krasni Rai

30. Crimean Tatar samozakhvat (self seized) settlement built by Crimean Tatar returnees out of simple brick. The banner before the stone houses reads "Beloved Homeland! The land of our fathers and forefathers is sacred." Since their return to the Crimea from exile the Tatars have built many such settlements in the Crimean countryside

31. Russian marchers in the Russian naval port city of Sevastopol carrying portraits of Stalin, the Soviet leader responsible for deporting the Tatars to Central Asia in 1944

32. Typical simple Crimean Tatar stone house known as samostroi (self construct) in Tatar settlement of Marino outside Simferopol

33. Elderly Crimean Tatar settlers who have returned from their place of exile in Uzbekistan to Crimea (settlement of Fontany outside Simferopol)

34. Crimean Tatar concrete mosque on hillside outside of Simferopol'

35. Simple mosque between Karasu Bazaar (Belogorsk as the town was renamed in Russian) and Simferopol

36. Newly erected Tatar grave in Baidar Valley featuring the Tarak Tamgha national symbol the Tatars

RETURN

The Chirchik Riots and the Radicalization of the Return Movement

The tension resulting from failed expectations of return among the Crimean Tatar community of Central Asia came to head in the year 1968, in the city of Chirchik, located thirty kilometers to the north east of the Uzbek SSR capital Tashkent in the foothills of the Chaktal mountains. Chirchik was an industrial city, in which a large Crimean Tatar population had been settled during the deportations. It was typical of many of the Uzbek factory towns in which the Tatars found themselves after 1944. Chirchik's large population of Crimean Tatar factory workers was also among the most restive of the places of exile and it is not surprising that the first outbreak of mass dissent took place here. According to eyewitnesses, several thousand Crimean Tatars from the neighboring communities drove to this city and met in the central park of Chirchik to celebrate Lenin's ninety-eighth birthday on April 21, 1968 (Lenin was seen as a supporter of Crimean Tatar nationhood and was adopted as a national hero by the exiled Tatars) and the traditional May festival of *Tepresh*. In spite of its innocent appearance, this gathering soon turned into a protest against the unsatisfactory nature of the recent decree and the authorities quickly moved in to arrest the protesters.[16] As the rally progressed, MVD (The Ministry of Interior Affairs) and para-military divisions from the surrounding areas converged on the Crimean Tatars in a resounding display of force. Police units attacked protesters with poisonous spray, batons, and high-pressure hoses, and arrested more than 300 of them in the subsequent melee.[17]

In the aftermath, activists smuggled news of the attack to the West and so, for the first time in over two decades, many in the West heard word of the exiled Crimean Tatars. The whole event was a public relations coup for the struggling Crimean Tatars and the first major post-World War II ethnic disturbance in the normally quiescent Central Asian republics.

Similar outbreaks of violence also occurred among restive Crimean Tatar populations in the Uzbek cities of Bekabad, Andijan, Fergana and in Tashkent proper during this period and there seemed to be no end in sight to their agitation. The growing intensity of the struggle may have had something to do with Khrushchev's increasing emphasis on calls for *slianiie* (the "blending" of nationalities) and *sblizheniie* ("rapprochement" between the peoples of the Soviet Union). These policies were seen by most national minorities as a euphemism for Russification. As a people without a state-sanctioned homeland-republic, the Crimean Tatars felt themselves to be particularly vulnerable to losing their ethno-national identity through this policy.

In this environment, the Crimean Tatar activists became increasingly outspoken in their calls for a return to the Crimea as a means of preserving their identity. In 1969 during a May Day parade in Tashkent, for example, a group of bold Crimean Tatars unfurled a banner that read "The Crimean Tatars have been in exile for twenty five years—Communists! Return our people to their Homeland" and hundreds of Tatars began protesting at the trials of well-known activists. The Crimean Tatars throughout Central Asia also made a point of commemorating the annual anniversary of the disbanding of the Crimean ASSR.

Perhaps the most noteworthy effort to overcome the effects of the 1967 decree was the mass uncontrolled migration of Crimean Tatars to the peninsula in the following years. The attempt by many to return without the permission of the authorities resulted in the re-deportation of as many as 6,000 Crimean Tatars in 1968 alone. As the Crimea was an All-Union health resort with a strict passport regime, it was easy for the local authorities to deport Crimean Tatars who did not have residence permits in their passports.

There were many incidences of arrests, beatings and the destruction of squatter settlements, as the local Crimean militia forces attacked squatter camps and forcefully expelled Tatars beyond the peninsula's borders. There were, for example, at least three reported cases of protest related self-immolation among the Crimean Tatars. The self-immolation of Musa Mahmut in particular became known to Crimean Tatars everywhere. Having returned with his family to settle in the Crimean *oblast* without the permission of the authorities, Musa Mahmut was repeatedly harassed, arrested by Crimean officials, refused a job and on several occasions his house was attacked.

Finally, when the police came to deport his family back to Central Asia for not possessing *propisky* (official residence permits) for the Crimea, a desperate Musa Mahmut covered his body with gasoline and set himself on fire. When news of Musa Mahmut's death was carried back to Central Asia he became a modern *Milli Shehit* (National Martyr) for his people. The story of his, and his nation's, suffering at the hands of the Soviets was told in a *samizdat* (underground "self-publication") work by Crimean Tatar activist Reshat Dzhemilev, which was smuggled to the USA and published by the American Crimean Tatar diaspora in New York. The funeral of Musa Mahmut in the Crimea was also a scene of protest for other desperate Crimean Tatars who gathered for the event despite police efforts to prevent a protest action commemorating Mahmut's death.

In light of events such as Musa Mahmut's death and the continuing arrests of Crimean Tatar activists, an increasing number of Crimean Tatars became involved in the struggle for their homeland by defending friends and neighbors who had been arrested for opposing their continued exile. This was not, however, a spontaneous outburst of frustration, as in the case of the Palestinian *intifada*. The Tatars strictly abstained from violence, their activists skillfully manipulated Soviet law to demonstrate the illegality of their continued exile, and the leaders of the movement were highly educated white-collar workers. Time and time again the trials of Crimean Tatar nationalists became forums for eloquent dissidents to disseminate their message demanding the right to return to the Peninsula to wider audiences.

Perhaps the most important show trial of Crimean Tatar dissidents during this period was the sentencing of the "Tashkent Ten", a group of dissidents comprising Izzet Khairov, Roland Kadiev, Ismail Yaziciev, Riza Omerev, Reshat Bayramev, Munire Halil, Svetlina Ahmet, Haydar Bariev, Ridvan Gafarev and Ruslan Eminev. Soon thereafter Ayshe Seytmuartova was sentenced for "slandering the Soviet system" and in 1973 a combative Reshat Dzhemilev was sentenced for attacking the Soviet system that had exiled his people after publicly labeling it a "totalitarian regime".[18]

The Case of Mustafa Dzhemilev "Kirimoglu"

Perhaps the dissident most representative of this new parallel leadership among the Crimean Tatars was a leader from Yangi Yul (Tashkent vicinity) named Mustafa Dzhemilev. Dzhemilev earned a Mandela-like status among Central Asians for his heroic, three decade long struggle to see his nation returned to its homeland.[19] Dzhemilev, a physically unimposing man who, decades later, was still suffering from health problems resulting from sixteen years spent in prison and labor camps, was exemplary of a new generation of average Crimean Tatars who made great personal sacrifices to bring about the return of their nation to its ancestral lands.

Dzhemilev was initially sentenced to prison in 1966 for his "anti-Soviet" activities and upon release joined with other famous Soviet dissidents, such as Andrei Sakharov, to form the "Initiative Group for the Defense of Human Rights in the USSR". Such activities earned the unrepentant Dzhemilev five more sentences (including one hard labor sentence) over the next two decades. Dzhemilev used his sentencing to draw attention to his people's plight and on one occasion went on a widely publicized 275 day hunger strike.

Dzhemilev also used his trials as a platform for issuing fiery speeches denouncing Soviet policies towards his people and calling for a return to "correct Leninist policies". In these speeches the "illegal" dissolution of the Crimean ASSR and the 46 per cent mortality rate of the Crimean Tatar deportees were constantly evoked. When asked the place of his birth during trials, Dzhemilev always made a point of stating "the Crimean ASSR" much to the chagrin of the state prosecutors who refused to acknowledge that the Crimea had ever been an autonomous republic. When asked if he had any prior arrests or sentences during his first trial in Uzbekistan, a young Dzhemilev answered in the affirmative and claimed he had been sentenced without a trial as an infant to a life of exile in Central Asia.

Dzhemilev was released from jail in 1988 (due in part to pressure from US President Ronald Reagan), at a time when the informal Crimean Tatar "Action Groups", made up of activist cells throughout Central Asia and other places of exile, were beginning to take advantage of the Gorbachev thaw and openly organize. In light of his growing reputation beyond Central Asia, it was not surprising that the newly established Organization of the Crimean Tatar National Movement (OCTNM), which emerged in 1989, chose Dzhemilev as its first elected chairman.[20]

Soon thereafter, Dzhemilev migrated to the Crimea in 1989 and was recognized in the second Crimean *Kurultay* (Congress) in June of 1991 for his sacrifices on the behalf of his people. He was officially given the honorary title, Kirimoglu—"The Son of the Crimea". This historic *Kurultay* (the first held by the Tatars on Crimean soil since 1917) was pointedly known by its organizers as the Second *Kurultay* to stress continuity with the first Crimean Tatar government crushed by the Bolsheviks during the Russian Civil War. In this *Kurultay*, Dzhemilev was also elected chairman of the *Mejlis*, the permanent thirty-three member parallel government or governing assembly of the *Kurultay*.

Mustafa Dzhemilev has been eloquently described as a "Moses leading his people back to the Promised Land" and one must know this extraordinary man in order to understand the Crimean Tatar national movement. In my 1997 interviews with Dzhemilev, I found that the youthful ardor of the fight for his people's repatriation had been tempered by a sobering realization of the formidable logistic, bureaucratic, financial, political, economic and legal obstacles he and his people had to confront as they attempted to reestablish themselves in a generally unwelcoming post-Soviet Crimea

Dzhemilev, who lived in a modest, vine-covered house guarded by one bodyguard on a hillside overlooking the old Crimean Khanate capital of Bahcesaray, was plagued with unexpected problems at the time of my visit. This tireless scourge of state prosecutors, the KGB, militiamen and the Communist *nomenklatura* (bureaucratic elite) had suddenly found himself confronted with the most daunting challenges of his career. Unforeseen hurdles appeared from every direction, and many of them now came from his own people. Dzhemilev's detractors cast accusations that he had been misusing the funds in a newly formed Crimean Tatar financial organization known as *Imdat* Bank; the old "veterans" of the movement, such as Reshat Dzhemilev and Ayshe Seytmuartova, complained to me about his imperious ways; a fraction in the *Mejlis* (Crimean Tatar parliament) headed by Lilia Bujurova, Izzet Khairov and others was maneuvering to oust him from power; and thousands of Tatars living in what can best be described as squatter camps were counting on "The Son of the Crimea" to provide them with Ukrainian citizenship, bring electricity and water to their settlements, and help in repatriating loved ones from Central Asia.

Calm, soft-spoken and prematurely aged by his long incarceration in the *Gulag*, Dzhemilev downplayed his years spent in Soviet prisons and dismissed the recent difficulties since arriving in the peninsula as typical examples of perpetual Crimean Tatar in-fighting. With a wave of his cigarette stained hand, one of the most widely known Soviet-era dissidents in the West told me:

> The KGB underestimated our people's determination during this early period, it was the unity forged during the 1960s and 1970s that allowed us to bring the people here when the conditions were right. It is this sense of unity that we developed in Central Asia that will allow us to rebuild our lives from the ground up here as our parents did in Uzbekistan after the war. There is something in the Crimean Tatar spirit that allows us to survive.[21]

Far from quelling the Crimean Tatars' Homeland Movement, the repeated arrests of Dzhemilev and scores of other dissident-activists, whose names are unrecorded, in the 1960s, 1970s and 1980s deepened the average Tatar's sense of grievance. These acts instilled the sense of unity of purpose to which Dzhemilev referred in our interviews. The state sponsored clamp down on the movement in fact appears to have increased the involvement of the average Crimean Tatar in it. Local Uzbek officials trying to quash the growing movement found themselves confronted with a multi-headed hydra. The arrest of one leader led to the rise of new organizers who were even harder to track. For Soviet officials who discounted the significance of the Soviet Union's internal republican borders and genuinely believed in the eventual rapprochement and blending of Soviet nations (such as the future president, Mikhail Gorbachev), the actions of Soviet citizens of Crimean Tatar background were incomprehensible. One frustrated Soviet official asked:

Why cannot Uzbekistan be a homeland for representatives of all nationalities living here? Why do they consider that only the Crimean Peninsula is their homeland, and that it belongs only to them? The Soviet Union is the homeland of all Soviet nations and national groups. National boundaries within this common homeland are relative, and with the development of productive forces these boundaries can and should change.[22]

Soviet Attempts to Find a Territorial Solution to the "Crimean Tatar Problem"

While the Soviet authorities did manage, to a certain degree, to decapitate the Crimean Tatar national movement through a series of arrests beginning in 1969 and continuing until the late 1970s, they appear to have realized that this people's aspirations could not be permanently muted by force alone. It was at this time that the Kremlin hit upon another solution that once again demonstrated its true lack of understanding of the real importance of an emotional link between a territory constructed as a "Fatherland" and a nation that considered itself to have been forged upon this territory.

Beginning in the early 1980s, the Soviet authorities began a project to create an ersatz homeland for the Crimean Tatars in two sparsely inhabited Uzbek *raions* (administrative regions) in the dry steppe lands south of Samarkand and Bukhara. The undeveloped Mubarek and Baharistan *raions* located in the Kashka Darya *oblast* were selected as a region of special settlement for them in an attempt to divert their drive to return to the forbidden Crimea.

In my interviews with Mustafa Dzhemilev, the leader informed me that Crimean Tatars who settled in the region were to receive schooling in their native tongue, were to be given prime administrative posts, would obtain preferential work treatment and would, in general, receive many of the benefits of state-sponsored, positive discrimination (i.e. *korenizatsiia*) so long deprived them. Uzbek authorities argued that much of the Crimean Tatars' national aspirations could be filled in a new homeland to be known as the "Mubarek Republic". At this time, Crimean Tatar students graduating from Tashkent's Nizami Pedagogical Institute were ordered to move to the region in order to receive their diplomas. Some illegal Tatar settlers who had been re-deported from the Crimea were also forcefully transferred to this area. An all-out effort was made to attract Crimean Tatars from throughout Central Asia to settle in the Mubarek, Baharistan region.

Abdulla Balich, the Crimean Tatar vice rector of the Nizami Institute (one of the highest ranking Crimean Tatars in Uzbekistan) further informed me that he was flown to the region and shown fully furnished houses, schools, administrative buildings etc. waiting for Tatar settlement in the city of Mubarek. He was then ordered to convince Crimean Tatar graduates to move to this ghost town and fulfill their "socialist duty" in developing the area. This source claimed that he was, however, skeptical, for in his words "This was the Uzbeks' homeland, and they would certainly be displeased to see their lands carved up for the creation of a homeland for another people."[23]

The majority of the Crimean Tatars appear to have agreed with Balich, and they began a series of protests, sit-ins at the Nizami and other institutes, and marches designed to show their displeasure with the state's attempts to provide an unsatisfactory territorial solution to their national problem. One Crimean Tatar *samizdat* source summed up their skepticism, claiming "They probably propose that Crimean Tatars, tempted by this carrot, would throng to the Qarshi steppes having forgotten about their native land, where institutions of higher learning in the native land existed many centuries before they appeared in Russia."[24]

In their history of the national movement, Guboglo and Chervonnaia state that "Any attempt to reconcile the Crimean Tatars with their status quo, to settle them in other republics or to search for means for their rebirth on 'foreign' land was perceived as provocative and hostile to the fundamental interests of the nation."[25] Dissident leader Mustafa Dzhemilev and other Tatar nationalists considered settlement in this region to be a betrayal of their people's desire to return to their native homeland, and the few Tatars who moved to the Mubarek Republic were stigmatized as traitors to the national cause. Dzhemilev summed up his people's disposition, saying "...it was completely clear to all Crimean Tatars that they had the prospect to revive their national culture in their Homeland, and that only there could they survive as a distinct people... For the Crimean Tatars, there was no Homeland other than the Crimea."[26] Most considered the whole Mubarek project to have been nothing more than another scheme by the crafty Uzbekistan SSR party boss, Sharaf Rashidov, to fleece Moscow of money for the development of a backward Uzbek region!

The failure of the "Mubarek Republic" to gain adherents among the Crimean Tatars has many parallels with the failure of the Kremlin's attempts to convince Soviet Jews to settle in their artificially created Jewish homeland-republic in the Soviet Far East, known as Birobidzhan, or the failed British attempts to create a Jewish homeland in Uganda in 1908. The failure of these related projects vividly demonstrates the importance of an emotional or imaginary link to a specific territory among a people or nation if this place is to be constructed as a "Motherland".

One can only speculate on the problems that would have arisen between the Uzbeks and Crimean Tatars in post-Soviet Republic of Uzbekistan if the latter had indeed accepted some sort of autonomy on Uzbek soil. For the most part, relations were cordial between the common Uzbeks and Crimean Tatars during the exile period; the Mubarek scheme was not given the chance to damage this stable relationship. In my interviews in Uzbekistan, I found the Uzbeks to be generally sympathetic to the Crimean Tatars' plight and to have respected this people who were often described by the Russians and Uzbeks as *trudolyubivii* (hard working). Although Uzbek party officials were known for clamping down on the Crimean Tatars' nationalist agitators, some members of the Uzbek intelligentsia supported the exiles. Uzbek writer, Temir Pulatov, for example, showed his support for them during the Gorbachev period, writing:

> They were able to survive with the understanding and sympathy of the native Uzbek and Kazakh populations which, in spite of the scorn and severity of the Stalinist officials, did not once in word or deed hurt the settlers, but made room for them not only at their hearths but on their land and territory. In spite of the total Stalinesque propaganda about the "enemy of the people" and the "nation of traitors", (our people) understood that the Crimean Tatars were first of all hard workers, honorable and that they, like the Uzbeks, work for their daily bread with the sweat of their brow.[27]

The Return to the Homeland Movement

By the mid 1980s, it became increasingly apparent that even Crimean Tatars who had never seen the Crimea had not "taken root" in Central Asia in any sense. Thousands had begun to move to the Ukrainian provinces bordering the Crimea to the north, especially the Kherson *oblast*, or to the Krasnodar *Krai* (territory) in the neighboring Caucasus region of Russia, to position themselves closer to what they considered their Motherland. In addition, Crimean authorities increasingly had to forcefully deport determined Crimean Tatar families attempting to illegally settle in the peninsula. The majority, it would seem, had never grown to accept Uzbekistan, Tajikistan, Kyrgyzstan, Kazakhstan or Russia as homelands (despite their cultural similarities with the Uzbeks and others). Unlike the Soviet Koreans and Uighurs, who were to be found in large numbers in Central Asia, they refused to consider these republics their permanent home. The Crimean Tatars refused to accept the Kremlin's assertion that the strategically located Crimea was already overcrowded with Slavs and holiday resorts. They could not be dissuaded from their ultimate goal: the physical repatriation of their entire people to their historical home.

What was astounding, in retrospect, was that the Crimean Tatars did not lose their collective determination to challenge the authorities during this period. They never put aside their objective of the physical return of their people to their ancestral lands in a real sense. While the Palestinians continued to publicly maintain a national mission of returning to their lost lands in the state of Israel many had, by contrast, come to see their people's return in the abstract and this was no longer seen as a realistic goal by the late 1970s and early 1980s.[28]

Although the Soviet state in comparison may have (from the comfortable position of hindsight) seemed destined to weaken and allow the Crimean Tatars to return, for those Crimean Tatars serving lengthy jail terms for merely agitating within the system for their people's right to return to the Crimea, the collapse of the all-powerful KGB, entrenched Soviet ruling elite and of the very totalitarian Soviet regime itself was simply unimaginable. It is easy today to underestimate the real risks these bold activists faced by directly confronting the police state with their demands for the "right of return". Crimean Tatar activists were still being arrested by the KGB in the late 1980s for such "seditious anti-Soviet" activities as sending appeals for support to the Crimean Tatar diaspora in Turkey and the USA, launching protest marches in the Krasnodar region and conducting demonstrations in Moscow. As late as 1988 an article in *Pravda Vostoka* (Truth of the East) announced the sentencing of a Crimean Tatar national activist, Reshat Ablaev, for his efforts to establish contacts with Fikret Yurter and Memet Sevdiyar, leaders of the American Crimean Tatar diaspora. The self-sacrifices made by jailed activists such as Rolan Kadiyev, Reshat Dzhemilev, Izzet Khairov, Ayshe Seytmuratova, Yuri Osmanov, Nariman Kadirov, Mustafa Dzhemilev and other dissidents on behalf of their people were in every respect tremendous.

The other two exiled groups remaining in Central Asia, the Volga Germans and Meshketian Turks, were by comparison much less active in directly challenging the Soviet regime and more willing to compromise on the issue of repatriation to their former administrative homelands. By the 1970s movements had arisen among the Meshketian Turks calling for permission to emigrate to Turkey, while the exiled Volga Germans had, by the 1980s, begun what was to become a mass migration to West Germany. This is not surprising when one considers that neither of these groups had experienced a strong national-territorial construction process during the late Imperial period, nor had they come to imagine their administrative republics as a *Vaterland* or *vatan* during the 1920s and 1930s (although the Volga Germans did undergo *korenizatsiia* and some territorialization of identity, the heterogeneous Meshketian Turks had no titular territorial unit within the Georgian SSR). As "Turks", many Meshketians viewed Turkey as a homeland after spending a generation in exile, while the Volga Germans considered themselves to be a diaspora of the larger *Volksdeutsche*.

The nationally-developed Crimean Tatars of Central Asia, by contrast, thought of themselves as uniquely "Crimean" and never conceptualized Turkey as an "alternative" homeland despite their ancestors' long history of emigration to this holy land. One of the nine tactics adopted by the Crimean Tatar movement in its struggle for repatriation explicitly called on activists to "Eschew references to our Islamic faith, even though it is an important part of our national identity, and do not demand to emigrate to Turkey, that is, do not seek to follow the well-trodden path of our ancestors of the last two centuries."[29]

It should be noted that the Crimean Tatars' drive for repatriation was not, however, simply based on typical nationalistic emotions. While the activists looked back to the days of the fabled Crimean Tatar Khanate (1443–1783) and their pre-Mongol *koreny* (roots) in the Crimea to legitimize their claim to the region, it is interesting to note that the *Leninshchina* (the period in which Lenin allowed national construction under *korenizatsiia* in the Crimean ASSR) was also considered a halcyon period and worthy of commemoration during meetings and rallies. This intense nostalgia for the period of the Crimean ASSR meant that emotional requests for the physical repatriation of the Tatar people to their ancestral homeland were always combined with more pragmatic calls for the reconstitution of the Crimean Autonomous Soviet Socialist Republic—with the Crimean Tatars as the obvious recipients of state sponsored, *koretiizatsiia*-style affirmative action within "their" administrative unit.

The Crimean Tatars' comparatively obscure struggle for repatriation did not come to the attention of any but a few nationality specialists in the West until the advent of new Soviet leader Mikhail Gorbachev's policies of *glasnost* (openness) and *perestroika* (restructuring) began the process of ending much of the Brezhnev era's repression. By the late 1980s Soviet authorities began to allow the repatriation of several thousand Crimean Tatars who were known to be uninvolved in the national movement to return in organized levies known as *orgnabor* (organized labor).

All of the *kolkhozes* where these early state-sponsored settlers were given land in the Crimea by the Soviet government were located in the dry steppe. This meant they were far from the more valuable southern land prized by the local Crimean Communist authorities and cherished in the Tatars' collective memory. Most of these early settlers experienced considerable difficulty in an area that was markedly different from the coast and mountains of their youth or their second hand childhood stories of the Green Isle. With the breakdown of Soviet authority many of these early settlers, however, moved to buy houses and land to the south around Simferopol, Bahcesaray, Karasu Bazar (Belogrosk) and in villages in the northern foothills of the Yaila. These settlers proved to be a vanguard for the vast waves of Crimean Tatars returning after 1989.

This slow pace of settlement was, however, seen by the Crimean Tatar leadership as unsatisfactory and, taking advantage of the new relaxed political environment, in April 1987 approximately 2,000 activists launched their most daring call for repatriation yet. They did so by holding a bold protest in the heart of Moscow on Red Square itself. Here they were seen by Western tourists and journalists with banners reading "Motherland or Death".

News of this unprecedented act, the largest mass demonstration in Red Square since the Russian Revolution, electrified the country. In response to this rally, which was reported throughout the world, the ageing Soviet president Andrei Gromyko agreed to establish a commission to deal with the Crimean Tatars' demands. There can be little doubt that other nationalist movements and fronts springing up in the Baltic republics and Transcaucasus at this time learned from the Crimean Tatars' successful methods of gaining the Kremlin's attention.

The so-called Gromyko Commission, however, found that since the population of the Crimea had doubled since World War II, the Tatars needed to look at the situation in "in a realistic way", taking into account the interests of all peoples in the Crimea and give up their selfish, un-Soviet dreams of returning to the peninsula. While the commission emphasized that the Crimean Tatars had been unjustly accused of treason against the Soviet homeland, it continued to forbid their return.

1989 and the Beginning of the Return Migration

By the year 1989, however, the situation in the USSR had changed dramatically as nationalist fronts appeared in the Baltics, radical nationalist movements that presaged war appeared in Armenia and Azerbaijan, and rising national movements arose throughout the USSR. In 1989, the Crimean Tatar singer Susana Memetova was permitted to sing on the central Moscow Television station and her song had a great symbolic impact among the Crimean Tatars in Central Asia. In her song Memetova asked "Why have our fountains been ruined? Why have our graves been destroyed" and ended by singing "I want to return to my homeland, but cannot find my way home." In this environment of nationalist expression, openness and restructuring, the continued insistence on keeping the increasingly vocal Crimean Tatars in exile in Central Asia became untenable. Events in Uzbekistan also vividly demonstrated the fact that non-Uzbeks were increasingly unwelcome in that republic. The Crimean Tatars' forty-five-year *modus vivendi* with the native Uzbek population was threatened by events that took place in the Fergana Valley in 1989. In June of that year, Uzbeks in the Fergana Valley cities of Kuvasai, Margilan, Fergana and Kokand went on a rampage of violence that targeted another of the deported peoples forced to remain in exile, the Meshketian Turks.[30] Scores of Meshketians were killed in the violence, their homes were burnt and as many as 40,000 Meshketians were hurriedly evacuated from the republic by the Soviet government with a tremendous loss of property. While relations between the Meshketians and Uzbeks had not been as cordial as those between the Crimean Tatars and Uzbeks (the Meshketians were often stereotyped as "Caucasian Mafiosi", for example), few had expected such a savage outbreak of violence. A wave of panic swept over all non-Uzbek minorities in Uzbekistan.

Although the Crimean Tatars were not directly targeted in the violence, Mustafa Dzhemilev informed the author that several members of his nation were killed by the Uzbek mobs. Many fled the Fergana Valley to escape the violence. According to Dzhemilev, panicked Crimean Tatars and Meshketian Turks were flown out of their burning villages by the Soviet army on Soviet Mil-18 helicopters to neighboring Tajikistan in order to save their lives. Other sources claim that hundreds of Crimean Tatars' houses were set ablaze or robbed in this violence.

Rumors were rife in Uzbekistan that dates had been set for attacks on other outsiders including the Crimean Tatars, according to local newspapers. While there had always been a "pull" operating in the Tatar community's desire to return to the Crimea, the Fergana Valley events certainly provided a new "push" factor in compelling many to consider leaving Uzbekistan. When asked what percentage of the Crimean Tatars wished to return to the Crimea in the aftermath of the Fergana Valley events, representative Aider Kurkchi, for example, claimed "It used to be about three quarters, but now it's practically all of them. After the events in Fergana, people don't believe that the authorities in Uzbekistan are capable of protecting them from possible pogroms."[31] Several Crimean Tatars interviewed by the author recalled the rhyming chant that was heard in many parts of the Uzbek republic at this time *"Russkii doloi, Tatarskii domoi, Koreetsii Hanoi!"'* (Down with the Russians, home with the Tatars, and to Hanoi with the Koreans). For a people that had already experienced one mass displacement in the twentieth century, the prospect of another was frightening.

Fortunately for the Crimean Tatars, in 1989 the dream of returning to the "Green Isle" became a reality. The Kremlin commission dealing with the Tatars finally granted them the right to return in a planned fashion to the Crimea and even contemplated the re-establishment of the Crimean ASSR.

The permission to return eventually came in a small article published on the front page of the Soviet Union's two major newspapers, *Izvestiia* and *Pravda*, on November 24, 1989. The article called the expulsion of the Crimean Tatars and other punished peoples from their homelands "a barbaric act on the part of the Stalinist regime" and declared that "The USSR Supreme Soviet considers it necessary to take the relevant legislative steps for the unconditional restoration of the rights of all Soviet citizens subjected to persecution."[32] Crimean Tatar interviewees described the wave of excitement that swept through the Central Asian diaspora as its members heard of the government's decree. The way was finally being paved for tens of thousands of them to return to a distant *vatan* on the Black Sea that most had only heard of from a disappearing generation that had been uprooted from their homes forty-five years earlier.

The Return to the Homeland

Many of the Soviet Union's estimated 500,000 Crimean Tatars saw this moment as a window of opportunity similar to the one that had been missed after the release from the special settlement camps in 1956. They quickly made preparations to return to the Crimea. Tatar activists went throughout the diaspora communities of Central Asia encouraging their compatriots to take advantage of the opportunity to return to the land of their ancestors. Although officials were sent by the Crimean authorities to discourage repatriation to the largely Russified Crimea, these efforts could not dispel the euphoria that swept through the Crimean Tatar settlements in 1989 and 1990.

THE CRIMEAN TATARS

In my interviews with Crimean Tatars in Central Asia and in the Crimea it soon became apparent that the migration was a highly organized event. Whole collective farms, neighborhoods or extended families migrated together and were met by Tatar leaders awaiting them in the peninsula. Parties of migrants would arrive in tent camps set up for them in advance in the main square in Simferopol (the Crimean capital) and would join in *samozakhvat* (self-seizure) "raids" on unused land belonging to state or collective farms in the Crimean countryside. In this fashion Crimean Tatar settlements appeared overnight throughout the countryside. Leaders were democratically elected from these settlements to represent their community in the Tatars' parallel parliament known as the *Mejlis*.

This was an exciting period in Crimean Tatar history, as older members of the community showed younger generations their former villages and haunts, local parallel governments known as mini-*Mejlises* were elected, settlements were built and the community celebrated its return to its home place.

The return of thousands of Tatars to the Crimea, not surprisingly, caused tension with the Russian population. The roots of this tension between the returning Crimean Tatars and local Slavic population in the Crimea were complex and go back to a failed deal made at this time.

Several Crimean Tatar leaders informed the author that, as the Tatars began their repatriation, they were approached by members of both the KGB and the GRU (Military Intelligence), who offered them legal, logistical and financial support in their repatriation if they would take a pro-Russian stance in the Russian dominated Crimea. The KGB's aim appears to have been to forge an alliance with the returning Crimean Tatars and to use this highly mobilized people as leverage in working for the separation of the Crimea from the Ukrainian SSR.

In any event, the offer was refused by the Crimean Tatar leaders, who instead turned to Kiev for support and took a pro-Ukrainian stance. For its part Kiev initially supported them as a counterweight to Russian secessionist movements in the region. But the Ukrainian government has been less interested in supporting the Tatars since the Crimean Russian population's breakaway movement was quelled in 1995 with the removal of the secessionist Crimean leader Yuri Meshkov.

In light of the Crimean Tatars' pro-Ukrainian stance, it is not surprising that their land seizures were strongly resisted by the conservative Russian Communist authorities (many of whom had ordered the expulsion of Crimean Tatar illegal settlers in the 1960s, 1970s and 1980s). In one of its most calculated blows against the returnees, the Crimean *oblast*'s authorities organized a referendum on reestablishing the Crimea as an autonomous republic in an effort to preempt the Crimean Tatars' own calls for the reestablishment of the Crimean ASSR (with prerogatives for its officially recognized *korennoi narod*). In 1991 the Ukrainian government responded to this vote and established the the Autonomous Republic of the Crimea (ARC), with no mention of the Crimean Tatars in the republican constitution or allowances for Crimean Tatar as an officially recognized language.

Clashes between well-organized Crimean Tatar groups and local Russian MVD and OMON (Special Police) units were commonplace at this time. Former *Mejlis* member Lilia Bujurova showed the author a video of the clash between Crimean Tatar squatters on the peach *kolkhoz* of Krasnii Rai in Alushta (October 1, 1992) and local security forces that captured some of the returnees' determination to seize land in the Crimea. The Krasnii Rai squatters had surrounded their settlement with trenches, barbed wire and stakes and had raised a banner proclaiming "homeland or death" over the settlement. When the local OMON units attacked the camp, the outnumbered Crimean Tatar defenders fought back desperately against bulldozers, helmeted police, and tear gas with sticks and Molotov cocktails.

When the wounded inhabitants of Krasnii Rai were arrested by the Crimean authorities, tens of thousands of Tatars converged on the Crimean Parliament building in Simferopol (locally known as the Pentagon) and stormed its lower floors as those inside fired upon them. The highly mobilized Crimean Tatars refused to leave their positions around the Parliament on the Central Square until their compatriots were released. After a tense standoff in which OMON special troops clashed with the protesters, the twenty-six Krasnii Rai settlers were released to a hero's welcome as thousands of cheering Tatars celebrated their newfound political assertiveness.

Another example of this astounding political unity took place in June of 1995 when two Crimean Tatar vendors in the city of Kurotne (Feodosiia vicinity) were killed by members of the Crimean mafia belonging to the Bashmak gang for refusing to pay protection bribes.[33] When the local militia refused to arrest the guilty party (in the Crimea the lines between the mafia and militia are often blurred), hundreds of Crimean Tatars began to attack and burn businesses owned by the Bashmak gang. In the process, the head of the local police militia was taken hostage and convoys of Crimean Tatars from throughout the Crimea's settlements mobilized to drive to the region to support their beleaguered countrymen as they had done during the Krasnii Rai incident three years earlier.

As the Crimean Tatar columns approached Feodosiia, they were blocked by a Ukrainian special force division known as the *Berkuts* (Golden Eagles). Mustafa Dzhemilev informed the author that in the ensuing confrontation the elite *Berkut* units fired on his people, killing several unarmed Crimean Tatars in the process. As the tension mounted in the Crimea, Dzhemilev and Crimean Tatar leader Refat Chubarov arrived at the scene and agreed to return the columns to their villages if the guilty parties in the Kurotne slayings were apprehended. Perhaps the most dangerous ethnic conflict in the post-Soviet Crimean Republican (if not post-Soviet Ukrainian) history was thus averted by the Crimean Tatars' traditionally moderate leadership.

The Construction of the Crimean Tatars as the Korennoi Narod in the Crimea in the Post-Soviet Context

The "return" to the Crimean Peninsula of tens of thousands of Crimean Tatars who had spent their entire lives in Central Asia, and their forceful seizures of land, offered a fascinating spectacle for political scientists, historians and anthropologists studying the phenomena of migration, homeland construction and mass-based nationalism. While it is easy to interpret this event as an obvious manifestation of late twentieth-century nationalism, I found it to be a more complex process.

Many of those returning to the Crimea from Central Asia were city dwellers (estimates of the percentage of city dwellers among the Crimean Tatars prior to the repatriation vary from 62 per cent to 80 per cent) and the majority of this once-thoroughly agrarian people appear to have become urbanized during the exile period.[34] To many, the "Return to the Homeland" meant a move from life in a dreary, industrial, urban setting in Central Asia to the smaller towns and villages of the often romanticized Crimean countryside. On many occasions, the romanticized images of the Crimean Tatar repatriates' youth (or, more commonly, their parents' or grandparents' youth) were, however, confronted by the harsh reality of life in the late twentieth-century Crimea. Describing the orchards of his home village an elderly returnee, for example, pointed out that "In our village of Buyuk Muskomiia in the Balaklava district, there were apple orchards. Such an abundance of varieties in them. Gul'pempe, Chelebi, Kandil, Sinai, Cary Sinai, Kara Sinai, Bal Alma, Pamyk Alma and many others I don't remember...Thanks to the power of the [Communist] party *nomenklatura* many of these have been lost forever."[35] The comparison between the Crimea of the late 1930s and the Crimea of the late twentieth century (which suffered from the typical environmental degradation that came with the Soviet Union's drive for industrialization) caused much disillusionment among the Crimean Tatars who were returning to localized micro-homelands that had been altered in their absence. One wrote "In the time of Pushkin, our Salgir was a stormy, deep, and most of all a clear river. The contemporary poet cannot say anything of the sort about it."[36] According to this source "great damage was done to the Crimea's eco-system" when newcomers arrived and constructed concrete canals that siphoned off water from the Salgir and did not follow the Tatars' time-honored canal building techniques. Another source writes of the villages of Tarak Tash (Comb Rock) in the Sudak valley:

> As an old traveler once wrote "The valleys of the big and little Tarak Tash abound with brooks and the water is so abundant here it nourishes all the Sudak fields." Alas, the water in this village was sufficiently strained that the numerous springs and brooks demanded careful expert care. The knowledge and skill was passed from one generation to the next, but right after the deportation, as a result of the unskilled activities of the new-comers to the village, the valley became dry.[37]

Such reconstructions of communal links to the Crimean land on the basis of "indigenousness" by Crimean Tatar settlers serve to reinforce this people's beliefs in their rights to the peninsula as the region's *korennoi narod* or *oz sahipleri* (true owners). This is in some respects a holdover from the communal memory of the *korenizatsiia* period of the 1920s and 1930s, which constructed this people as the Crimea's most legitimate nation on the basis of its indigenous "roots" there. The Crimean Tatar *Kurultay's* maximalist demands for quotas of up to one third of the seats in the Crimean parliament during the early 1990s (even though they only made up 10 per cent of the Crimea's 1995 population of 2,685,000) also stemmed from this belief that the Tatars had special rights and political prerogatives in the peninsula that resulted from their indigenous roots there. Since their repatriation in the late 1990s, the Crimean Tatars have fought to be recognized in international forums on national rights as the Crimea's officially recognized indigenous ethnic group.[66] In the convoluted language of the Ukrainian *Verkhovna Rada* (Supreme Parliament), EU, UN, the Council of Europe and the Minority Rights Organization, the Crimean Tatar leadership, for example, places great importance on having their people defined not as a "minority", but as an "indigenous people" with native rights to their land. One of the *Kurultay's* objectives has been to "Strive to have the Crimean Tatars recognized as the indigenous people of the Ukraine and the Crimea." There is a Crimean Tatar organization, headed by

Mejlis member Nadir Bekirov, known as the Foundation for Research and Support of Indigenous Peoples in the Crimea, which supports the formulation of special rights for the Tatars that resemble those given, for example, to the Sami Lapplanders in the Norwegian Assembly. In response to this movement, the Ukrainian government has declared the Crimean Tatars an indigenous people and has stated:

> The issue of the rights of indigenous peoples has a certain distinctiveness which distinguishes it from the general issue of minority rights and, in particular, the rights of national minorities…A principal difference is that although indigenous groups are not titular or dominant ethnic groups, they have lived on the territories of modern independent states since time immemorial, consider these territories their homeland, and have maintained especially strong spiritual links to these territories.[38]

As the self-proclaimed indigenous people of the Crimea, the Crimean Tatars stress their unique claim to the land that had for two centuries been taken from them by Russian *pomeshchiks* and the Soviets. A declaration made at the second *Kurultay* held in Simferopol in June of 1991 proclaimed:

> The land and natural resources of the Crimea, including its therapeutic and recreational potential, are the basis of the national wealth of the Crimean Tatar people and cannot be utilized without its will or its clearly expressed approval. Any actions which harm the ecological status of the Crimea, including its offshore Black Sea waters, must be halted. Damage to nature and the resources of the Crimea must be compensated by the perpetrators.[39]

This emphasis on the Crimean Tatars' unique indigenous claim to the peninsula has led to an often uncompromising approach by their leadership. It has been pointed out that, at its most extreme, the Crimean Tatar ideologues have developed "a complete ethnological theory which claims that no one besides the Crimean Tatars has the right to be called 'Crimean people.'"[40] This is an example of the exclusionary legal rights to national territory which was firmly encapsulated in Soviet national theory and which has been perpetuated in the post-Soviet context by native populations in the Baltics, Central Asia, Buryatia, Abkhazia, the Crimea and elsewhere."[41] Guboglo and Chervonnaia cite as further proof of this tendency the demand made by Crimean Tatar nationalists for Russians and Ukrainians to "release the Crimea which should be returned to the only people having a legal, historical right to it, the Crimean Tatars."[42] The Tatars bolster their exclusive claims to the peninsula with the oft repeated mantra that "the Crimean Tatars have only one homeland, the Crimea, and, unlike other nationalities, they have nowhere else to emigrate to avoid endless discrimination and violence."

Crimean Tatar Settlement Patterns

While Soviet nation building policies of the 1920s and 1930s still shape many of the Crimean Tatars' actions in the Autonomous Republic of the Crimea that was formed in 1991, one must also understand the role of the communal memory in shaping these activities. In particular, the Crimean Tatars' links to the Yaila Mountains and Yaliboyu coast micro-homelands must be understood in order to comprehend their current settlement patterns.

Many of those former exiles migrating to the peninsula intended to "return" to the very village or region from whence their parents or grandparents had been deported in 1944. To a certain extent this impulse was a holdover from this people's pre-nationalist, agrarian ties to the land, which were passed down to new generations in stories of the fields of one's home village, the mountains of one's specific region, and so forth. This desire to migrate to the *kucuk vatan* (micro-homeland), which had been described in detail as a paradise by the older generations, re-enforced an already powerful sense of attachment to the larger Crimean homeland, which was defined in typically modern, nationalistic terms.

While the Crimean Tatars have been largely kept off the Yaliboyu coast by the powerful Crimean mafia, the Crimean *nomenklatura* (bureaucratic elite), local city councils, large business-resort interests and the Crimean MVD security forces, many still dream of moving to this region, which was endlessly described to them in the stories of their childhood. The first tentative Tatar settlements have appeared in the Sudak Valley (southeastern coast), in the Feodosiia vicinity and on a hillside overlooking the resort coastal town of Yalta. These hard won coastal footholds are considered by the *Mejlis* to be the first step in the eventual return of Crimean Tatars to this historically Tatar zone. Most have, not surprisingly, settled in other historically Tatar, but less contentious, zones. These can be found in the northern foothills of the Yaila Mountains, with the Bahcesaray district, Simferopol district and Belogorsk district (still known as Karasu Bazar to the Crimean Tatars) receiving the most settlers. The strip between Simferopol and Belogorsk, in particular, has seen considerable Tatar settlement. On a more practical level, many have also attempted to settle in the cities in order to find jobs, but most have been excluded from the urban areas and live in sprawling squatter suburbs outside its major towns.

While one can debate the Crimean Tatars' motives for leaving their places of exile in Central Asia, where most had finally prospered and become socially integrated, few can argue as to the results: in spring of 1987 there were a mere 17,400 Crimean Tatars in the peninsula. By June of 1991 the number had risen to 135,000, and by May of 1992 to 173,000. By the end of 1993, approximately 259,000, or just over half of the Crimean Tatar nation of 500,000, had returned to the Crimea.[43] This was to be the largest migration in Crimean Tatar history, surpassing even the Great Migration of 1860 in its scale. On this occasion, however, the Crimean Tatars were, for the first time, migrating to the Crimea instead of leaving it.

If it was NKVD-KGB transport trains described as "crematoria on wheels" that brought the Crimean Tatars to Central Asia, it was the trusty Soviet *Lada*—the automotive badge of success for most exiles—that carried the Crimean Tatars back to their homeland. In the early 1990s whole villages and extended families formed convoys of cars and migrated to the peninsula on either the southern route (From Turkmenistan to the Caspian Sea, across the Caspian Sea to Baku by ferry, Baku to the Northern Caucasus, and then, finally, to the Crimea) or the northern alternative across the plains of Kazakhstan and the northern Caucasus. The stories of cars being attacked by bandits in Kazakhstan, of heavy "fines" being levied on Tatars by GAI (*Gosudarstvennaya Avtomobilnaya Inspektsiya*—state auto police) officials in Turkmenistan and of the general risks invoked in moving across a crumbling empire with all one's possessions, demonstrate the courage and determination of the Crimean Tatar migrants to reach the romanticized "Green Isle".

The sacrifices made by Tatars to fulfill their dreams of once again living in their Crimean homeland have been great. Most were forced to sell their houses and apartments in Central Asia at deflated prices, and the quality of living of many declined dramatically as they then had to build primitive brick houses covered with corrugated tin roofs (usually on scrubby unwanted land in the countryside) in order to live in the peninsula.

In spite of these hardships, the following interview with a returnee from exile is typical of the hardy settler mentality that has developed among the repatriates:

> Saniye, now 65, and her husband, Seidjalil Asanov, 71, left behind a six-room house in Tajikistan. "There was a garden, an orchard with grapes and figs, an aisle of flowers-it was so beautiful" she recalled. Now they live in a flimsy shack made of sheet metal, burlap and wood, surrounded by dust, mud and weeds, they couldn't be happier. "We're living in the homeland" she beamed.[44]

Reasons for the Decline in Migration to the Crimea

By 1994 the pace of the migration had, however, tapered off for a number of reasons, the most obvious being problems with integrating this large population into the resource-scarce Crimea. With over two-and-a-half million largely unwelcoming Russians and (to a much lesser extent) Russified Ukrainians, there were very few jobs, there was almost no health care, and there was constant anti-Tatar discrimination and poor standards of living. For many Crimean Tatar repatriates, the idealized image of the Crimean homeland was dispelled by the harsh realities of attempting to find work in one's profession and trying to build a niche for one's family in a land where they were largely unwanted.

Few Crimean Tatars have been able to settle in the cities, where jobs are available, and most live in *samozakhvat* (self seizure) settlements built in the countryside, or in the outskirts of larger cities. Most Crimean Tatars in the region have been forced to live in primitive settlements such as those located between Simferopol and Belogorsk-Karasu Bazar such as Lazovoe, Sary Su, Kamenka, Aromatnaya, Svetochnaia, Khosh Geldi, and Bogatoe. Other Tatar pockets can be found in the Simferopol area, such as the settlements of Stroganovka, Marino, Belaya, Fontany, and in the Evpatoriia district in such settlements as Ismail Bey and Yar Kaya or in the settlements of Ak Kaya (Yalta), Verhnaya Ku-tuzhova (between Alushta and Simferopol), Koktebel and Primorskoye (Feodosiia area) and numerous settlements around Bahcesaray, such as Skalistoye.

These settlements often lack basic amenities, such as paved roads, running water, or electricity, and conditions in the simple squatter villages are particularly bleak in winter.[45] Health conditions have deteriorated dramatically as a result and illnesses, such as tuberculosis and nerve problems, are widespread among the Crimean Tatar settlements. Few settlements have access to medical facilities and many illnesses go untreated.

In addition, the problems associated with de-urbanization have been particularly acute as the large number of Crimean Tatar white collar workers and intelligentsia (doctors, engineers, professors, teachers) are forced to sell goods in the market, grow their own food and build their own houses in the primitive squatter settlements surrounding the cities. The Tatars' traditional agricultural skills in viniculture, step terrace farming, fruit production and tobacco growing had of course been lost when their "roots" to the Crimea were sundered during the exile period. Most repatriates have encountered problems adapting to the rural conditions in the land of their parents and grandparents. While Crimean Tatar leaders were able to optimistically claim in 1989 that "99% of the Crimean Tatars were ready to move to the Crimea", most now admit that the poor social, political and material conditions there have halted the return migrations for the foreseeable future.[46]

The slowing pace of return was in part due to events surrounding the collapse of the Soviet Union in 1991. The Soviet state initially planned to organize the repatriation of the Tatars in a planned fashion. The so-called "State Program for the Return of the Crimean Tatars to the Crimean Oblast" aimed to assist them in the construction of housing, finding of employment and development of social and cultural infrastructures. Financial and material resources were also promised to the Crimean Tatar repatriates from the Uzbek SSR, Tajik SSR, Ukrainian SSR and the Russian Federation.

With the collapse of the Soviet Union, the very state that had initially done so much to destroy this people, the Crimean Tatars, ironically, lost an important source of funding. Many Crimean Tatars could not afford to return to the peninsula when hyper-inflation swept the post-Soviet republics in the early 1990s. In addition, as many as 80,000 returning Tatars were denied Ukrainian citizenship until 1999 due to the fact that they had arrived in the Ukraine after the passing of the 1991 Ukrainian citizenship law granting citizenship only to those living in the country at that time. This lack of citizenship excluded many repatriates from medical facilities, pensions, schooling, voting etc. When combined with first hand reports of the dismal political and socioeconomic conditions of the Crimean Peninsula, the depletion of this peoples' life savings related to post-Soviet hyper-inflation convinced approximately half of the Crimean Tatar nation to remain in their places of exile.

In addition, although several CIS (Commonwealth of Independent States) countries signed an agreement in Bishkek, Kyrgyzstan on October 9, 1992 calling for the lifting of bureaucratic barriers to the repatriation of citizens of those newly independent countries with Crimean Tatar origins, red tape and bureaucratic hurdles remained for those attempting to emigrate to the Ukraine and renounce their previous citizenship. In particular it should be noted that, although the Ukrainian and Uzbek governments signed a protocol in the fall of 1998 on the "facilitation of the decision of citizenship for deportees, their children and grandchildren," other CIS countries have failed to make such agreements. The approximately 30,000 Crimean Tatars living in the Russian Federation, in particular, faced numerous obstacles in emigrating to the Ukraine.

It should also be stated that the Crimean Tatars appear to have lost out in the privatization of land that took place in the peninsula as a result of a 1999 decree privatizing collective farms. This was largely a result of local government policies deliberately designed to exclude them from land. Only 16,000 of the more than a quarter of a million Crimean Tatars living in the region belonged to collective farms at this time. Those who did not, failed to receive land when these collective areas were privatized.

As the indigenous people of the Crimea, the Crimean Tatars have called on the Crimean Parliament to allot them "reservations" for returning generations, but this concept has yet to be fully implemented. For the returning Tatars of today, the land issue is as burning as it was for the Young Tatar leader Abdureshid Mehdi at the beginning of the twentieth century. As Mustafa Dzhemilev explained it "Around 200,000 more Tatars are getting ready to return to the homeland. What should we tell them when they return and there's nothing for them?"[47] It is also interesting to note that in March 2000, the local *Mejlis* of Bahcesaray, headed by Ilmi Umerov, has begun calling for the return of the *vakif* lands following the example of other indigenous groups who have fought to regain their lost lands. There, however, appears to be little real chance of this happening in the near future. Thus the process of depriving the indigenous Crimean Tatar population of its lands that began in 1783 continues to this very day.

The Socio-Cultural Effects of the Central Asian Exile

Those exiles who have managed to return to their imagined homeland are still closely linked to their former places of exile in Central Asia. Many aspects of Crimean Tatar society and culture have been drastically affected by their half-century sojourn in Central Asia. At the time of the deportation, for example, the Crimean Tatar people had made great strides in coalescing around a distinct Crimean Tatar national identity, but local sub-national regional-linguistic cleavages between Nogai, and Yaliboyu and Yaila Tat were still present and important.

In reminiscing on his childhood in the peninsula prior to World War II, the great Crimean Tatar writer Cengiz Dagci informed the author that there were still major differences between the Nogais and the Tats even at this late date.[48] According to this source, very few Tats, who considered themselves more cultured than the Nogais, intermarried with these plain-dwellers from the northern Crimea in his youth. The exile experience in Central Asia, however, appears to have had a considerable homogenizing influence on the Crimean Tatars and these cleavages have been largely subsumed since the deportation and return. In many ways the exile has thus broken down the regional linguistic differences that had for centuries divided the various groups comprising the Tatars of the Crimea. This homogenizing experience acted as the final catalyst in the forging of the unified Crimean Tatar nation of today. Most Crimean Tatars who do still speak their native language speak the Middle Path Kipchakized Oghuz Tatar, which became widespread during the 1920s and 1930s, and have little interest in sub-ethnic affiliations. This experience was, interestingly, also found among the eclectic Meshketian Turks or Ahiska, who did not unite to form a nation until the exile period.

While Crimean Tatars are still aware of their original sub ethnic-geographic origins and all can tell you whether they are a Yaila Tat, Yaliboyu Tat or Nogai, their contemporary identities are more profoundly shaped by their exile experience. Those who lived in Tashkent, for example, consider themselves to be cosmopolitan and talk of this great Central Asian city's restaurants, efficient subway system, museums and so forth. Those from Samarkand have a certain nostalgia for that city's *chaihanas* (traditional tea shops), and longing for the soil which grew "Uzbekistan's best grapes". The Crimean Tatars who were settled in the Fergana Valley speak of the mountains and rich piedmont soil found there, whiles those from Siberia, Kazakhstan, Kyrgyzstan or Tajikistan have completely different geographic and cultural points of reference. Geographically-based identities that were forged during the exile years now appear to be more salient than the previous sub-ethnic identities, which were forged over hundreds of years in the Crimea's three distinct zones. A Tat Tatar from Tashkent is, for example, more likely to hire a fellow *Tashkentli* (Tashkenter) who is a Nogai on the basis of this shared background than a fellow Tat whose family lived in Dushanbe (Frunze) Tajikistan during the exile period.

Talk in the primitive Crimean Tatar settlements is also laced with nostalgia for life in Uzbekistan. Crimean Tatar officials estimate that approximately 72 per cent of the returnees are from Uzbekistan, with 16 per cent coming from Russia (predominately the Krasnodar *Krai* near Sochi, and Moscow) and the rest hailing from Kyrgyzstan, Tajikistan, Kazakhstan and the Ukraine.[49] Crimean Tatars from the large "Soviet" capital city of Uzbekistan, Tashkent (which has a Russophone population that is roughly equal to that of the entire Crimea), miss its urban culture and amenities. Many Crimean Tatars from Tashkent were whitecollar workers who shopped in the city's massive stores such as *Detskii Mir* (Children's World), *GUM* (the State Universal Shopping Mall), or the colorful Charsou Bazaar. These Sovietized Tatars spoke to their Russian and Uzbek colleagues and neighbors in the *lingua Sovietica* of Russian, enjoyed performances at the Navoi Theater and have found that they miss the amenities of life in a large city. It is also interesting to note that, while in the Crimea in the Fall of 1997, the author ate at several Crimean Tatar restaurants with names like "The *Markanda*" (The Samarkand) which served Uzbek *laghman* (noodles), Uzbek-style *plov* (rice), Uzbek *manty* (meat "raviolis") and other examples of Central Asian cuisine which have now become a part of the Crimean Tatar diet.

Much of this nostalgia for Central Asia is certainly a reflection of the general post-Soviet longing for the financial and political security and stability that marked the Soviet Union from the 1960s to early 1980s, but it is also based on the truly stark position many Crimean Tatar repatriates find themselves in today. For most Crimean Tatars in the post-Soviet Crimea the quality of housing, schooling and medical attention has declined drastically. The returnees have faced considerable social, economic and political marginalization in their cherished "Zion".

Tatar men (the traditional providers in Muslim societies) frequently cannot find work in the Crimea and divorce, which was previously unheard of in this culturally Muslim society, has begun to rise as a result. Life is so harsh in the Crimea that some Crimean Tatars have been forced to leave the "Green Isle" to return to Central Asia. Others have built crude cinder block houses in the peninsula (as a means of staking a claim to plots seized from the government), but continue to live in Central Asia and the adjacent Krasnodar *Krai* until conditions improve there. The Tatar settlements today are filled with half-finished houses that belong to Tatars who continue to live and work in Central Asia and elsewhere. All Crimean Tatar settlements are littered with rough hewn, spongy yellow building blocks carved from the limestone of the Yaila Mountains used to build houses that may never be completed. In many instances Tatars live in the first floor of houses while the second floor remains unfinished or dwell in simple, one-room structures with a toilet and modest cooking facilities.

In spite of the hardship, most Crimean Tatars in the Crimea are determined to remain in their homeland. When I asked settlers in the *samozakhvat* settlements I lived in why they made such sacrifices to return to the peninsula, interviewees invariably answered with the simple expression *"rodina eta rodina"* (the homeland is the homeland). A sixty-year-old returnee perhaps best summed up her people's unwavering, deep-rooted determination to live in their ancestral lands when she said "I sold everything for pennies, packed up, gathered my family and moved here. My father recently died, at the age of ninety-one, but he was happy to die here in our homeland."[50]

Despite the obvious feelings of disillusionment, most Crimean Tatars in the Crimea feel a sense of partaking in something larger than themselves, namely the rebuilding of a nation and the reversing of centuries of expulsion from the land.

This makes the hardships bearable for many. In the Crimean Tatar settlements, there is thus, mixed with the sadness of financial loss, a feeling of triumph.

Lilia Bujurova, Crimean Tatar national poet, a popular television host on the Crimean language news and commentary program known as *Ana Yurt* (Motherland) and a former member of the *Mejlis*, explained this mixed emotion to me in 1997. Reminiscing on her youth in Central Asia Bujurova explained "We spent our entire lives promising ourselves that we would, at all cost, return to this place. No one thought it would be easy, and in truth it has been hard. But we are all of us happy to be in the place we grew up loving. This place is who we are as a people. No one will take this away from us again, we are a hardworking people and sooner or later we will flourish here."

This spirit of optimism and a strong communal will to succeed, in spite of the immense obstacles, is best captured in Lilia Bujurova's celebration of homeland. Written the year the Crimean Tatars' mass return movement began in 1989 it is titled "What is the Homeland's Scent?":

> Of what does the homeland smell?
> Of a dry blade of grass,
> Caught in a child's hair,
> Of a pine branch, of bitter wormwood,
> Or, of a separation, buried in the heart?
> Or, of a lamb's wool, of aromatic coffee,
> Tinkling as it pours into thin little cups
> Of mountain tea, of almonds, fragrant with mint,
> Of today's reality, of yesterday's dream?
> Or of the searing cry of a lone seagull?
> Or, of the snowy peak of Cadir Dag?
> Or, of the distant music of an ancient song?
> Oh no, my homeland smells of hope.[51]

The Crimean Tatar Diaspora in Central Asia Today

While all Crimean Tatars in the Crimea harbor a deep-seated hope that the portion of their nation still in *surgun* (exile) will return to join in the rebirth of their nation, the author found little evidence in Central Asia of any future mass migrations to the peninsula from this region. Conditions in the Crimea are so bleak that the *Mejlis* now believes it is irresponsible to encourage further migration from Central Asia.

There will doubtless be a trickle of migration as Crimean Tatars move to join family members, but it will in all probability not assume the vast scale of the second *Buyuk Goc* (Great Migration) of 1989–1993. Only an external catalyst (such as the breakdown of general security and rising anti-outsider nativism in Uzbekistan, perhaps following the death of Uzbek president Islam Karimov) could call forth such a massive movement to the Crimean Peninsula from Central Asia.

It should, however, be stated that there is increasing uneasiness among the Crimean Tatar community of the Krasnodar *Krai* in the northern Caucasus resulting from rising anti-Islamic sentiment in this region. The rise in anti-Islamism is, in part, a backlash resulting from the unsuccessful outcome of the first Russo-Chechen War (1994–96) and continuing violence in neighboring Chechnya and Dagestan related to the 1999–2009 Russo-Chechen War. As local Russian politicians with nationalist agendas continue to discriminate against Muslims here, this may cause the remaining population of less than 15,000 Crimean Tatars still living there to migrate to the Crimean Peninsula in the near future.

Most Crimean Tatars remaining in Central Asia or the Krasnodar Krai, however, simply cannot afford to make the costly migration to the Crimea. The financial position of those Crimean Tatars remaining in Central Asia is not much better than that of their kin in the peninsula, according to Izzet Khairov, the former representative of the Crimean Tatar *Mejlis* in Uzbekistan. Khairov informed me that the comparatively well off Tatars of the Central Asian diaspora have already left for the Crimea.

Many of those who have remained suffer in economic terms from the general post-Soviet economic collapse. According to this source:

> Today [1995] in the Central Asia region there are close to 200,000 Crimean Tatars, among whom 140–160,000 continue to live in Uzbekistan, for the most part concentrated in the industrial regions of the republic. 70 to 80 per cent of families are incomplete and divided [between Central Asia and the Crimea], the level of life among the average Crimean Tatar family in Uzbekistan is significantly lower (by up to two times) than in the Crimea …In relation to the Crimean Tatars, the government institutions and organizations of Uzbekistan consider them to be minions (*vremenshchiky*), or at best, potential non-citizens of Uzbekistan. For this reason they are unable to better their living conditions or rise up the work ladder. Their poor financial position does not allow them to return to the homeland with their compatriots.[52] Naturally, the Crimean Tatar *Mejlis* fears that this half of their nation, which remains scattered in its places of exile, will not benefit from the national renaissance which is taking place among the compactly settled Tatar population of the Crimea. A 1995 declaration by the Crimean Tatar *Mejlis*, for example, warned of the threat of the "complete degradation of the people" who remained in Central Asia without a Crimean Tatar press, schools or radio to help them sustain their identity.[96]

While in Uzbekistan, I found this to be a very real threat as some urbanized Crimean Tatars in Tashkent (the largest center of Crimean Tatar inhabitation) considered themselves to be "internationalists" in the old Soviet sense. Many were unwilling to make the sacrifices necessary to maintain their national identity (most notably selling their apartments, quitting their jobs and moving to the Crimea). Although the Crimean Tatars have opened a cultural center in Tashkent, it is difficult to imagine this having a considerable impact on the Tatars who are dispersed in towns throughout Uzbekistan and greater Central Asia. In addition, exiles who are forced to remain in Central Asia find themselves politically marginalized by the Crimean Tatar *Mejlis* which focuses its activities on those Tatars who have returned to the peninsula.

While it is risky to make assumptions concerning the fate of this nation which now sees itself divided between the Central Asian diaspora and the Crimean homeland, it is safe to make a few cautious predictions. Firstly, it can be argued that the portion of the Crimean Tatar population compactly settled in the Crimean homeland will certainly maintain and rebuild a much more dynamic and active national identity than the segment of the nation scattered throughout Central Asia. It is also safe to argue that, barring any reoccurrence of events similar to the 1989 Fergana Valley pogroms, a sizable portion of the Crimean Tatar people will, by circumstance or by choice, remain in Central Asia, perhaps permanently.

The most nationally active and energetic portion of this nation has of course migrated to its homeland. Many Crimean Tatars in Central Asia, however, continue to identify with the peninsula and this may help them sustain some form of a distinct diasporic national identity, even if this population does lose its native language and many of its distinctive national traits. This community may maintain a diasporic link with the *yesil ada* ("Green Isle") in much the same way that many in the Crimean Tatar communities of the Dobruca and Turkey did in the twentieth century. Popular Crimean Tatar journals that make their way to Central Asia, such as *Avdet* (Return), *Golos Kryma* (Voice of the Crimea), *Vatan*, and *Salgir* (the name of a cherished river in the Crimea), are replete with descriptions of the homeland and full of articles on the region's history, geography, culture, and archeology. The constantly recurring theme of the Crimea certainly serves to keep the dream of migrating alive in the minds of those left behind in the places of exile. In many ways then, these publications may serve the same role among the Crimean Tatar diaspora of Central Asia that the journal *Emel* did in the Romanian Dobruca and Turkish diasporas, namely it will contribute to the maintenance of Crimean Tatar identity in this region.

RETURN

With the re-establishment of a Crimean Tatar presence in the Crimea, the history of migration that began with the 1783 mass emigration of Tatar *muhajirs* to the imagined homeland of the Muslim Ottoman Empire by Crimean Muslims has come full circle. The Crimean Tatars' unique, territorialized national identity, developed during a half century-long process of nation building begun by Ismail Bey Gasprinsky, Abdureshid Mehdi, Numan Celebi Cihan, and Veli Ibrahimov, has allowed this people to begin the process of reversing over 200 years of out-migration and expulsion and has enabled them to rebuild their ethnie on the lands lost by their forbears.

Today there are more Crimean Tatars in the Crimean Peninsula than at any time since the Great Migration of 1860. As of December 31, 1999 the long struggle to acquire Ukrainian citizenship for approximately 80,000 Crimean Tatars who had not been granted citizenship rights in 1991 was solved by the Ukrainian *Verkhovna Rada* (Parliament) with its decree entitled "On Measures Concerning Resolving the Problems with the Citizenship of Formerly Deported Peoples and Their Descendants Returning to the Ukraine from the Republic of Uzbekistan." The attacks on Crimean Tatar *samozakhvat* settlements of the early 1990s have, since 1994 (when the Ukrainian government reigned in pro-Russian secessionist leaders in the Crimea), largely ceased. Most Crimean Tatars are now struggling to overcome high unemployment and their lack of political representation, rather than struggling to defend their hard won settlements from attacks. The secular, politically aware nation that the early twentieth-century Tatar nationalist Numan Celebi Cihan dreamed of is now a reality in the Crimean *vatan*.

This rebirth of Crimean Tatar parent community in the "Green Isle" will also perpetuate the existence of Crimean Tatar identity in the Central Asian, Balkan and Turkish diasporas in the future by providing its members with a living focus for their diasporic identity. As the Tatars in the Crimea partake in the general reconstruction of identity that is occurring throughout the former Soviet Union, their struggle to rebuild their people will be aided by their bonds to this larger diasporic "nation" that is spread from the mountains of Tajikistan to the Danube delta region of Dobruca.

Although the Russian Communist-dominated Crimean government has largely brought a halt to its campaign to expel the Crimean Tatars since 1994, the potential for violence in this region nevertheless remains real. The Tatars' political struggle for, among other things, a voice in local Crimean Republic affairs, greater rights and freedoms, desperately needed job opportunities, land, restitution, the return of their fellow countrymen from Central Asia, the rebirth of their culture and an end to anti-Tatar discrimination continues.

In January 1999 the Crimean Tatar *Mejlis* building in Simferopol was firebombed by unknown assailants and considerable damage was done to the offices of Mustafa Dzhemilev. In the spring of 1999 a Crimean Tatar mosque in the Yalta vicinity was also firebombed by unknown assailants, and tensions ran high. Most recently, in January 2000, the Crimean militia raided the renovated *Mejlis* building and confiscated documents, leading to the growing potential for conflict between the Crimean Tatars and local authorities.

Perhaps the greatest cause of tension between the local authorities and the Crimean Tatars, however, is the continued exclusion of the latter from the Crimean *Verkhovna Rada* (Parliament). They have no voice in the Crimean government despite the fact that they make up between 10 and 11 per cent of the autonomous republic's population. In many ways then the Crimean Tatars' position has deteriorated in the peninsula since the mid 1990s, when they had fourteen quota seats in the government. In the spring of 2000 Oxana Shevel wrote "The Crimean Tatars quest for greater political rights in the Crimea have met with virtually a deaf ear…Anti-Tatar prejudice is still widespread among the population and elites and some members of the Crimean parliament openly voice their opinion that 'Tatars are good for nothing other than trading goods in the market'."[53]

While the ethnic tension between Russians and Tatars in the Crimea hardly resembles the tension found in early 1990s, Dzhemilev is quick to point out that the potential for real violence lies just below the surface in this volatile region. The political and economic marginalization of the Tatars and their deepening economic plight may lead to a radicalization of the historically peaceful Crimean Tatar national movement in the future.

Certain elements in the Crimean Tatar society, such as Server Karimov's nationalist *Adalet* (Justice) party, or the newly established *Vatan* party, have already begun to move in a more radical, nationalist direction. Karimov informed the author in an interview held in offices in the *Mejlis* that were subsequently destroyed in a January 1999 firebombing, that his organization was gaining adherents who were increasingly disillusioned with the meager results stemming from the Crimean Tatars' traditionally peaceful approach. Writing in the spring of 2000, Ukrainian political analyst Natalya Belitser warned:

> The Crimean Tatar community represents the most organized, easily mobilized force in the ARC (Autonomous Republic of the Crimea), and a further delay in the adoption of legislative and normative acts for securing the full restoration of their rights is fraught with the danger of a more radicalized movement. This would result almost inevitably in a serious ethno-political conflict which might develop into something more severe than ever before.[54]

RETURN

The rising level of tension among the community was clearly manifested in the spring of 1999. On April 8, 1999 as many as five thousand Crimean Tatars converged on Simferopol's parliament building to commemorate Russia's annexation of the Crimean Khanate on April 8, 1783. The frustrated Tatars demanded the resignation of the Crimean Republic president Leonid Grach, burned copies of the Crimean constitution and annexation manifesto of 1783, waved blue banners emblazoned with the *tarak tamgha* national symbol and demanded Ukrainian citizenship for the approximately 80,000 Crimean Tatar repatriates who had been excluded from it up to that point.

While this protest was not as volatile as a protest held in the previous year, in which thousands of Crimean Tatars clashed with Crimean militia forces, this was largely due to the Tatar leadership's successful efforts to mute any violence. It is, however, not known how long Mustafa Dzhemilev-Kiriimoglu, Refat Chuborov and other moderate politicians can keep the increasingly desperate Crimean Tatars from the path to greater assertiveness, and perhaps violence, in future.

From Annexation to Annexation. The Crimean Tatars Return to Russian Rule

The February 27, 2014 seizure of the Crimean parliament building by mysterious masked Russian soldiers alarmed the Crimean Tatars who had fought them the day before in the main square of Simferopol to demonstrate their loyalty to Ukraine. Two people were killed and thirty five injured in that confrontation between Tatars chanting "Glory to Ukraine!" and Russians chanting "Russia!" The Crimean Tatars feared any talk of the Russian majority's call for secession of the Crimea from the Ukraine and its annexation by their historical nemesis, Russia (Russians make up 60 per cent of the Crimea's population). The fears of the Crimean Tatars that the Russian majority of the peninsula might move against them were considerably heightened by the March 2, 2014 Russian invasion by 6,000 troops. The subsequent annexation of the Crimea by Russia in spring of 2014 caused tremendous dismay among Crimean Tatars as they and their homeland were transferred overnight from democratic, Western-leaning Ukraine to Putin's authoritarian Russia.

The loudest voices in the Crimea opposing Vladimir Putin's unilateral surprise invasion of the peninsula on March 2, 2014 came from Tatar crowds that marched to protest the arrival of Russian troops, not the local Ukrainians. The Crimean Tatars had turned down a deal to work with Russians back in 1991 in favor of cooperating with the Ukrainian government. They subsequently supported the pro-Western Orange Revolution in Ukraine in 2004, which overthrew a pro-Russian government, and they continued to support Kiev until 2014. The *Washington Post* stated in March 2014 "Whatever the Tatar grievances against the Ukrainian state may be, when faced with the choice of being under either Russian or Ukrainian control, the Crimean Tatar leadership has consistently and unequivocally chosen Ukraine."[55]

Not surprisingly, the Crimean Tatar *Mejlis* has refused to recognize the new Crimean government put in place by the Russians since their invasion. One member of the *Mejlis* stated "We are occupied territory. It is foreign invasion. So we ask our people to be calm and not to go for provocations. We cannot call people to go to streets and to organize meetings in front of political terrorists, you know? These political terrorists, they control government buildings now."[56]

Tatar leader Mustafa Dzhemilev who had previously given up control of the *Mejlis* to his successor Refat Chubarov (but was still a member of the Ukrainian parliament), stubbornly refused to accept the Russian conquest and annexation of his homeland, despite efforts by the Putin administration to negotiate with him. The Russians went so far as to offer to release his son who was being held in jail if Dzhemilev would only formerly endorse the annexation. He, however, stuck to his guns and refused to publicly back the "illegal" annexation of the Crimea.

In return, the Russians banned Dzhemilev from entering Russia, including the Crimea, for five years. This has everything to do with the fact that the principled Dzhemilev refused to compromise with Putin and was thus described in the Western media as "the voice that carries most authority in challenging the referendum under which the people of Crimea are said to have voted overwhelmingly to join Russia."[57] Dzhemilev would subsequently claim that he told Putin "the territorial integrity of our homeland [Ukraine] is very important."[58] He also said "I was polite with him [Putin]. I said, 'We are not opposed to help, and Russia certainly owes us for [the Soviet deportations], but first you have to remove your troops.'"[59]

Vladimir Putin himself telephoned Dzhemilev in March 2014, soon after the Russian conquest of the peninsula, and promised him language rights for the Crimean Tatars if he recognized the Russian annexation. But Dzhemilev, having suffered so much at the hands of Putin's former employer, the KGB, would not back down.[60] Putin also met with Crimean Tatar representatives in Sochi in the spring to discuss their concerns and publicly condemned the

1944 deportation of the Crimean Tatars. He later announced "Today we must all realise that the interests of the Crimean Tatars today are tied to Russia."[61]

But the new pro-Russian Crimean authorities sent mixed signals by flying helicopters over Crimean Tatar commemorations marking the seventieth anniversary of the deportation on March 18, 2014 and calling for the return of all land illegally taken in the peninsula. This latter edict has tremendous ramifications for the Crimean Tatars, most of whom are squatters illegally living on land they seized in the late 1980s and early 1990s. Local Cossacks have also been calling for the "return of the Tatars to Tatarstan" and this has had a chilling impact on the Crimean Tatars, as has the rise of Russian "self defense" units.

Matters came to head again in September 2014 when Russian forces raided the Tatar *Mejlis* building in Simferopol as well as the houses of key Crimean Tatar leaders and several mosques. Fears were also stoked when Tatar houses were daubed with swastikas. At the time, the Crimea's pro-Russian prime minister, Sergei Aksyonov, stated of the *Mejlis* "From a juridical perspective, there is no such organization for me. What *Mejlis*? The organization was not registered properly. It does not exist."

As strong supporters of Western-leaning Ukraine's rule in the Crimea, Tatars feared the arrival of Vladimir Putin's Russian troops, whom they equated with Moscow's historical oppression of their people. One Crimean Tatar from Fontany, a settlement outside the capital of Simferopol, expressed his fears of the Russian invasion as follows "We want to live in peace. But Russian troops have entered our territory—Ukrainian territory—and armed men are walking around. It scares us—not just me, but all of us."[62] Another from Bahcesaray stated "If there is a conflict, as the minority, we will be the first to suffer. We are scared for our families, for our children. This could be a new Yugoslavia."[63]

Putting the latest Russian invasion in its historical context, another Crimean Tatar said "From the moment Russian Empress Yekaterina II sent her troops here to annex this territory, our sorrows began."[64] Most Tatars saw the March 2, 2014 Russian invasion of the Crimea through the prism of history and related it to their own experiences. National Public Radio reported an interview with a Crimean Tatar on March 3, 2014 as follows "71-year-old Asan Sait Asanov, who was 10 months old when his parents bundled him up for more than a half century of exile in Uzbekistan, says whatever the future holds, nothing will force the Tatars from their homeland again. When asked if the younger generation understands their history, he nods firmly."[65]

Another Crimean Tatar from the settlement of Khosh Geldi (Welcome) similarly said "Our people are peaceful, but if they threaten us, our men will defend the community. It is better to die here than leave again."[66] A Crimean Tatar named Rustem Mustafayev, whose father was deported at the age of seven, said "They almost wiped us out. There are few of us left now. This is our homeland. We have nowhere else to go."[67] Finally, a Tatar named Mamut said, "What we can say definitively as Tatars is there is nowhere else for us to go. We were removed once before by force. We endured genocide. We came home again. And we will never leave again."[68]

Having sacrificed so much to return to the Crimea from their scattered places of exile, the Tatars were understandably made nervous by the March 2014 arrival of armed Russian troops, which had echoes of the earlier deportation of their nation seventy years previously. As a mere 12 per cent of the peninsula's population of just over two million, they fear for their future under Vladimir Putin, who came to power in 1999–2000, crushing the Chechens' bid for independence. Despite the professed resolutions of many Tatars to never again leave the Crimea, thousands have already fled to the Ukraine. Those that remain face the prospect of living under the rule of their people's historical "Other". It remains to be seen how this small nation adjusts, as it once again finds itself under Moscow's rule.

NOTES

PROLOGUE

1. For more on this fascinating, but little studied, chapter in European history see. Brian Glyn Williams. *The Sultan's Raiders. The Military Role of the Crimean Tatars in Ottoman History*. Washington DC; Jamestown Foundation. 2013. Available online at: brianglynwilliams.com under "Publications."

1. THE PEARL IN THE TSAR'S CROWN

1. Harry de Windt. *Russia as I know it*. Philadelphia; JB Lippincott. 1917. Page 187.
2. Peter Pallas. *Travels in 18th Century Russia*. London; Studio Editions. 1990. Page 135–6.
3. Charles Scott. *The Baltic, the Black Sea and the Crimea*. London; Richard Bentley. 1854. Page 306.
4. F.A. Feodorov. *Krym s Sevastopolem Baliklavoiu*. St. Petersburg; 1855. Page. 37.
5. Edward Clarke. *Travels in Various Countries of Europe and Asia. Part one. Russia, Tahtary and Turkey*. London; T. Cadell and W. Davies. 1816. Page 239.
6. F.A. Feodorov. *Krym s Sevastopolem Balaklaviou*. St. Petersburg. Korableva and Sirakova. 1855. Page 38.
7. Laurence Oliphant. *The Russian Shore of the Black Sea*. New York; St. Arno Press. 1970 (First published 1854). Page 169.
8. Evgenii Markov. *Ocherkii Kryma*. Simferopol; Tavria. Reprint 1995. Page 210–211.
9. B. Kuftin. "Iuzhnoberezhnye Tatary Kryma." *Zabveniiu ne Podolzhit*. Kazan; Tatarskoe Knizhnoe Izdatel'stvo. 1992. Page 44.
10. Evgenii Markov. *Ocherkii Kyrma*. Page 212.
11. Charles Scott. Op cit. no. 3. Pages 232–233.
12. Edward Clarke. *Travels in Various Countries of Europe and Asia. Part one. Russia, Tahtary and Turkey*. London; T. Cadell and W. Davies. 1816. Page 234.

13. Ebenezer Henderson. *Biblical Researches and Travels in Russia, Including a Tour in the Crimea*. London; James Nisbet. 1826. Pages 300–301.
14. Meriel Buchanan. *Recollections of Imperial Russia*. New York; George Doran and Co. 1924. Page 228.
15. Edward Clarke. *Travels in Various Countries of Europe and A*sia. Page 173.
16. Ibid. Page 145.

2. DISPOSSESSION: THE LOSS OF THE CRIMEAN HOMELAND

1. E.I Druzhinina. *Severnoe Prichernomor'e 1775–1800 g.g*. Moscow; 1995. Page 109.
2. G. Bliumsfeld. *Krymsko-Tatarskoe Zemlevladenie*. Odessa; Odessa Vestnik. 1888. Page 35.
3. Ibid. Page 29.
4. Edward Lazzerini. "The Crimea Under Russian Rule. 1783 to the Great Reforms." *Russian Colonial Expansion to 1917*. Ed. Michael Rywkin. London; Mansell Publishing. Page 126. And Arsenii Markevich. "Peresleniia Krymskikh Tatar v Turtsiiu v Sviazi s Dvizheniem Naseleniia v Krymy." *Izvestiia Akademii Nauk SSR*. 1928. Page 388.
5. Alexandre Bennigsen. "Several Nations or One People. Ethnic Consciousness Among Soviet Central Asian Muslims." *Central Asian Survey*. Summer 1979. Vol. 24, no. 3. Page 53.
6. Mary Holderness. *New Russia. A Journey from Riga to the Crimea*. London; Sherwood Jones and co., 1823. Page 28.
7. Alan Fisher. "Enlightened Despotism and Islam Under Catherine II." *Slavic Review*. Vol. 27, no. 4. December 1968. Page 547.
8. Mohammad Reza Djalili. "Dar al Harb." *The Oxford Encyclopedia of the Modern Islamic World*. Oxford; Oxford University Press. 1995. Page 338.
9. Bernard Lewis. *The Political Language of Islam*. Chicago; University of Chicago Press. 1988. Page 105.
10. W. Montgomery Watt. *Muhammad at Mecca*. Oxford; Oxford University Press. 1953. Page 110.
11. Hakan Kirimli. *National Movements and National Identity Among the Crimean Tatars*. Leiden; EJ Brill. 1996. Page 8.
12. Ibid. Page 150.
13. E.I. Totleben. "O Vyselenii Tatar iz Kryma v 1860 gody." *Russkaia Starina*. June 1893. Page 535.
14. G.I. Levitskii. "Pereslenie Tatar iz Kryma v Turtsiiu." *Vestnik Evropy*. No. 10. October 1882. Page 600.
15. Mark Pinson. "Russian Policy and the Emigration of the Crimean Tatars to the Ottoman Empire, 1854–1862." *Guney-Dogu Avrupa Arastimalari Dergisi*. No. 1, 1972. Page 40.

16. Charles Koch. *The Crimea from Kerch to Perekop*. London; Routledge. 1855. Page 23.
17. G.I. Levitskii. "Pereslenie Tatar iz Kryma v Turtsiiu." Op. cit. footnote 28. Page 600.
18. Gavin Hambly. *Central Asia*. London; Morrison and Gibb Ltd. 1969. Page 193.
19. M. Goldenberg. "Krym i Krymskie Tatary." *Vestnik Evropy*. No. 6, 1883. Page 80.

3. *DAR AL HARB*: THE NINETEENTH-CENTURY CRIMEAN TATAR MIGRATIONS TO THE OTTOMAN EMPIRE

1. Alexander Kinglake. *The Invasion of the Crimea. Its Origins and an Account of its Progress*. New York; Harper and Brothers. 1874. Vol. 1. Pages 422–423.
2. Arsenii Markevich. "Peresleniia Krymskikh Tatar v Turtsiiu v Sviazi s Dvizheniem Naseleniia v Krymy." *Izvestiia Akademii Nauk SSR*. 1928. Page 393–394.
3. E.I. Totleben. "O Vyselenii Tatar iz Kryma v 1860 gody." *Russkaia Starina*. June 1893. Page 532.
4. G.I. Levitskii. "Pereslenie Tatar iz Kryma v Turtsiiu." Op. cit. footnote 28. Page 605.
5. Evgenii Markov. *Ocherkii Kryma*. Simferopol; Tavria. Reprint 1995. Page 115.
6. V.E. Vozgirin. *Istoricheskie Sud'by Krymskikh Tatar*. Moscow; Misl. 1992. Page 325.
7. Alexander Herzen. "Gonenie na Krymskikh Tatar." *Kolokol*. Dec. 22, 1861. No. 117. Page 973.
8. Mark Pinson. "Russian Policy and the Emigration of the Crimean Tatars to the Ottoman Empire, 1854–1862." *Guney-Dogu Avrupa Arastimalari Dergisi*. No. 1, 1972. Page 44.
9. G.I. Levitskii. "Pereslenie Tatar iz Kryma v Turtsiiu." *Vestnik Evropy*. No. 10. October 1882. Page 604.
10. Evgenii Markov. *Ocherkii Kryma*. Simferopol; Tavria. Reprint 1995. Pages 112 and 114.
11. V.E. Vozgirin. *Istoricheskie Sud'by Krymskikh Tatar*. Moscow; Misl. 1992. Page 323.
12. Arsenii Markevich. "Peresleniia Krymskikh Tatar v Turtsiiu v Sviazi s Dvizheniem Naseleniia v Krymy." *Izvestiia Akademii Nauk SSR*. 1928. Page 395.
13. E.I. Totleben. "O Vyselenii Tatar iz Kryma v 1860 gody." *Russkaia Starina*. June 1893. Page 538.
14. For more on modern Europe's first case of genocide see Walter Richmond. *The Circassian Genocide*. Rutgers University Press. 2012.
15. M. Goldenberg. "Krym i Krymskie Tatary." *Vestnik Evropy*. no. 6. 1883. Page 69.
16. N. Shcherban'. "Pereselenie Krymskikh Tatar." *Russkit Vestnik*. 1860. vol. 30. H-12. Page 38.
17. M. Goldenberg. "Krym i Krymskie Tatary." *Vestnik Evropy*. no. 6. 1883. Page 73.
18. B.M. Vol'fson. "Emigratsiia Krymskikh Tatar v 1860 g." *Istoricheskie Zapiski*. No. 9. 1940. Page 187.
19. Arsenii Markevich. "Peresleniia Krymskikh Tatar v Turtsiiu v Sviazi s Dvizheniem Naseleniia v Krymy." *Izvestiia Akademii Nauk SSR*. 1928. Page 402–403.

20. Vol'fson, B. M. "Emigratsiia Krymskikh Tatar v 1860 g.'*Istoricheskie Zapiski*. no. 9. 1940. Page 192.
21. E.I. Totleben. "O Vyselenii Tatar iz Kryma v 1860 gody." *Russkaia Starina*. June 1893. Page 541.
22. B.M. Vol'fson. "Emigratsiia Krymskikh Tatar v 1860 g." *Istoricheskie Zapiski*. No. 9. 1940. Pages 187–88.
23. Arsenii Markevich. "Peresleniia Krymskikh Tatar v Turtsiiu v Sviazi s Dvizheniem Naseleniia v Krymy." *Izvestiia Akademii Nauk SSR*. 1928. Page 396.
24. Hamdi Giray. *Hicret*. Istanbul. 1927.
25. Ia. S. Smirnova. *Nogaitsy. Istoriko-Etnografcheskii Ocherk*; Cherkesk; Stavropol'skoe Knizhnoe Izdatel'stvo. 1988. Page 37.
26. N.P. "Iz Vospomianii Byvshago Krymskogo Pomeschchika." *Russkaia Starina*. Vol. 131. 1907. Page 164.
27. E.I. Totleben. "O Vyselenii Tatar iz Kryma v 1860 gody." *Russkaia Starina*. June 1893. Page 357.
28. P. V. Maslov. et. al. *Krym. Khrestomatiia po Istorii Kraiia*. pt. 1. Simferopol; Krymskoe Gosudarstvennoe Izdatel'stvo. 1930. Page 240.
29. S.B. Efetov and B.I. Filonenko. "Pesni Krymskikh Tatar." Izvestiia Tavricheskogo Obshchestvo Istorii Arkheologi i Etnografi. No. 1. (58). Simferopol. 1927. Page 71.

4. *VATAN*: THE CONSTRUCTION OF THE CRIMEAN FATHERLAND

1. Alan Fisher. "A Model Leader for Asia. Ismail Gaspriali." *The Tatars of the Crimea. Return to the Homeland*. Durham; Duke University Press. 1998. Page 34.
2. "Bliznost Russkikh." *Tercuman*. No. 29, July 28, 1903. Page 124.
3. Edward Lazzerni. *Ismail Bey Gasprinskii and Muslim Modernism in Russia. 1878–1914*. Unpublished doctoral dissertation. Department of History. University of Washington. 1973. Page 36.
4. Hakan Kirimli. *National Movements and National Identity Among the Crimean Tatars*. Leiden; EJ Brill. 19996. Page 92.
5. Brian Glyn Williams. *The Crimean Tatars. The Diaspora Experience and the Forging of a Nation*. Leiden; 2001. For a chapter on this emigration of 1874 which was caused by efforts to recruit Crimean Muslims into the Russian army.
6. Robert Lyall. *Travels in Russia, the Krimea. the Caucasus and Georgia*. London: Routledge. 1812. Page 349.
7. Anatole Leroy-Beaulieu. *The Empire of the Tsars and Russians*. London; G. Putnam and Sons. 1893. Page 93.
8. Alan Fisher. *The Crimean Tatars*. Stanford; Hoover Institution Press. 1978. Page 101.
9. Edward Lazzerini. "Ismail Gasprinskii (Gaspirali): The Discourse of Modernism and the Russians." *The Crimean Tatars. Return to the Homeland*, ed. Edward Allworth. Durham; Duke University Press. 1998. Page 53.

10. Hakan Kirimli. *National Identity and National Movements Among the Crimean Tatars*. Leiden: E.J. Brill. 1997. Page 37.
11. Edward Lazzerini. "Ismail Gasprinskii (Gaspirali): The Discourse of Modernism and the Russians." *The Crimean Tatars. Return to the Homeland*, ed. Edward Allworth. Durham; Duke University Press. 1998. Page 23.
12. Alexandre Bennigsen and Chantal Lemercier Quelquejay. *La Presse et le Mouvement National Chez les Mussulmans de Russia Avant 1920*. Paris. Mouton. 1964. Page 41.
13. Hakan Kirimli. *National Identity and National Movements Among the Crimean Tatars*. Leiden: E.J. Brill. 1997. Page 41.
14. Edward Lazzerini. "Ismail Bey Gasprinskii's Perevodchik/Tercuman. A Clarion of Modernism." Central Asian Monuments. Ed. Hassan Paksoy. Istanbul; Isis Press. 1987. Page 154. Karl Deutsch. *Nationalism and Social Communication*. Boston; MIT Press. 1962. Pages 86–105.
15. V. Iu. Gankevich. *Ocherk Istorii Krymskotatarskogo Narodnogo Obrazovaniia*. Simferopol; Tavria. 1997. Page 115.
16. Iu. Kandymov. *Ismail Bei Gasprinskii (Gaspirali) Iz Zaslediia*. Simferopol. Tavria. 1991. Page 12.
17. Ismail Gasprinsky. *Rossia i Vostok. (Russkoe Musulmanstvo i Russko-Vostochnoe Soglashenie)*. Kazan; Fond Zhien. 1993. Pages 28–29.
18. This was of course an inflated number. Edige Kirimal. "The Crimean Tatars." *Studies on the Soviet Union*. (new series). Vol. X. no. 1. 1970.
19. Ismail Gasprinsky. *Tercuman*. September 15, 1903. No. 36. Page 155.
20. Ismail Gasprinsky. "Ob Emigratsiia." *Tercuman*. May 7, 1902. No. 17. Page 3.
21. Ismail Gasprinsky. *Tercuman*. November 11, 1902. No. 43. Page 65.
22. Richard Pipes. *The Formation of the Soviet Union*. Cambridge MA; Harvard University Press. 1954. Page 189.
23. Hakan Kirimli. *National Identity and National Movements Among the Crimean Tatars*. Leiden: E.J. Brill. 1997. Page 93.
24. E. Seitbekirov. "Sviashchennaia Bor'ba Krymskikh Tatar." *Golos Kryma*. November 4, 1997. Page 5.
25. Hakan Kirimli. *National Identity and National Movements Among the Crimean Tatars*. Leiden: E.J. Brill. 1997. Page 88.
26. Ibid. Page 109.
27. A.K. Bochagov. *Milli Firka*. Simferopol; Gosudarstvennoe Izdatel'stvo. 1930. Page 27.
28. Hakkan Yavuz. "The Patterns of Political Islam: Dynamics of National and Transnational Loyalties and Identities." *Central Asian Survey*. 1995. 14 (3). Page 352.
29. Ibid. Page 97.
30. Shamil Aliadin. *Teselli*. Moscow; Sovetskii Pisatel. 1985. Page 307.
31. Hakan Kirimli. *National Identity and National Movements Among the Crimean Tatars*. Leiden: E.J. Brill. 1997. Page 103.

32. Ibid. Page 173.
33. Memet Sevdiyar. *Etiudy ob Etnogenze Krymskikh Tatar*. New York; Fond Kryma. 1997. Page 201.
34. Shamil Aliadin. *Teselli*. Moscow; Sovetskii Pisatel. 1985. Page 276.
35. Ibid. Page 263.
36. Zsuzsa Kakuk. *Kirim Tatar Sarkiliari*. Ankara; Turk Dil Kurumu Yayinlari. 1993. Page 37.
37. V.E. Vozgirin. *Istoricheskie Sud'by Krymskikh Tatar*. Moscow; Misl. 1992. Page 51.
38. A.I. Kliachin. "Dinamika Ethnicheskikh Sistem Rasseleniia v Krymy." *Etnograficheskoe Obozrenie*. No. 2. March–April. 1992. Page 27.
39. Baron Pierce Balthazar von Campenhausen. *Travels Through Several Provinces of the Russian Empire*. London; Richard Philips. 1808. Page 52.
40. V.E. Vozgirin. *Istoricheskie Sud'by Krymskikh Tatar*. Moscow; Misl. 1992. Page 309.
41. Alexandre Bennigsen. "Islamic or Local Consciousness Among Soviet Nationalities?" *Soviet Nationality Problems*. Ed. by Edward Allworth. New York; Columbia University. 1971. Page 176.
42. Galina Yemelianova. "The National Identity of the Volga Tatars at the Turn of the 19th Century: Tatarism, Turkism and Islam." *Central Asian Survey*. 1997. 16 (4). Page 562.

5. SOVIET HOMELAND: THE NATIONALIZATION OF THE CRIMEAN TATAR IDENTITY IN THE USSR

1. V.N. Sagatovskii. "Tavrida Internatsional'naia." *Krymskaia ASSR. 1921–1945. Voprosy, Otvety*. Simferopol; Tavria. 1990. Page 36.
2. R.I. Muzafarov. "ASSR Natsional'naia." *Krymskaia ASSR. 1921–1945. Voprosy, Otvety*. Simferopol; Tavria. 1990. Page 28.
3. Ibid.
4. Robert Kaiser. *The Geography of Nationalism in Russia and the Soviet Union*. Princeton; Princeton University Press. 1994. Page 94.
5. A.K. Bochagov. *Milli Firka. Natsional'naia Kontrerevolutsiia v Krymy*. Simferopol; Krymskoe Gosudarstvennoe Izdatel'stvo. 1930. Page 40.
6. M.F. Bunegin. *Revolutsiia i Grazhdanskaia Voina v Krymu (1917–1920 gg.)*. Simferopol; Krymgosizdat. 1927. Page 89.
7. Ibid. Pages 89–90.
8. Ibid. Page 326.
9. B. G. Zarubin and A. G. Zarubin. "Krymskotatarskoe Natsianol'noe Dvizhenie v Nachale 1918 g." *Istoriia i Arkeologiia Iugo-Zapadnogo Kryma*. Ed. Iu. M. Mogarchev. Simferopol; Tavria. 1993. Page 205.
10. M.F. Bunegin. *Revolutsiia i Grazhdanskaia Voina v Krymu (1917–1920 gg.)*. Simferopol; Krymgosizdat. 1927. Page 45.

11. Charles Hostler. *The Turks of Central Asia*. Westport Connecticut; Praeger. 1993. Pages 44–45.
12. B. G. Zarubin and A. G. Zarubin. "Krymskotatarskoe Natsianol'noe Dvizhenie v Nachale 1918 g." *Istoriia i Arkeologiia Iugo-Zapadnogo Kryma*. Ed. Iu. M. Mogarchev. Simferopol; Tavria. 1993. Pages 209–210.
13. M.F. Bunegin. *Revolutsiia i Grazhdanskaia Voina v Krymu (1917–1920 gg.)*. Simferopol; Krymgosizdat. 1927. Page 45.
14. Alan Fisher. *The Crimean Tatars*. Stanford; Hoover Institution. 1978. Page 120.
15. *Bol'shaia Sovetskaia Entsiklopediia*. Vol. 35. Moscow; 1937
16. For chapters on the Crimean Tatar communities of the Bulgarian and Romanian Dobruca see: Brian Glyn Williams. *The Crimean Tatars. The Diaspora Experience and the Forging of a Nation*. Leiden, Cologne, Boston. 2001.
17. M.F. Bunegin. *Revolutsiia i Grazhdanskaia Voina v Krymu (1917–1920 gg.)*. Simferopol; Krymgosizdat. 1927. Page 329.
18. Alan Fisher. *The Crimean Tatars*. Stanford; Hoover Institution. 1978. Page 127.
19. V.E. Vozgirin. *Istoricheskie Sud'by Krymskikh Tatar*. Moscow; Mysl'. 1992. Page 423.
20. I. Katerina. "Bor'ba Krymskih Tatar Protiv Vrangelia." *Istorik Marksist*. No. 5. 93. 1944. Page 75.
21. Joseph Castagne. "Le Bolchevisme et l'Islam: Les Organizations Sovietiques de la Russie Musulmane." *Revue de Monde Musulmane*. No. 51. 1922. Page 5–6.
22. Richard Pipes. *The Formation of the Soviet Union*. Cambridge Massachusetts; 1967. Page 190.
23. Interview with Memet Sevdiyar. New York. February 1999.
24. Robert Conquest. *Soviet Nationalities Policy in Practice*. London; The Bodley Head. 1967. Page 54.
25. Yuri Slezkine. "The USSR as a Communal Apartment, or How a Socialist State Promoted Ethic Particularism." *Slavic Review*. Vol. 53. No. 2. Summer 1994. Page 420.
26. A. Skachko. "Vostochnye Republiki na S. Kh. Vystavke v 1923 Godu." *Novyi Vostok*. No. 4. 1923. Pages. 482–484.
27. M. N. Morav. *The Crimea. Pearl of the Soviet Union*. Moscow; Intourist. 1934. Page 147.
28. *Bol'shaia Sovetskaia Entsklopediia*. Vol. 35. 1937. Page 302.
29. Aleksander Solzhenitysn. *The Gulag Archipelago*. Vol. 5–7. New York; Harper and Row Publishers. 1976. Page 386.
30. R.I. Muzafarov. "Kak Osushchetvlialos' Obuchenie Krymskotatarskogo Naseleniia v Respublike?" *Krymskaia ASSR (1921–1945)*. Simferopol; Tavria. 1990. Page 165.
31. B. Vroshevan and P. Tygliiants. *Izganie i Vozvrashenie*. Simferopol; Tavrida. 1994. Page 33.
32. Paul Kostoe. *Russians in the Former Soviet Republics*. Bloomington IN; Indiana University. 1995. Page 191.

33. Mikhail Gubogolo and Svetlana Chervonnaia. "The Crimean Tatar Question and the Present Ethnopolitical Situation in the Crimea." *Russia Politics and Law*. Vol. 33, no. 6. Page 44.
34. Allan Kagedan. "Territorial Units as Nationality Policy." *Soviet Nationality Policies*. Ed. by Henry Huttenbach. London; Mansell. 1990. Page 164.
35. Edige Kirimal. *Dergi* (Munich). 1955. No. 1. Pages 55–57.
36. Alexandre Bennigsen and Chantal Lemercier-Quelquejay. *Islam in the Soviet Union*. London; Paul Mall Press. 1967. Page 150.
37. Robert Kaiser. *The Geography of Nationalism in Russia and the Soviet Union*. Princeton; Princeton University Press. 1994. Page 104.
38. Philip Groder. "Soviet Federalism and Ethnic Mobilization." *World Politics*. Vol. 43. October 1990–July 1991. Pages 196–232.
39. Edige Kirimal. "The Tragedy of the Crimea." *The Eastern Quarterly*. Vol. 4, no. 1. 1951. Page 42.
40. Alan Fisher. *The Crimean Tatars*. Stanford; Hoover Institution Press. 1978. Page.
41. Zainulla Bulushev. V.M. Broshevan and A.A. Formanchuk. *Krymskaia Respublika: God 1921. (Kratkii Istoricheskii Ocherk)*. Simferopol; Tavria. 1992. Page 110.
42. *Bol'shaia Sovetskaia Entsiklopediia*. Vol. 35. 1937. Page 317.
43. Robin Cohen. *Global Diasporas, An Introduction*. Seattle; University of Washington Press. 1997. Page 53.
44. Ann Sheehy and Bohdan Nahylo. *The Crimean Tatars, Volga Germans and Meshketians. Soviet Treatment of Two Minorities*. London; Minority Rights Group. 1971. Page 7.
45. Ronald Wixman. "Manipulating Territory, Undermining Rights." *Cultural Survival Quarterly*. Winter 1992. Vol. 16, no. 1.
46. Alexandre Bennigsen. "Sultan Galiev. The USSR and the Colonial Revolution." *The Nationality Question in the Soviet Union*. Ed. Gail Lapidus. New York; Garland Publishing Inc. 1992. Page 120.
47. Ibid.
48. Zh. N. Mona. "Kak Byl Realizovan v Krymy Leninskii Dekret o Zemle?" *Kryamaskaia ASSR (1921–1945)*. Simferopol; Tavrida. 1990. Page 71.
49. A.I. Kliachin. "Dinamika Etnicheskih Sistem Rasseleniia v Krymy." *Ethnogrficheskoe Obozrenie*. No. 2. March–April 1992. Page 25.
50. Hakan Kirimli. *National Movements and National Identity Among the Crimean Tatars*. Leiden; EJ Brill. 1997. Page 20.
51. For a description of this plan see. Salo Brown. *The Russian Jews under the Tsars and Soviets*. New York; Macmillan Co. 1964.
52. Zh. N. Mona. "Kak Byl Realizovan v Krymy Leninskii Dekret o Zemle?" *Kryamaskaia ASSR (1921–1945)*. Simferopol; Tavrida. 1990. Page 62.
53. I.S. Chirva, V.P. Volkhov et. al. *Bor'ba Bol'shevikov za Yprochenie Sovetskoi Vlasti Vosstanovlenie i Razvite Naradnogo Khoziastva Kryma*. Krymizdat. 1958. Page 304.

54. Edige Kirimal. "The Crimean Tatars." *Studies on the Soviet Union*. Vol. 10. No. 1. 1970. Page 83.
55. Yuri Slezkine. "The USSR as a Communal Apartment." *Slavic Review*. Vol. 53. No. 2. Summer 1994. Page 420.
56. Ricks Smeets. "Circassia." *Central Asian Survey*. Vol. 14, no. 1. Mar. 1995. Page 116.
57. Shrin Akiner. "Melting Pot, Salad Bwol, Cauldron? Manipulation and Mobilization of Ethnic and Religious Identities in Central Asia." *Ethnic and Racial Studies*. Vol. 20, no. 20. Page 377.
58. Yuri Slezkine. "The USSR as a Communal Apartment." *Slavic Review*. Vol. 53. No. 2. Summer 1994. Page 445.
59. Bruce Franklin. *The Essential Stalin. Major Theoretical Writings, 1905–52*. London; Croom Helm. 1973. Page 6.

6. *SURGUN*: THE CRIMEAN TATAR EXILE IN CENTRAL ASIA

1. "Ob Utverzhdenii Ukazov Prezidiuma Verkhovnogo Soveta RSFSR." *Izvestiia*. June 26, 1942. Page 2.
2. Edige Kirimal. "The Tragedy of the Crimea." *Eastern Quarterly*. Vol. 4, no. 1. 1951. Pages 45–46.
3. Nikolai Bugai. *Iosif Stalin-Levrentiiu Berii "Ikh Nado Deportirovat"."Dokumenty, Fakty, Kommentarii*. Moscow; Druzhba Narodov. 1992. Page 131.
4. B. Broshevan and P. Tygliiants. *Izganie i Vozvrashenie*. Simferopol; Tavrida. 1994. Page 34.
5. Nikolai Fedorovich Bugai. Iosif Stalin-Lavrentiiu Berii: "Ikh Nado Deportirovat." Dokumenty, Fakty, Kommentarii. Moscow; Druzhba Narodov. 1992. Page 133.
6. Edige Kirimal. *Der National Kampf der Krimturken*. Emsdetten; Verlag Lechte. 1952. Page 32. Also Joachim Hoffman. *Der Ostlegion 1941–1943. Turkotataren, Kaukasier and Wolfganinnen in Deutschen Herr*. Freiburg; Verlag Rombach. 1976. Pages 39–50.
7. Mark Elliot. "Soviet Military Collaborators During World War II." *Ukraine During World War II. History and its Aftermath*. Edmonton; Canadian Institute of Ukrainian Studies. 1986. Page 92.
8. Edige Kirimal. "The Crimean Tatars." *Studies on the Soviet Union*. Vol. 10, no. 1. 1970. Page 93.
9. Alexander Nekrich. *The Punished Peoples. The Deportation of Soviet Minorities at the end of World War II*. New York; W.W. Norton and Co. 1978. Page 21.
10. Alan Fisher. *The Crimean Tatars*. Stanford; Hoover Institution Press. 1978. Page 159.
11. B. Broshevan and P. Tygliiants. *Izganie i Vozvrashenie*. Simferopol; Tavrida. 1994. Page 19.
12. Ibid. Page 36.

13. Svetalana Alieva. *Tak Eto Bylo. National'noe Repressi v SSSR*. Vol 3. Moscow; Pisan. 1993. Page 99.
14. Gerald Reitlinger. *The House Built on Sand. The Conflicts of German Policy in Russia, 1939–1945*. London; Weidenfeld and Nicolson. 1960. Pages 185–186 and 304.
15. Letter from National Center for Crimean Tatars to Sadoka Ogata UNHCR provided to the author by Fikret Yurter.
16. N.F. Bugai. *Iosif Stalin-Lavrentiiu Beriu: "Ikh Nado Deportirovat". Dokumenty, Fatky, Kommentarii*. Moscow; Druzhba Narodov. 1992. Page 131.
17. N.F. Bugai. "K Voprosy o Deportatsii Naradov SSSR v 30–40 godax." *Istoriia SSSR*. No. 6. Nov.–Dec. 1989. Page 137.
18. Shmuel Spector. *Encyclopedia of the Holocaust*. Vol. 2. New York; Macmillan Publishing Co. 1996. Page 786.
19. Alexander Nekrich. *The Punished Peoples. The Deportation and Fate of the Soviet Minorities at the end of the Second World War*. New York; W.W. Norton and Co. 1978. Page 19.
20. Nurie Bilazova. "Pamiati Zhertv Genotsida Posviaschaetssia." *Golos Kryma*. May 17, 1996. Page 5.
21. Edige Kirimal. "The Crimean Tatars." *Studies on the Soviet Union*. Vol. 10. No. 1. 1970. Page 89.
22. N.F. Bugai. *Iosif Stalin-Lavrentiiu Beriu: "Ikh Nado Deportirovat". Dokumenty, Fatky, Kommentarii*. Moscow; Druzhba Narodov. 1992. Page 134.
23. An alarmed Turkey in return planned for full mobilization. Galia Golan. *Soviet Policies in the Middle East from World War Two to Gorbachev*. Cambridge; Cambridge University Press. 1990. Page 32. George Harris. "The Soviet Union and Turkey." *The Soviet Union and the Middle East. The Post-World War II Era*. Stanford; Stanford University Press. 1974. Page 27.
24. From 1941 to 1942 the Nazis executed 91,678 people in Crimea, mainly Jews, Gypsies and Communists.
25. Reshat Dzhemilev. *Musa Mahmut. Human Torch*. New York; Crimea Foundation. 1986. Page 20.
26. Alexander Solzhenitsyn. *Gulag Archipelago*. Vol. 5–7. New York; Harper and Row Publishers. 1976. Page 389.
27. Osman Tukay. "The Tragedy of the Crimean Tatars." *Index on Censorship*. 3, no. 1. (1974). Pages 71–72.
28. Svetalana Alieva. *Take to Blyo. National'noe Repressi v SSSR*. Vol. 3, Moscow; Pisan. 1993. Page 99.
29. N.F. Bugai. "K Voprosy o Deportatsii Narodov SSR v 3040 godax." *Istoriia SSR*. No. 6.
30. Michael Rywkin. *Moscow's Lost Empire*. Armonk NY; Sharpe. 1994. Page 67.
31. Nicholas Poppe. *Introduction to Altaic Linguistics*. Wiesbaden; Otto Harrassowitz. 1965. Page 44.

32. B. Broshevan and P. Tygliiants. *Izganie i Vozvrashenie*. Simferopol; Tavrida. 1994. Page 46.
33. *Tashkentskii Protsess*. Amsterdam; The Herzen Foundation. 1976. Page 590.
34. Reshat Dzhemilev. *Musa Mahmut. Human Torch*. New York; Crimea Foundation. 1986. Page 20.
35. *The Crimean Review*, vol. 1 no. I May 18, 1986. Page 10.
36. B. Broshevan and P. Tygliiants. *Izganie i Vozvrashenie*. Simferopol; Tavrida. 1994. Page 45.
37. Ibid. Page 103.
38. Svetalana Alieva. *Tak Eto Bylo. National'noe Repressi v SSSR*. Vol 3. Moscow; Pisan. 1993. Page 12.
39. "Crimean Diary." *Institute of Current World Affairs*. July 20, 1995. Page 3.
40. B. Broshevan and P. Tygliiants. *Izganie i Vozvrashenie*. Simferopol; Tavrida. 1994. Page 49.
41. Ibid.
42. B.L. Finogeev et. al. *Kiymskotatarskie Zhenshchiny: Tryd, Byt, Traditsii*. Simferopol; Crimean State Committee for National Affairs. 1994. Page 15.
43. M. Guboglo and S. Chervonnaia. *Krymskotatarskoe jXatsional'noe Dvizhenie*. vol. 12. Moscow; Russian Academy of Science. 1992. Page 76.
44. Alexander Nekrich. *The Punished Peoples. The Deportation of Soviet Minorities at the end of World War II*. New York; W.W. Norton and Co. 1978. Page 137.
45. Ann Sheehy and Bohdan Nahylo. *The Crimean Tatars, Volga Germans and Meshketians. Soviet Treatment of Some National Minorities*. London; Minority Rights Group. 1980. Page 8.
46. B. Broshevan and P. Tygliiants. *Izganie i Vozvrashenie*. Simferopol; Tavrida. 1994. Page 106.
47. Ibid.
48. R.J. Rummel. *Lethal Politics. Soviet Genocide and Mass Murder Since 1917*. New Brunswick; Transaction Publishers. 1990. Page 158.
49. M. Guboglo and S. Chervonnaia. *Krymskotatarskoe Natsional'noe Dvizhenie*. vol. 1 Moscow; Russian Academy of Science. 1992. Page 238.
50. Lemercier Quelquejay. "The Tatars of the Crimea, A Retrospective Summary." *Central Asian Review*. Vol. 6, 1968. no 1. Page 25
51. B. Broshevan and P. Tygliiants. *Izganie i Vozvrashenie*. Simferopol; Tavrida. 1994. Page 74.
52. Ibid. Page 80.
53. Mikhail Guboglo and Svetlana Chervonnaia. "The Crimean Tatar Question and the Present Ethnopolitical Situation in the Crimea." *Russian Politics and Law*. vol. 33, no. 6. Page 39.
54. Viktora Nekipelova. "Spuchitsiia i Tleet vo Mne." *Kirim*. 1997. August 23. Page 3.
55. Andrew Bell-Fialkoff. "A Brief History of Ethnic Cleansing." *Foreign Affairs*. vol. 72. no. 3. Page 115.

56. A. Shuster. *Krym*. Kiev; Ministerstva Kulturi U.R.S.R. 1961. Page 6.
57. Alexandre Bennigsen and Marie Broxup. *The Islamic Threat to the Soviet State*. Aew York; St. Martin's Press. 1983. Page 18.

7. RETURN: THE CRIMEAN TATAR MIGRATIONS FROM CENTRAL ASIA TO THE CRIMEAN PENINSULA

1. Robert Kaiser. *The Geography of Nationalism in Russia and the USSR*. Princeton. Princeton University Press, 1994. Page 30.
2. Lilia Bujurova. "Govori" *Tak eto Bylo. Natsional'nye Repressi v SSSR 1919–1952 gody*. vol. 3. Moscow; Pisan. 1993. Page 122.
3. *Emel. Staty i Dokumenty ob Istorii, Literature i Kulture Krymskikh Tatar*. New York; Fund Krym. 1978. Page 43.
4. David Waines. *A Sentence of Exile. The Palestine/Israel Conflict, 1897–1977*. Wilmettc, Illinois, The Medina Press. 1977. Page 117.
5. *The Crimean Review*, vol. VII. Special Issue. 1995. Page 37.
6. B.L. Finogeev et. al. *Krymskotatarskie Zhenshchiny: Tryd, Byt.Traditsii*. Simferopol; Crimean State Committee for National Affairs. 1994. Page 15.
7. Reuters. "Thousands in Ukraine Mark Date of Expulsion. Crimean Tatars Reunite for a 50th Anniversary." *Boston Globe*. May 19, 1994. Page 3.
8. Gavin Hambly *Central Asia*. London; Dell Publishers. 1969. Page 242.
9. Elizabeth Bacon. *Central Asians Under Russian Rule*. Ithaca; Cornell Univ. 1966. Page 172.
10. Walker Connor. "Nation-Building or Nation Destroying?" *World Politics*. Vol. XXI. Oct. 1971–July 1972. Page 350.
11. Azade-Ayse Rorlich. "One or More Tatar Nations?" *Muslim Communities Reemerge. Historical Perspectives on Nationality, Politics, and Opposition in the Former Soviet union and Yugoslavia*, ed. Edward Allworth. Durham: Duke University Press, 1994. Page 172.
12. Bohdan Nahylo and Ann Sheehy. *The Crimean Tatars, Volga Germans and Meskhetians. Soviet Treatment of Some National Minorities*. London; Minority Rights Group. 1971. Page 14.
13. Mikhail Guboglo and Svetlana Chervonnaia. *Krymsko-Tatarskoe Natsional' noe Dvizhenie. Istoria. Problemy, Perspektivy*. Moscow: Rossikaia Akademiia Nauk. 1992. Page 112.
14. There was a large Volga Tatar diaspora in Central Asia formed over the previous century by migration to this region. The Volga Tatars were much more mobile than the Crimean Tatars and for over a century served as trading intermediaries between the Central Asian peoples and Russia.
15. Azade-Ayse Rorlich. "One or More Tatar Nations?" Muslim Communities Reemerge. Historical Perspectives on Nationality, Politics and Opposition in the

Former Soviet Union and Yugoslavia. Ed Edward Allworth. Durham; Duke University Press. 1994. Page 69.
16. Interviewees in Chirchik informed the author that the local Uzbek mayor, who spoke Crimean Tatar in order to communicate with the large Crimean Tatar population of Chirchik, did not order the subsequent attack on the peaceful protesters. Rather it was MVD (Ministry of Interior) commandeers from nearby areas.
17. Peter Potichnyj. 'The Struggle of the Crimean Tatars." *Canadian Slavonic Papers*. vol. XVII. no. 2–3.' Page 315.
18. In my interview with Izzet Khairov in Tashkent, this source claimed that he and the other members of the Tashkent Ten and an earlier student organization had underestimated the ability of the KGB to infiltrate and move against their group. From this time forward the Crimean Tatars tended to avoid the creation of easily identifiable organizations which could be broken up by the authorities.
19. For more on Dzhemilev see. Brian Glyn Williams. "Mustafa Jemilev." *Encyclopedia of Nationalism*, vol. 2. ed. Alexander Motvl. Academic Press. 2000.
20. The Organization of the Crimean Tatar National Movement was the first Crimean Tatar political movement since the disbanding of the Milli Firka by the Soviets. This organization was. for a brief time, challenged by Yuri Osmanov's less popular Crimean Tatar National Movement (CTNM) which sought to com promise with the authorities. This opposition organization collapsed with the as sassination of Yuri Osmanov, a well known Soviet dissident, in November 1993.
21. Author's interview with Dzhemilev, Crimea, November 1997.
22. *A Chronicle of Human Rights in the USSR*, no.'s 5–6. Nov.–Dec. 1973. Page 32.
23. Interview with Abdullah Balich. Vice Rector Nizami Institute. Tashkent. Uzbekistan. April 1997.
24. Edward Allworth. *The Tatars of the Crimea*. Durham; Duke University Pres. Pages 347–348.
25. Mikhail Guboglo and Svetlana Chervonnaia. *Krymsko-Tatarskoe Natsional' noe Dvizhenie. Istoria. Problemy, Perspektivy*. Moscow: Rossikaia Akademiia Nauk. 1992. Page 95.
26. Mustafa Dzhemilev. "The Crimean Tatars' Thorny Path to their Homeland."* *Central Asia. Tlie Rediscovery of History*, ed. H.B. Paksov. Armonk XY: M.E. Sharpe. 1994. Pages 171–172.
27. Temir Pulatov. "Vsem Mirom Pomoch' Brat'iam!" *Druzhba Narodov*. no. 2. 988. Page 203.
28. George Bishrat. "Displacement and Social Identity; Palestinian Refugees in the West Bank." *Population Displacement and Resettlement: Development and Conflict in the Middle East*. New York: Center for Migration Studies. 1994. Page 181.
29. Edward Allworth. *Tatars of the Crimea. Return to the Homeland*. Durham; Duke University. Press. 1998. Page 198.
30. "Pravda o Kuvasae" *Pravda Vostoka*. no. 137. June 11, 1989. Page 3.

31. *The USSR Today. Perspectives from the Soviet Press*. Columbus Ohio; Current Digest of the Soviet Press. 1985. Page 135.
32. "Deklaratsiia Verkhovnogo Soveta Soiuza Sovctskikh Sotsialisticheskikh Respublik" *Izvestiia*. Nov. 24, 1989 p.l and *Pravda* Nov. 24, 1989. Page 1.
33. Returning Crimean Tatars in general refused to pay protection money. Viktor Tkachet et. al. *The Crimea, Chronicle of Separatism (1992-1995)*. Kiev; Ukrainian Center for Independent Research. 1996. Pages 152-155. Interview with Mustafa Dzhemilev. Bahcesaray. 1997.
34. Emil Payin. "Population Transfer: The Crimean Tatars Return Home." *Cultural Survival Quarterly*. Winter 1992. Vol. 16. no. 1. Page 34. A. I. Kliachin. "Dinamika Etnichesskikh Sistem Rasseleniia v Krymu." *Etnograftcheskoe Obozrenie*. no. 2. March-April. 1992. Page 32.
35. Midat Iunusov. "Vozrodit Starve Sorty" *Golos Kryma*. Feb. 2. 1996. Page 5.
36. Ekaterina Urskaia. "Berega Voselye Salgir." *Golos Kryma*. Jan. 13, 1996. Page 5.
37. Taliat Ilias. "Sto Let i Vsia Zhizhn' Krvma." *Golos Kryma*. Aug. 16. 1996. Page 2.
38. *Verkhovna Rada*. "Draft Concept of the National Policy of the Ukraine in Relation to Indigenous Peoples." Page 4.
39. James Critchlow. *"Punished Peoples" of the Soviet Union*. New York; Helsinki Watch. 1991. Page 42. Two hundred and eighty Crimean Tatar delegates from throughout the USSR represented the Crimean Tatars in all their places of exile in the 1991 Kurultay.
40. M. Guboglo and S. Chervonnaia. *Krymskotatarskoe Natsional'noe Dvizhenie*. vol. 1 Moscow; Russian Academy of Science. 1992. Page 238.
41. According to Guboglo and Chervonnaia, the Crimean Tatar nationalist leaders consider all other nationalities in the Crimea to be "'non-Tatars' or 'cultures'. 'diasporas'. 'enclaves', 'Slavic masses', 'colonists' or anything you wish, but not 'people of the Crimea.'" The Crimean Tatars also claim to have an exclusive right to self-determination in the region. Ibid.
42. Ibid. Page 237.
43. M. Guboglo and S. Chervonnaia. *Krymskotatarskoe Natsional'noe Dvizhenie*. vol. 1 Moscow; Russian Academy of Science. 1992. Page 9.
44. Fred Kaplan. "After Decades in Exile, Crimean Tatars Reclaim Home."*Boston Globe*. Sept. 6, 1992. Page 14.
45. According to Crimean Tatar sources, of the 291 Crimean Tatar settlements in the Crimea, a full 70 per cent are without running water and 25 per cent without electricity and 90 per cent are without tarmac roads. *Dokumenty Kurultaia Krmskotatarskogo. Naroda. 1991-1998 gg*. Simferopol: Medzhlis Krymskotatarskogo Naroda. 1999. Page 123.
46. *The Crimean Review*, vol. IV. No. 2, 18. Dec. 1989. Page 3. "Vosstanavlivia Spravedlivost." *Pravda*. May 17, 1990. no. 147. Page 2.
47. Lily Hyde. "Crimean Tatars Demand Ancestral Lands." *Radio Free Europe/Radio Liberty.World Monitor*. March 26, 2000.

48. Conversation with Cengiz Dagci, London, England. January 2000. While this source stressed the differences between the Tats and Nogais he made a point of stating that "both groups were good Crimean Tatar patriots."
49. *Spektr. Informaslionanno-Analiticheskii Biuleten*. Simferopol; Crimean Center for Ethno-Social Investigation. 1996. no. 5 (13).pt. 2. Page 21.
50. Urszula Doroszewska. "Crimea: Whose Country."* *Uncaptive Minds*, vol. 5. no. 3. (21). Fall 1992. Page 44.
51. Lilia Bujurova. "Kak Pakhnet Rodina?" *Tak eto Bylo*. Moscow; Pisan. 1993. Page 123.
52. Svetlana Chervonnaia. *Krymskotatarskoe Natsional'noe Dvizhenie 1994–1995*. Moscow; Russian Academy of Sciences. 1997. Page 10.
53. Oxana Shevel. "The Crimean Tatars and the Ukrainian State." *Paper given at the 5th Annual World Convention of the Association for the Study of Nationalities*. Columbia University, NY. April 15, 2000.
54. Natalie Belitser. "The Constitutional Process in the Autonomous Republic of the Crimea in the Context of Interethnic Relations and Conflict Settlement." *Paper presented at the University of Birmingham, England*. March 10, 2000.
55. Oxana Shevel. "Who are the Crimean Tatars and why are They Important?" *Washington Post*. March 1, 2014.
56. "As Russians Return, Tatars Fear Repeat of History." *NPR*. March 3, 2014.
57. "Mustafa Dzhemilev. The Man who Might Clip Putin's Wings." *The National*. March 27, 2014.
58. Crimean Tatar leader tells Putin secession would break post-Soviet pact." *Reuters*. March 12, 2014.
59. Threatened, Raided, And Exiled: Opposing Putin In Crimea." *Buzzfeed*. September 27th 2014.
60. Ibid.
61. "Vladimir Putin Tells Crimea's Tatars Their Future Lies with Russia." *The Guardian*. May 16, 2014.
62. "Fear is in the air Among Crimean Tatars." *Voice of America News*. March 3, 2014.
63. "Loyal to Ukraine. Tatars lie Low as Russia Seizes Crimea." *Reuters*. March 2, 2014.
64. Ibid.
65. "As Russians Return, Tatars Fear Repeat of History." *NPR*. March 3, 2014.
66. "Crimean Tatars Ponder Return of Russian Rule." *New York Times*. March 1, 2014.
67. "Tensions Flaire as pro-Russians, Crimean Tatars Clash. *Bloomberg.com*. February 26, 2014.
68. "Russian Stealth in Crimea Leaves Ethnic Tatars, Ukrainians on Verge of Panic." *The Star*. March 4, 2014.

BIBLIOGRAPHY

A Chronicle of Human Rights in the USSR. No. 5-6. November-December. 1973.

Abdoulline, Yahya. "Histoire et Interpretations Contemporaines du Second Reformise Musulman (ou Djadisme) Chez les Tatars de la Volga et de Crimee." *Cahiers du Monde Russe et Sovietique.* Vol. 27. Nos 1-2. January-June. 1996. pp. 65-79.

Abdulhamitoglu, Necip. *Türksiiz Kirim. Yuz Binlerin Surgiin.* Istanbul; Bogazici Yayin-lari. 1974.

Abkazian. T. "Literature on Abkhazia and the Abkhazian-Abazian." *Caucasian Review.* Vol 16. No. 3. (1968). pp. 217-222.

Abrahamovic, Zygmunt. "Turkology in Poland: Achievements and Some Problems for Future Developments." *International Journal of Turkish Studies.* Winter 1984-1985. Vol. 3. No. l. pp. 123-139.

Adzhi, Murat. "Polovetskoe Pole." *Kirim.* Oct. 4, 1997. p. 3.

Akchura, Iskender. *Genocide Behind the Iron Curtain. A Short History of Repressions by the Soviet Government Aimed at the Extermination of Pious Moslems of the Crimea.* New-York; Raussen Bros. 1963.

Akiner, Shirin. "Melting Pot. Salad Bowl-Cauldron? Manipulation and Mobilization of Ethnic and Religious Identities in Central Asia." *Ethnic and Racial Studies.* Vol. 20, No. 2. pp. 362-394.

———. *The Formation of Kazakh Identity. From Tribe to Nation-State.* London; Royal Inst. of International Affairs. 1995.

Aksan, Virginia. "The 1768-1774 Russo-Turkish War: A Comparative Analysis of Russian and Ottoman Campaign Preparedness." *Turkish Studies Bulletin.* April 1992. Vol. 16. No. 1. pp. 21-24.

———. *An Ottoman Statesman in War and Peace. Ahmed Resmi Effendi, 1700 to 1783.* Leiden; EJ. Brill. 1995.

Al Aboudi, Nasir. "Muslim Experience in Eastern Europe. A First Hand Report." *Journal of Muslim Minority Affairs*, Vol. 17. No. 1. Jan. 1986. pp. 88-116.

Albion, Adam Smith. "Crimean Diary." *Institute of Current World Affairs.* July 20, 1995.

BIBLIOGRAPHY

Alcxeyeva, Ludmilla. "Mustafa Dzhemilev, His Character and Convictions." *Tatars of the Crimea. Return to the Homeland*. Durham; Duke University Press. 1998. pp. 206–226.

———. *Soviet Dissent. Contemporary Movements for National, Religious, and Human Rights*. Middleton Conn; Wesleyan University Press. 1985.

Alexiev, Alexander and Enders Wimbush. *Ethnic Minorities in the Red Army*. Boulder; Westview Press. 1988.

Aliadin, Shamil. *Teselli*. Moscow; Sovetskii Pisatel.' 1985.

Allworth, Edward. *Tatars of the Crimea. Return to the Homeland*. Durham; Duke University Press. 1998.

Altan, Mubeyyin Batu. "Sevki Bekotre (1888–1961)." *Crimean Review*, Vol. 3. No. 2. December 18, 1988. p. 5.

———. "Plight of the Crimean Tatar People." *Crimean Review*, Vol. 1. No. l. May 18, 1996. p. 6.

———. "Structures. The Importance of Family-A Personal Memoir." *Tatars of the Crimea. Return to the Homeland*. Durham; Duke University-Press. 1998. pp. 99–110.

Altay, Deniz. "Kirikkale'de Kirim Du§unmek." *Emel*. March–April. 1994.

Amit, Emil'. "Nikto Ne Zabyt, Nichto ne Zabyto. Vospominaniia." *Tak elo Bylo. Natsional'nye Repressii v SSSR 1919–1952 Gody*. Vol. 3. Moscow; Rossiiskii Mezhdunaraodny Fond Kultury. 1993.

Anderson, Benedict. *Imagined Communities. Reflections on the Origin and Spread of Nationalism*. New York; Verso. 1979.

Andreev. A.R. *Istoriia Kryma*. Moscow; Izdatel'stvo Mezhregional'ny Tsentr. 1997.

Andrews, Peter Alford. *Ethnic Groups in the Republic of Turkey*. Wiesbaden; Ludwig Reichert Verlag. 1989.

"Appeal to the People of Fergana." *Report on the USSR*. Radio Liberty, Vol. 1. No. 24. June 16, 1989. pp. 26–27.

Arash, Altan. "Kirim Tiirklerinin Muhacir Tiirkuleri ve Halk Destanlari." *Emel*. Jan.–Feb. No. 56. 1970.

Arbitailo, LB. *Ves' Gorod kak Volshebny Krai. Bakhchisarai v Isskustve*. Simferopol; Tavriia'. 1993.

Arbore, Al. P. *La Dobrudja*. Bucarest; Academie Roumaine. 1938.

Armstrong, T.B. *Journal of Travels in the Seat of War During the Last Two Campaigns of Russia and Turkey*. London; A. Seguin. 1831.

Azrael, Jeremy and Emil Payin. *Cooperation and Conflict in the Former Soviet Union: Implications for Migration*. Santa Monica: Rand Cooperation. 1996.

Bacon, Elizabeth. *Central Asians Under Russian Rule*. Ithaca; Cornell University. 1966.

Baddley, John. *The Russian Conquest of the Caucasus*. London: Longman Greens and Co. 1908.

BIBLIOGRAPHY

Badian, V. V. "Torgovlia Kaffy v XII-XV w." *Feodal'naia Tavrika*. ed. S.N. Bibi-kov. Kiev; Naukova Dumka. 1973. pp. 174–189.

Bainbridge, Margret. *The Turkic Peoples of the World*. London; Kegan Paul. 1993.

Baker, James. *Turkey in Europe*. London; Casscll Petter and Galpin. 1877.

Bala, Mirza. "Kirim" *Islam Ansiklopedisi*. Vol. 6. Istanbul; Milli Egitim Basimevi. 1967. pp. 756–59.

Baranow I. A. "O Vosstanii Ioanna Gotskogo." *Feodal'naia Tavrika*. ed. S. N. Bi-bikov. Kiev; Naukova Dumka. 1974. pp. 151–162.

Barker, Thomas. *Double Eagle and Crescent*. Albany; State University of New York Press. 1967.

Barkley, John. *Between the Danube and the Black Sea (Or Five Tears in Bulgaria)*. London; John Murray. 1876.

Barret, Thomas. "The Frontiers of the North Caucasus.'" *Slavic Review*. Fall 1995. pp. 578–602.

Bates, Daniel. "The Ethnic Turks and Bulgarian elections of October 1991" *Turkish Review of Balkan Studies*, pp. 193–204.

Bayar, Hamdi and Namik Kemal Bayar. "Sakarya (Tirnaksiz) Koyu." *Emel*. September–October. 1993. p. 35.

Baytugan, Barsabi. "The North Caucasus.'" *Studies on the Soviet Union*. (New Series). Vol. 11. No. 1, 1971. pp. 1–38.

Bccattini, Francesco. *Storia Delia Crimea, Piccola Tataria*. Rome; Prcsso Leonardo Bassaglia. 1785.

Beldiceanu-Steinher, Irene et al. "La Crimee Ottomane et ['institution du Timar" *Annali (Aion). Instituto Orientate di.Vapoli*. Vol. 39. (new series 29). 1979. pp. 523–563.

Bennigsen, Alexandre and Chantal Lemercicr-Quelquejay. *Islam in the Soviet Union*. London; Pall Mall Press. 1967.

Bennigsen, Alexandre and Chantal Lemercier-Quclquejay. *La Presse el Le Alouve-menl National Chez les Musulmans de Russie Avant 1920*. Paris; Moulon. 1964.

Broshevan, B. and P. Tygliiants *Izganie i Vozvrashchenie*. Simferopol; Tavrida. 1994.

Brown, Salo. *The Russian Jew Under the Tsars and Soviets*. New York; Macmillan Co. 1964.

Buchanan, Meriel. *Recollections of Imperial Russia*. New York; George Doran and Co. 1924.

Bugai, Nikolai Fedorovich. "K Voprosy o Deportatsii Narodov SSSR v 30-40-x Godax." *Istoriia SSSR*. No. 6. 1989. Nov.–Dec. 1989. pp. 135–144.

Bugai. Nikolai Fedorovich. *Iosif Stalin-Lavrentiiu Berii: "Ikh Xado Deportirovat". Dokumentj, Fakty, Kommentarii*. Moscow; Druzhba Narodov. 1992.

———. "Pravda o Deportatsii Chechenskogo i Ingushkogo Narodov." *Voprosy Istorii*. No. 7. 1990. pp. 32–44.

Bujurova, Lilia. "Govori" *Tak eto Bylo. NatsionaVnye Repressi v SSSR 1919–1952 gody*. Vol. 3. Moscow; Pisan. 1993. p. 122.

BIBLIOGRAPHY

———. "Kak Pakhnet Rodina?" *Tak eto Bylo. NatsionaPnye Repressi v SSSR 1919–1952 gody*. Vol. 3. Moscow; Pisan. 1993. p. 123.

Bukharaev, Ravil. *Islam in Russia. The Four Seasons*. London; Curzon Press. 2000.

Bunegin, M.F. *Revoliutsia i Grazhdanskaia Voina v Krymu (1917–1920 gg.)*. Simferopol; Krymgosizdat. 1927.

Cacavellas, Jeremiah. *The Siege of Vienna by the Turks*. London; Cambridge University Press. 1925.

Campenhausen, Baron Pierce Balthazar von. *Travels Through Several Provinces of the Russian Empire*. London; Richard Phillips. 1808.

Castagne, Joseph. "Le Bolchevisme et l'Islam: Les Organisations Sovietiques de la Russie Musulmane." *Revue du Monde Musulman*. No. 51. 1922. pp. 1–12.

Cevik, Celebi. "Sungurlu'dan: Koyum Bilemivorum." *Emel*. September–October. 1994. No. 204. p. 29.

Chervonnaia, Svetlana. *Krym 97. Kurultai Protiv Raskola*. Moscow; Rossiiskaia Akademiia Nauk. 1998.

———. "Ismail Gasprinskii-V'vdaiushchiicia Krymskotatarskii Prosvetitel' i Gumanist." *Etnograficheskoe Obozrenie*. Jan.–Feb. No. 1. 1992. pp. 158–165.

———. *Krymskotatarskoe Natsional'noe Dvizhenie (1994–1996)*. Moscow; Rossiskaia Akademiia Nauk. 1997.

———. *Krymskotatarskoe XatsionaVnoe Dvizhenie 1994–1995*. Moscow; Russian Academy of Sciences. 1997.

Chirva, I.S. and V.P. Volkhov, et. al. *Bor'ba Bol'shcvikov za l'prochenie Sovetskoi Vlasti, Vosstanovlenie i Razvitie Narodnogo Klwzyaistva Kryma*. Simferopol; Krvmizdat. 1958.

Chuborov. Refat. "Krymskotatarskaia Problema v Zerkalc Ukrainskoi Pressy." *Avdet*. July 14, 1997. p. 3.

Clarke, Edward. *Traveb in Various Countries of Europe and Asia. Part one. Russia, Tahtary and Turkey*. London; T. Cadell and V. Davis. 1816.

Clot, Andre. *Suleiman the Magnificent*. London; Saqi Books. 1992.

Cohen, Robin. *Global Diasporas. An Introduction*. Seattle; University of Washington Press. 1997.

Collins, Leslie. "On the Alleged 'Destruction' of the Great Horde." *Byzantine Forschungen*. Vol. 16. 1991. pp. 361–399.

———. "The Military Organization and Tactics of the Crimean Tatars, 16th-17th Centuries." *War, Technology and Society in the Middle East*. cd. V.J. Parry and M.E. Yapp. London; Oxford University Press. 1975. pp. 257–276.

Connor, Walker."Nation-Building or Nation Destroying?" *World Politics*. Vol. 24. Oct. 1971–July 1972.

Conquest, Robert. *Soviet Nationalities Policy in Practice*. London; The Bodlev Head. 1967. Conquest. Robert. *The Nation Killers. The Soviet Deportation of Nationalities*. New York; Macmillan. 1970.

BIBLIOGRAPHY

Critchlow. James. *'Punished Peoples' of the Soviet Union. The Continuing Legacy of Stalin's Deportations*. New York; Helsinki Watch. 1991.
Dagci, Ccngiz. *Hatiralarda*. Istanbul; Otuken. 1998.
———. *Korkunc Yiillari*. Istanbul; Otuken. 1989.
———. *0 Topraklar Bizimdi*. Istanbul; Varlik Yayinevi. 1972
Danesco, Gregoire. *Dobrogea*. Bucharest; Independance Roumaine. 1903.
Deccei, Aurcl. "Le Probleme de la Colonisation des Turcs Seljoukides dans la Dobrogea au XHIe siecle. *Tarih Arastirmalari Dergisi*. vi, 1968. pp. 85–111.
de Hartog, Leo. *Russia and the Mongol Yoke*. London; British Academic Press. 1996.
de Hell, Xavier Hommaire. *Travels in the Steppes of the Caspian Sea*. London; Chapman and Hall. 1847.
de Jong, Fredrick. "The Turks and Tatars of Romania." *Turcica. Revue d'Etudes Turques*. Vol. 18. 1986. pp. 165–189.
———. "The Muslim Minorities in the Balkans." *Islamic Studies*, Vol. 36: 2. No. 3. 1997. pp. 413–427.
de La Primaudic, Elie. *Etudes sur le Commerce au Moyen Age. Histoire du Commerce de la Mer Noire et Colonies Genoises de la Krimee*. Paris; Comptoir des Imprineurs-Unis. 1848.
de Tott, Baron. *Memoirs of Baron de Tott*. London; G. G.J. Robinson. 1785. Vol. I
de Windt, Harry. *Russia as I Know It*. Philadelphia; J.B. Lippincott co. 1917. p. 187.
Detrez, Raymond. *Historical Dictionary of Bulgaria*. London; Scarecrow Press. 1997. Deutsch, Karl. *Nationalism and Social Communication. An Inquiry into the Foundations of Nationality*. Cambridge; MIT Press. 1962.
Djalili, Mohammad Reza. "Dar al-Harb." *The Oxford Encyclopedia of the Modern Islamic World*. Oxford; Oxford University Press. 1995. p. 338.
Dominion, Leon. *The Frontiers of Language and Nationality in Europe*. New York; American Geographical Society. 1917.
Doroszewska, Urszula. "Crimea: Whose Countrv." *Uncaptive Minds*, Vol. 5. No. 3. (21). Fall 1992. pp. 39–58.
Dokumenty Kurultaia Krymskotatarskogo Naroda. Simferopol; Medzhlis Krymskotatarskogo Naroda. 1999.
Druzhinina. E.I. *Severnoe Prichernomor'e v 1775–1800g.g.* Moscow; Akademiia Nauk. 1959.
Dzhcmilev, Mustafa. "The Crimean Tatars' Thorny Path to their Homeland." *Central Asian Monuments*, ed. H.B. Paksoy. Armonk, NY; M.E. Sharpe. 1994. pp. 171–176.
Dzhemilev, Mustafa. "Vostanovlenie Prav Krvmskikh Tatar." July 24. 1997.
Dzhemilev. Reshat. *Musa Mahmut, Human Torch*. New York: Crimea Foundation. 1986.
Efetov, S.B. and B.I. Filonenko. "Pesni Krvmskikh Tatar" *Izvestiia Tavricheskogo Obshchestvo Istorii Arkheologii i Etnografii*. No. 1. (58). Simferopol. 1927. pp. 69–85.
Eller, Jack and Reed Coughlan. "The Poverty of Primordialism; The Demystification

of Ethnic Attachements." *Ethnic and Racial Studies*, Vol. 16. No. 2. April 1993. pp. 183–203.

Elliot, Mark. "Soviet Military Collaborators During World War II." *Ukraine During World War II. History and Its Aftermath*. Edmonton: Canadian Institute of Ukrainian Studies. 1986. pp. 89–104.

Emel editorial committee. "Rusya'nin Kinm' Ilkhakinm 200 Yil DSnumu." *Emel* 129. March–April. 1982. pp. 42–43.

Emel. Staty i Dokumenty ob Istorii, Literature i Kulture Krymskikh Tatar. New York; Fund Krym. 1978. p. 43.

Emin, Mehmed. "Anadoludan Bir Ses Yahut Cenge Giderken." *Ttirkce Siirler*. Istanbul; 1900. p. 37.

Eminov, Ali. *Turkish and other Muslim Minorities in Bulgaria*. New York; Routledge. 1997.

———. "Turks and Tatars in Bulgaria and the Balkans." *Nationalities Papers*. Vol. 28. No. 1. 2000. pp. 130–166.

Engin, Arin. *The Voice of Turkism*. Istanbul; Ataturkist Cultural Publications. No. 18. 1964. pp. 32–43. Eren, Ahmet. *Tiirkiye'de Goc ve Gocmen Meseleleri Tanzimat Devri*. Istanbul; Nurgok Matbaasi. 1966. Eren, Nermin. "Crimean Tatar Communities Abroad." *The Tatars of the Crimea.Return to the Homeland*, ed. Edward Allworth. Durham; Duke University Press.1998. pp. 323–351.

Erer, Tekin. "Gunes ne Zaman Dogacak?" *Emel*. No. 107. p. 17–18.

Ersoy, Mehmet Aksif. "Chosen Traumas of the Alavis in Anatolia." *Mind and Human Interaction. History Myth and Mind*. Vol. 9. No. 1. 1998. pp. 38–51.

Esbenshade, Richard. "Remembering to Forget: Memory, History and National Identity in Postwar East-Central Europe." *Representations*. Winter 1995. No. 49. pp. 38–52.

Fedorov, F.A. *Krym s Sevastopolem' Balaklavoiu*. St. Petersburg; Korableva and Siriakova. 1855.

Finogeev, B.L. et al. *Krymskotatarskie ZJienshchiny: Tryd, Byt,Traditsii*. Simferopol; Crimean State Committee for National Affairs. 1994.

Fisher, Alan. "Azov in the Sixteenth and Seventeenth Centuries." *Jahrbiicher fur Geschichte Osteuropas*. Vol. 21. No. 2. (1972).

———. "Crimean Separatism in the Ottoman Empire." *Nationalism in a Non-National State. The Dissolution of the Ottoman Empire*, ed. William Haddad and William Ochenswald. Columbus; Ohio State University. 1977. pp. 57–76.

———. "Emigration of Muslims from the Russian Empire in the Years after the Crimean War." *Geschichte Ost Europas*. Vol. 35. No. 3. 1987. pp. 356–371.

———. "Enlightened Despotism and Islam Under Catherine II." *Slavic Review*. Vol. 27. No. 4. Dec. 1968. pp. 542–553.

———. "Sahin Girey, the Reformer Khan and the Russian Annexation of the Crimea." *Jahrbiicher fur Geschichte Osteuropas*. Vol. 15. 1967. pp. 341–364.

———. "Muscovite-Ottoman Relations in the Sixteenth Centuries." *Huma-niora Islamica*. I (1973). pp. 207–217.

———. "Muscovy and the Black Sea Trade." *Canadian American Slavic Studies*. 6. No. 4. 1972. pp. 575–594.

———. "Social and Legal Aspects of Russian-Muslim Relations in the Nineteeth Century. The Case of the Crimean Tatars." *The Mutual Effects of the Islamic and Judeo-Christian World; The East European Pattern*, ed. Abraham Ascher et al. New York; Columbia University Press. 1979. pp. 77–92.

———. "Sources and Perspectives for the Study of Ottoman-Russian Relations in the Black Sea Region." *International Journal of Turkish Studies*, Vol. 1. No. 2. 1980. pp. 77–84.

———. "The Crimean Tatars, the USSR, and Turkey." *Soviet Asian Ethnic Frontiers*, ed. Williams McCagg and Brian Silver. New York; Pergamon Press. 1979. pp. 1–24.

———. "The Ottoman Crimea in the Sixteenth Century." *Harvard Ukrainian Studies*, Vol. 5. No. 2. June 1981. pp. 135–143.

Fletcher, Giles. *Rude and Barbarous Kingdom*, ed. Lloyd Bern and Robert Crummcy. Madison; University of Wisconsin Press. 1968.

Foreign Office Archives (Public Record Office) F.O. 424/57. p. 129. No. 248.

Foreign Office Archives. F.O. 424/60. Confidential (3384). p. 198. No. 336/1.

———. F.O. 424/69. Confidential. (3625). p. 163. No. 279/1.

Franklin, Bruce. *The Essential Stalin; Major Theoretical Writings, 1905–52*. London; Croom Helm. 1973.

Franz, Erhard. *Population Policy in Turkey*. Hamburg; Deutsche-Orient Institut. 1994.

Gamzatov, Rasul. "Iazik." *Krymskie Tatary. Isloriko-Lingvisticheskii Ocherk*. Simferopol; Anayurt. 1993. pp. 34–36.

Gankevich, V. Iu. *Ocherk Istorii Krymskotatarskogo Narodnogo Obrazovaniia*. Simferopol; Tavria. 1997.

Gasprinsky, Ismail. *Rossia i Vostok. (Russkoe Musulmanstvo i Russko-Vostochnoe Soglashenie)*. Kazan; Fond Zhien. 1993.

Gasprinsky, Ismail. "Blizost Russkikh" *Terciiman*. No. 29 July 28, 1903. p. 124.

———. "Ob Emigratsiia." *Terciiman*. May 7, 1902. No. 17. p. 3.

———. "Pis'mo Emigranta." *Terciiman*. March 14, 1903. No. 10 p. 37.

———. *Terciiman*. Nov. 11 1902. No. 43. p. 65

———. *Terciiman*. Sept. 15, 1903. No. 36. p. 155.

Gibb, H.A.R. *The Travels o/Ibn Battuta*. Vol. 11. Cambridge; Cambridge University Press. 1962.

Gokbilgin, Ozalp. *1532–1577 Yillari Arasinda Kirim Hanligi'nin Siyasi Durumu*. Ankara; Sevin Matbaasi. 1973.

Gokbilgin, Tayib. *Rumeili'de Yiiriikler, Tatarlar, ve Evlad-i Fatihan*. Istanbul; Turkiyat Mecmuasi.1957.

Golan, Galia. *Soviet Policies in the Middle East from World War Two to Gorbachev*. Cambridge; Cambridge University Press. 1990.

BIBLIOGRAPHY

Golden, Peter. *An Introduction to the History of the Turkic Peoples*. Wiesbaden; Otto Harrowitz. 1992.

Goldenberg, M. "Krym i Krymskie Tatary." *Vestnik Evropy*. No. 6. 1883.

Gozaydin, Etham. *Kirim. Kirim Türklerinin Yerlesme ve Gocmeleri*. Istanbul; Vakit Matbaasi. 1948.

Grigorenko, Andrei. *A Kogda My Vernemsia*. New York; Fund Krym. 1977.

Groder, Philip. "Soviet Federalism and Ethnic Mobilization." *World Politics*. Vol. 43. Oct. 1990–July 1991. pp. 196–232.

Guboglo, Mikhail and Svetlana Chervonnaia. *Krymsko-Tatarskoe Natsional' noe Dvizhenie. Istoria, Problemy, Perspektivy*. Moscow; Rossikaia Akademiia Nauk. 1992.

———. "The Crimean Tatar Question and the Present Ethnopolitical Situation in the Crimea." *Russia Politics and Law*. Vol. 33. No. 6. pp. 31–60.

Guthrie, Marie. *A Tour Performed in 1795–6 Through the Taurida or Crimea*. London; T. Cadell. 1802.

Habioglu, Bedri. *Kafkasya'dan Anadolu'va Gocler ve Iskanlari*. Istanbul; Nart Yayincilik. 1993.

Hall, Mica. *Russian as Spoken by the Crimean Tatars*. Unpublished Dissertation, University of Washington. 1997. p. 37.

Halperin, Charles. *The Mongol Empire and the Golden Horde*. Bloomington; Indiana University Press. 1985.

Hambly, Gavin. *Central Asia*. London; Morrison and Gibb Ltd. 1969.

Harris, George. "The Soviet Union and Turkey." *The Soviet Union and the Middle East. The Post-World War II Era*. Stanford; Stanford University. Press. 1974. pp. 55–78.

Hart, B.H. Liddell. *History of the Second World War*. New York: Putnam and Sons. 1970.

Henderson, Ebenezer. *Biblical Research and Travels in Russia*. London; James Nisbet. 1826.

Henze, Paul. "Circassia in the Nineteenth Century. The Futile Fight for Freedom." *Turco-Tatar Past, Soviet Present*. Paris; Editions Peeters. 1986. pp. 243–275.

Herzen. Alexander. "Gonenie na Krymskikh Tatar." *Kolokol*. Dec. 22, 1861. No. 117. pp. 973–977.

Hoffman, Joachim. *Die Ostlegion 1941–1943. Turkotalaren, Kaukasier und Wolgafinnen im deutschen Heer*. Freiburg; Verlag Rombach. 1976. pp. 39–50.

Holderness, Mary. *New Russia. A Journey from Riga to Crimea*. London; Sherwood Jones and co. 1823.

Hooson, David. *Geography and National Identity*. Oxford; Institute of British Geographers. 1994

Hostler, Charles. *The Turks of Central Asia*. Westport Conneticut; Praeger. 1993.

Howorth, Henry. *History of the Mongols*. London; Longman Green and Co. 1880.

Hrushevsky, Michael. *A History of Ukraine*. New Haven; Yale University Press.

Huttenbach, Henry. "The Soviet Koreans." *Central Asian Survey*, Vol. 12. No. 1. 1993. pp. 59–71.

BIBLIOGRAPHY

Iakobson. A. *Krym v Srednie Veka.* Moscow; Izdatelstvo Nauka. 1973.
Iaremchuk, V.D. and V.B. Bezverkhii. "Tatari v Ukraini Istoriko-Politologichii Aspekt." *Ukrainskyi Istorychnyi Zhumal.* Vol. 5. 1994.
Inalcik, Halil. "Daulet Giray." *The Encyclopaedia of Islam*, ed. Bernard Lewis et al. Leiden; E.J. Brill. 1965. pp. 178–179. Inalcik, Halil. "Dobrudja." *The Encyclopaedia of Islam*, ed. Bernard Lewis et al.
———. 1965. pp. 611–612. Inalcik, Halil. "Giray." *The Encyclopaedia of Islam*. New Edition, Vol. II. Leiden; E.J. Brill. 1965. pp. 1110–1115. Inalcik, Halil. *Sources and Studies on the Ottoman Black Sea. The Customs Register of Caffa, 1487–1490.* Vol. 1. Cambridge Mass; Harvard University Press. 1996. p. 150. Inalcik, Halil. *The Ottoman Empire. The Classical Age, 1300–1600.* London; Leidenfeld and Nicolson. 1973. Inalcik, Halil. "The Rise of the Ottoman Empire." *A History of the Ottoman Empire to 1730.* ed. V.J. Parry, et al. Cambridge University Press. 1976. Inalcik, Halil. "Yeni Vesikalara Gore Kirim Hanliginin Osmanli Tabiligine Girmesi ve Ahidname Meselesi." *Belleten.* Vol. 8. No. 31. (1944). pp. 185–229.
Ipek, Nedim. *Rumeili'den Anadolu'ya Turk Gocleri.* Ankara; TTK. 1994.
Irwin, Zachary. "The Fate of Islam in the Balkans. A Comparison of Four States" *Religion and Nationalism in Soviet and East European Politics*, ed. Pedro Ramet. Durham; Duke University Press. 1989. pp. 379–497.
Iunusov, Midat. "Vozrodit Starye Sorty" *Golos Kryma.* Feb. 2. 1996. p. 5.
Ivanics, Mary. "Formal and Linguistic Peculiarities of 17th Century Crimean Tatar Letters Addressed to Princes of Transylvania." *Acta Orientalia Academiae Scien-tarum Hungaricae.* Vol. 29, (2). 1975. pp. 213–224.
Iz, Fakir. *Ebul-Hayr Rumi'nin Sözlu Rivayetlerden Topladigi Sari Saltuk Menakibi.* Cambridge. 1974–84.
Jackson, Peter. *The Mission of Friar William of Rubruck.* London; Hakluyt Society. 1990.
Kacha, R. "Genocide in the Northern Caucasus." *Caucasian Review*, No. 2. 1956. pp. 74–83.
Kafesoglu, Ibrahim. *A History of the Seljuks.* ed. Gary Leiser. Carbondale; Southern Illinois University Press. 1988.
Kagedan, Allan. "Territorial Units as Nationality Policy." *Soviet Nationality Policies.* ed. Henry Huttenbach. London; Mansell. 1990.
Kaiser, Robert. *The Geography of Nationalism in Russia and the USSR.* Princeton; Princeton University Press. 1994.
Kakuk, Zsuzsa. *Kirim Tatar Sarkiliari.* Ankara; Turk Dil Kurumu Yayinlari. 1993.
Kandymov, Iu. *Ismail bei Gasprinskii (Gaspirali). IzNaslediia.* Simferpol; Tavria. 1991.
Kaplan, Fred. "After Decades in Exile, Crimean Tatars Reclaim Homeland." *Boston Globe.* Sept. 6, 1992. p. 14.
Karpat, Kemal. "Ottoman Urbanism: The Crimean Emigration to Dobruca and the Founding of Mecidiye, 1856–1878." *International Journal of Turkish Studies.* Winter, 1984–1985. Vol. 3. No. 1. pp. 1–27.

BIBLIOGRAPHY

———. *Ottoman Population 1830–1914. Demographic and Social Characteristics.* Madison; University of Wisconsin Press. 1985.

———. "Ottoman Immigration Policies and Setdement in Palestine." *Settler Regimes in Africa and the Arab World.* ed. Ibrahim Abu-Lughod and Baha Abu-Laban. Wilmette Illinois; Medina University Press International. 1974. pp. 7–72.

———. "Population Movements in the Ottoman State in the 19th Century, An Outline." *Collection Turcica.* 1983. pp. 385–428.

———. "The *Hijra* from Russia and the Balkans." *Muslim Travelers. Pilgrimage, Migration, and the Religious Imagination,* ed. Dale Eickelman and James Piscatori. London; Routledge. 1990.

———. "The Status of the Muslim Under European Rule; The Eviction and Settlement of the Cerkes." *Journal of Muslim Minority Affairs,* Vol. 1. No. 2. Winter 1979. pp. 7–28.

———. "The Turks of Bulgaria: The Struggle for National-Religious Survival of a Muslim Minority." *Nationalities Papers,* Vol. 23. No. 4. 1995. pp. 725–749.

Katenina, L. "Bor'ba Krymskikh Tatar Protiv Vrangelia." *Istorik Marksist.* Vol. 93. No. 5. 1944. pp. 74–81.

Kazinski, Michel. *Les Goths Ier-VIIe Apres J.-C.* Paris; Editions Erance. 1991.

Khalimov, Said. No. 1. 1923. "Krymskaia Avtonomnaia Respublika." *Zhizn' Natsional'nostei.* pp. 119–127.

Khazanov, Anatoly. *After the USSR. Ethnicity, Nationalism, and Politics in the Commonwealth of Independent States.* Madison; University of Wisconsin Press. 1995.

Kiel, Michael. "The Turbe of Sari Saltuk at Bagadag-Dobrudja. Brief Historical and Architetonical Notes." *Studies on the Ottoman Architecture of the Balkans.* Hampshire; Variorum. 1990.

King, Charles and Neil Melvin. *Nations Abroad. Diaspora Politics and and International Relations in the Former Soviet Union.* Boulder Colorado; Westview Press. 1998.

Kinglake, Alexander. *The Invasion of the Crimea. Its Origin and and Account of its Progress.* Vol. I. New York; Harper and Brothers. 1874.

Kirim, Metin. "Kirim Hanligi Ilhaki ve 1944 Siirgiin." *Emel.* No. 130. 1982. Nov.–Dec. 1982. p. 40.

Kirimal, Edige. "Complete Destruction of National Groups as Groups. The Crimean Turks." *Genocide in the USSR.* New York; Scarecrow Press. 1959.

———. "The Crimean Tatars." *Studies on the Soviet Union,* (new series), Vol. 10. No. 1, 1970. pp. 70–97.

———. "The Tragedy of Crimea." *Eastern Quarterly,* Vol. 4. No. 1. 1951. pp. 38–46.

———. *Der National Kampf der Krimturken.* Emsdetten: Verlag Lechte. 1952. Kirimal, Edige. *Dergi.* (Munich) 1955. No. 1. pp. 55–57.

Kirimca, Seyit Ahmet. "Symbols. The National Anthem and Patriotic Songs by Three Poets." *Tatars of the Crimea. Return to the Homeland,* ed. Edward Allworth. Durham; Duke University Press. 1998. pp. 71–83.

BIBLIOGRAPHY

Kirimli, Hakan. *National Movements and National Identity Among the Crimean Tatars (1905–1916)*. Leiden; E.J. Brill. 1996.

Kliachin, A. I. "Dinamika Etnicheskikh Sistem Rasseleniia v Krymy." *Etnografi-cheskoe Obozrenie*. No. 2. March–April. 1992. pp. 23–35.

Klimovich, Liutsian. *Islam v Tsarskoi Rossii*. Moscow; State Ami-Religious Press.1936.

Koch, Charles. *The Crimea From Kertch to Perekop*. London; Routledge. 1855.

Kochaev, B. *Nogaisko-Russkie Otnosheniia*. Almaty: Nauka. 1988.

Kochaev, B. *Sotsial'no Ekonomicehskoe i Politicheskoe Razvitie Nogaiskogo Obshschestva*. Alamty; Nauka. 1973.

Kolarz, Walter. *Russia and Her Colonies*. New York; Archon Books. 1967.

Kongonashivili, K. *Kratkii Slovar' Istorii Kryma*. Simferopol; Biznes-Inform. 1995.

Kononov. A. N. *Istoriia Izucheniia Tiurkskikh Iazikov v Rossi*. Leningrad; Nauka. 1982.

Kortepeter, Carl Max. "Karasu Bazar". *Encyclopaedia of Islam*. New Edition, Vol. 4. ed. B. Lewis et al. Leiden; EJ Brill. 1978. pp. 629–630.

———. *Ottoman Imperialism During the Reformation*. New York: New York University Press. 1972.

Kostanick, Huey Louis *Turkish Resettlement of Bulgarian Turks 1950–1953*. Berkeley: University of California Press. 1957.

Kostoe, Paul. *Russians in the Former Soviet Republics*. Bloomington; Indiana University Press. 1995.

Kowalewski, David. *National Dissent in the Soviet Union: The Crimean Tatar Case*. Washington DC; U.S. State Dept. 1977. p. 13.

Krymsk'ski Studii. Informatsiinii Biuleten'. No. 1. 2000.

Kudusov. Ernst. *Istoriia Formirovaniia Krymskotatarskoi Natsii*. Simferopol: Kasavet. 1996.

Kuftin, B. A. "Iuzhnoberezhnye Tatary Kryma." *Zabveniiu tie Podlezhit*. Kazan: Tatarskoe Knizhnoc IzdatcPstvo. 1992. pp. 239–250. (originally published in *Obshestvenno-Nauchny Zhhurnal*. 1925.)

Kurat, Akdes. *Topkapi Saray Müzesi Arsivindeki Altin Ordu, Kirim ve Turkistan Hanlarina Ait Yarlik ve Bitikler*. Istanbul; Burhannedin Matabaasi. 1990.

———. *Turkiye ve Rusya*. Ankara; Ankara University. 1970.

Landau, Jacob. "Diaspora and Language." *Modern Diasporas in International Politics*. ed. Gabriel Sheffer. London; Croom Helm. 1986. pp. 75–103.

Landau, P. G. *Islam v Istorii Rossii*. Moscow; Vostochnaia Literatura. 1995.

Lashkov, F. *Shagin Girei. Poslednii Krymskii Khan*. Kiev; Tipografia Davedeniko. 1886.

Lazzerini, Edward. "Gadidism at the Turn of the Twentieth Century." *Cahiers du Monde Russe el Soviedque*. Vol. 15. No. 2. pp. 245–279.

Lazzerini, Edward. "Ismail Bey Gasprinskii's Perevodchik/Terciiman: A Clarion of Modernism." *Central Asian Monuments*, ed. Hasan Paksov. Istanbul: Isis Press 1992. pp. 143–156.

BIBLIOGRAPHY

———. "Ismail Gasprinkii (Gaspirali): The Discourse of Modernism and the Russians." *The Tatars of the Crimea. Return to the Homeland*, ed. Edward Allworth. Durham; Duke University Press. 1998. pp. 48–70.

———. *Ismail Bey Gasprinskii and Muslim Modernism in Russia, 1878–1914*. Unpublished doctoral dissertation. University of Washington. 1973.

———. "Local Accommodation and Resistance to Colonialism in Nineteenth Century Crimea." *Russia's Orient. Imperial Borderlands and Peoples, 1700–1918*. Bloomington; Indiana University Press. 1997. pp. 169–188.

Lecat, Cesar. *The Crimean Expedition*, Vol. 1. London; Sampson Low and Son. 1866.

Lemercier-Quelquejay, Chantal. "From Tribe to Umma." *Central Asian Survey*, Vol. 3. No. 3. pp. 11–31.

———. "The Crimean Tatars. A Retrospective Summary." *Central Asian Review*, Vol. 16. No. 1(1968).pp. 15–25.

Leroy-Beaulieu, Anatole. *The Empire of the Tsars and Russians*. London; G. Putnam and Sons. 1893.

Leskov. A.M. *Gorny Krym v I Tysiacheleii do Nashei Ery*. Kiev; Naukova Dumka. 1965.

Levi, Scott C. *The Indian Diaspora in Central Asia and Its Trade*. Unpublished dissertation. University of Wisconsin, Madison. 2000.

Levitskii, G. I. "Pereselenie Tatar iz Kryma v Turtsiiu." *Vestnik Evropy*. Vol. 5. pp. 596–639.

Lewis, Bernard. "Vatan." *Journal of Contemporary American History*, Vol. 26. (1991). pp. 523–533.

———. *The Political Language of Islam*. Chicago: University of Chicago Press. 1988.

Lyall, Robert. *Travels in Russia, the Krimea. the Caucasus and Georgia*. London; Routledge. 1812.

Lynch, David. *The Conquest, Settlement and Initial Development of New Russia (The Southern-Third of the Ukraine): 1780–1837*. Dissertation. New Haven; Yale University. 1965.

Maenchen-Helfen, J. Otto. *The World of the Huns*. Berkeley; University of California Press. 1973.

Magocsi, Paul. *A History of the Ukraine*. Seattle; University of Washington Press. 1996.

———. *The Blessed Land. Crimea and the Crimean Tatars*. Toronto; University of Toronto Press. 2014.

"Mahometan Subjects of Russia." *Times*. (London). Dec. 4, 1874. p. 8.

Mahmut, Nedret. *Bozcigit. Dobruca Tatar Masallari*. Bucharest; Kriterion. 1988.

Marcu, L. P. "The Tatar Patriarchal Community in the Dobrudja and its Disen-tigration." *Revue des Etudes Sud-Est Europeennnes*. vol. 5. 1967. No. 3–4. pp. 501–542.

Markevich, Arsenii. "Pereselenie Krymskikh Tatar iz Kryma v Tiurtsiiu v Sviazy s Naselenia v Krymu." *Izvestiia Akademii Nauk SSSR*. 1928. pp. 375–405.

Markov, Evgenii. *Ocherkii Kryma*. Simferopol; Tavria. 1995. (original printed 1884).

BIBLIOGRAPHY

Marples, David. "Food Versus Ecology: Building the North Crimean Canal." *News from the Ukraine*, No. 3 Jan. 1989. p. 4.

Mart'ianov, G. P. "Posledniaia Emigratsiia Tatar iz Kryma v 1874 g." *Istoricheskii Vestnik*. No. 6. pp. 698–708.

Martin, Janet. "Muscovite Relations with the Khanate of Kazan and the Crimea." *Canadian-American Slavic Studies*, Vol. 17, 1983.

Maslov, P. V. et al. *Krym. Khrestomatiia po Istorii Kraiia*. pt. 1. Simferopol; Kryms-koe Gosudarstvennoe Izdatel'stvo. 1930.

Masud, Muhammad Khalid. "The Obligation to Migrate: the Doctrine of Hijra in Islamic Law." *Muslim Travellers, Pilgrimage, Migration, and the Religious Imagination*. ed. Dale Eickelman and James Piscatori. London; Routledge. 1990.

McCarthy, Justin. "Age, Family, and Migration in Nineteenth-Century Black Sea Provinces of the Ottoman Empire." *International Journal of Middle East Studies*. Vol. 10. No. 3. August 1979. pp. 289–308.

———. "An Ottoman Document on the Refugees of the Crimean Period." *Turkish Studies Association Bulletin*, Vol. 6. No. 2. pp. 29–30.

———. *Death and Exile. The Cleansing of the Ottoman Muslim. 1821–1922*. Princeton; Darwin Press. 1995.

———. "Muslims in Ottoman Europe." *Nationalities Papers*, Vol. 28. No. 1. 2000. pp. 29–43.

McNeill, William. *Europe's Steppe Frontier 1500–1800*. Chicago; University of Chicago Press. 1964.

Mehmet, Iacub. *Prezente Musulmane in Romania*. Bucharest; Meridiane. 1976.

Melek, lytegun. *Altin Ordu, Kirim ve Kazan Sahasina ait Yarlik ve Bitiklerin Dil ve Aslip Incelemesi*. Ankara; Turk Dil Kurumu. 1996.

Melikoff, Irene."Qui Etait Sari Saltuk? Quelques Remarques sur le Manuscrits du Saltukname." *Studies in Ottoman History in Honour of V.L. Menage*, ed. Colin Heywood and Colin Imber. Istanbul; Isis Press. 1994. pp. 231–238.

Memetov, Aider. *Krymskie Tatary. lstoriko-Lingvisticheskii Ocherk*. Simferopol: Anaiurt. 1993. Memetov, A. "O Proiskhozhdenii Krymskikh Tatar i ikh Iazyka." *Kasavet. Sotsial'no Literaturny Zhurnal*. Feb. 3 1994. pp. 2–6.

Meyendorf, John. *Byzantium and the Rise of Russia*. Cambridge; Cambridge University Press. 1981.

Mikaelian. V.A. *Na Krymsko Zemle. Istoriia Armianskikh Poselenii v Krymy*. Erevan; Izdatelstvo Aiastan. 1974.

Miller, Phillip. *Karaite Separatism in Nineteenth-Century Russia*. Cincinnati; Hebrew Union College Press. 1993.

Milner, Thomas. *The Crimea, Its Ancient and Modern History*. London; Longman, Brown, Green and Longmans. 1855.

Mona, Zh. N. "Kak Byl Realizovan v Krymy Leninskii Dekret o Zemle?" *Krymskaia ASSR (1921–1945) Voprosy, Otvety*. Simferopol; Tavrida. 1990.

Moore, Margaret. "The Territorial Dimension of Self-Determination." *National Self*

BIBLIOGRAPHY

Determinalion and Secession. Oxford: Oxford University Press. 1998. pp. 134–158.

Morav, M. N. *The Crimea. Pearl of the Soviet Union*. Moscow; Intourist. 1934.

Munro. George. "The Annexation of the Crimea." *The Modern Encyclopedia of Russian and Soviet History*, Vol. 8. Gulf Breeze Florida: Academic International Press. 1978.

Munsie, Robert. *Peter the Great, His Life and World*. New York; Alfred Knopf. 1980.

Murvar, Vatro. *Nation and Religion in Central Europe and the Western Balkans-The Muslims in Bosnia, Hercegovina and Sandzak: A Sociological Analysis*. Brookfield Wisconsin; University of Wisconsin Press. 1989.

Mustafaev, Sh. U. "Evoliutsiia Samosoznaniia-Vzgliad Iznutri." *Krymskie Tatary: Problemy Repatriatsi*. ed. A.P. Viatkin and E.S. Kul'pin. Moscow; Rossiiskaia Akedemiia Nauk. 1997. pp. 20–37.

Muzafarov, R.I. "ASSR Natsional'naia." *Krymakaia ASSR (1921–1945). Voprosy, Otvety*. Simferopol; Tavria. 1990. pp. 24–30.

——— "Kak Osushchetvlialos' Obuchenie Krymskotatarskogo Naseleniia v Respublike?" *Krymskaia ASSR (1921–1945). Voprosy, Otvety*. Simferopol; Tavria. 1990. pp. 163–168. N.P. "Iz Vospominanii Bwshago Krvmskogo Pomeshchika." *Russkaia Slarina*. Vol. 131. July–September. 1907. pp.'155–182.

Nadinskii, P.N. *Ocherki po Islorii Kryma*. Vol. 1. Simferopol; Tavria. 1951.

Nahylo, Bohdan and Ann Sheehy. *The Crimean Tatars, Volga Germans and Meskhelians. Soviet Treatment of Some National Minorities*. London: Minority Rights Group. 1971.

Namitok. A. "The 'Voluntary' Adherence of Kabarda (Eastern Circassia) to Russia." *Caucasian Review*, No. 2 1956. pp. 17–34.

Natsuko, Oka. "Deportation of Koreans from the Russian Far East to Central Asia." *Migration in Central Asia: Its History and Current Problems*, ed. John Schoberlein et al. Osaka; Japan Center for Area Studies. 2000. pp. 127–147.

Nekrich, Alexander. *The Punished Peoples. The Deportation and Fate of Soviet Minorities at the end of the Second World War*. New York; WAV. Norton and Co. 1978.

Nogay, Sami. *Nogay Turkleri*. Ankara; 1997.

Nogay Haber Biilletini. Vol. 1. No. 1. 1999.

Norris. H.T. *Islam in the Balkans*. Columbia SC; University of South Carolina Press. 1993.

Novosel'skii, Aleksei. *Bor'ba Moskovskogo Gosudarstva s Tatarami v Pervoi Polovine XVII Veka*. Moscow; Academy of Sciences Press. 1948.

Obolensky, Dimitri. *Byzantium and the Slavs*. New York; St. Vladimir's Press. 1994.

Oliphant, Laurence. *The Russian Shores of the Black Sea*. New York; Arno Press. 1970.

Olkusal, Miistecip. "Crimean Turks. The Tragedy of the Crimean Turks and Their Cause of Independence." *The Voice of Turkism*. ed. Arin Engin. Istanbul; Ata-turkist Cultural Publications, No. 18. 1964. pp. 29–37.

Olkusal, Mtistecib Fazil. *Dobruca ve Turkler*. Ankara; Turk Kultiiriin Arastirma Enstitiisii. 1966.

BIBLIOGRAPHY

Olson, James. *An Ethno-Historical Dictionary of the Russian and Soviet Empires*. Westport Conn. Greenwood Press. 1994.

Osmanov, L. "Den' Deportatsii v Turtsii." *Avdet*. No. 10. May 26, 1994. p. 1.

Ostapchuk, Victor. "Five Documents from the Topkapi Palace Archive on the Ottoman Defence of the Black Sea Against the Cossacks (1639)." *Journal of Turkish Studies*. No. 11. 1987. pp. 49–104.

———. "The Publication of Documents on the Crimean Khanate in the Topkapi Saray." *Turcica*, Vol. 14. 1987. pp. 247–257.

Ostrowski. *Muscovy and the Mongols*. Cambridge: Cambridge University Press. 1998.

Ovod, Vladimir. *Migratsionnye Protsessy v Krymy; Istoriia, Problemy, Perspektivy*. Simferopol; Administration for Migration, Crimean Republic, 1997.

Ovseichika, V. et al. *Krym. Chrestomatiia po Istorii K'raia*. Simferopol; Krymskoe Gosudarstvennoc Izdatel'stvo. 1930.

Ozenbajh, Ahmet *Carlik Hakimiyetinde Kirim Faciasi Yahut Tatar Hicretleri*. Akmecit; Krymskoe Gosudarstvennoe Izdatel'stvo. 1925.

Ozhiganov, Edward. "The Crimean Republic: Rivalries for Control." *Managing Conflict in the Former Soviet Union: Russian and American Perspectives*. Cambridge Mass; MIT Press. 1997. pp. 83–137.

Pallas, Peter. *Travels in 18th Century Russia*. London; Studio Editions. 1990.

———. *Travels Through the Southern Provinces of the Russian Empire in 1793 and 1794*. London; T. N. Longman. 1802.

Parr)-, V.J. *A History of the Ottoman Empire to 1730*. Cambridge; Cambridge University Press. 1976.

Payin, Emil. "Population Transfer: The Crimean Tatars Return Home." *Cultural Survival Quarterly*. Winter 1992. Vol. 16. No. 1.

Perushkin, Viktor. "Yplyvet li Krym v Turtsiiu?" *Argumenty i Fakty*. October 1994. No. 40 (729). p. 6.'

Peyssonel, Claude. M. *Traite sur le Commerce de la Mer jYoire*. Paris; 1787.

Pierce, Richard. *Russian Central Asia 1867–1917. A Study in Colonial Rule*. Berkeley; University of California. 1960.

Pmson, Mark. "Ottoman Colonization of the Circassians in Rumili after the Crimean War." *Etudes Balkiniques*. No. 3. 1972. pp. 71–85.

———. "Russian Policy and the Emigration of the Crimean Tatars to the Ottoman Empire 1854–1862." *Guney-Dogu Avrupa Arastimalan Dergisi*. No. 1. (1972). pp. 37–55. and Nos 2–3 (1974) pp. 101–114

———. "The Ottoman Colonization of the Crimean Tatars in Bulgaria, 1854–1862." *Turk Tarihi Kongresi*. Vol. 2. 1973. pp. 1040–1058.

Pipes, Richard. *The Formation of the Soviet Union*. Cambridge Mass; Harvard University Press. 1957.

Pittard, Eugene. *Les Peuples de Balkans. Reserches Anthropologiques* Paris; Editions Leroux 1920.

BIBLIOGRAPHY

Pletneva. S.A. *Kochevniki Srednovekov'ya Poiski*. Moscow; Nauka. 1992.

———. *Steppi Evrazii Epokhu Srednevekov'ya*. Moscow; Nauka. 1981.

Pohl, J. Otto. *The Stalinist Penal System. A Statistical History of Soviet Repression and Terror 1930–1953*. Jefferson North Carolina; McFarland and Co. 1997.

Popovich, Alexander. "A Propos de la Revue Emel." *Altaica Collecta*. Weisbaden; Otto Harrassowitz. 1976. pp. 194–198.

Popovich, Andrei. *The Political Status of Bessarabia*. Washington D.C. School of Foreign Service. 1931.

Poppe, Nicholas. *Introduction to Altaic Linguistics*. Wiesbaden; Otto Harrassowitz. 1965.

Potichnyj, Peter. "The Struggle of the Crimean Tatars." *Canadian Slavonic Papers*. Vol. 27. Nos 2–3. pp. 302–319.

Poulton, Hugh and Suha Taji-Farouki (eds). *Muslim Identity and the Balkan State*. London; Hurst and Co. 1997.

Pravda. "Deklaratsiia Verkhovnogo Soveta." Nov. 24, 1989. p. 1.

———. "Vosstanavlivia Spravedlivost." No. 147. May 17, 1990. p. 2.

Pravda Vostoka. "Pravda o Kuvasae". No. 137. June 11, 1989. p. 3.

Pulatov, Temir. "Vsem Mirom Pomoch' Brat'iam!" *Druzhba Narodov*. No. 2. 1988 p. 203.

Radio Free Europe/Radio Liberty Newsline. "Turkish Premier in Kviv." Vol. 2. No. 30. Part II. February 1998.

Ramet, Pedro. "The Interplay of Religious Policy and Nationalities Policy in the Soviet Union and Eastern Europe." *Religion and Nationalism in Soviet and East European Politics*. Durham; Duke University Press. 1989. pp. 3–42.

Reitlinger, Gerald. *The House Built on Sand. The Conflicts of German Policy in Russia 1939–45*. London; Weidenfeld and Nicolson. 1960.

Rhinelander, Anthony. *Prince Michael Vorontsov. Viceroy to the Tsar*. London; McGill-Queen's University Press. 1990.

Roider, Karl. *The Reluctant Ally, Austria's Policy in the Austro-Turkish War 1737–1739*. Baton Rouge; Louisiana State University Press. 1972.

Rorlich, Azade-Ayse. "One or More Tatar Nations?" *Muslim Communities Reemer-ge. Historical Perspectives on Nationality, Politics, and Opposition in the Former Soviet Union and Yugoslavia*, ed. Edward Allworth. Durham; Duke University. Press, 1994.

Rubruck. William. *The Mission of Friar William of Rubruck*. London; Hakluyt Society. 1990.

Rummel, R.J. *Lethal Politics. Soviet Genocide and Mass Murder Since 1917*. New Brunswick; Transaction Publishers. 1990.

Safran, William. "Diasporas in Modern Societies: Myths of Homeland and Return." *Diaspora*, Vol. 1. No. 1. Spring 1991. pp. 83–100.

Sagatovskii, V. N. "Tavrida Internatsional'naia." *Krymakaia ASSR, 1921–1943. op rosy, Otvety*. Simferopol; Tavria. 1990.

Sahlieh, Sami Aldeeb Abu. "The Islamic Conception of Migration." *International Migration Review*, Vol. 30. No. 1. Spring. 1996. pp. 37–58.

Said, Edward, and C. Hitchens. *Blaming the Victims*. London; Verso. 1988.

Sanin, G.A. *Otnowheniia Rossii i Ukrainy s Krymskim Khanstvom v Seredetne XVI* Moscow; Nauka. 1997.

Saracoglu, Haydar. "Kulus. Gunesi Dogacaktir." *Emel*. No. 107. 1978. p. 7.

Schamiloglu, Uli. "The Qaraci Beys of the Later Golden Horde: Notes on the Organization of the Mongol World Empire." *Archivum Eurasiae Medii Aevi*. Vol. 4. 1984. pp. 283–299.

Schayfer, Daniel. *Building Nations and Building States. The Tatar-Bashkir Question in Revolutionary Russia, 1917–20*. Dissertation. University of Michigan. 1995.

Schoberlein, John et al. *Migration in Central Asia: Its History and Current Problems*. Osaka; The Japan Center for Area Studies. 2000.

Schulz, Friedrich. *The Battle for Crimea. Attack on Sevastopol*, (translated from German War Report). Historical Division, HQ, US Army, Europe. 1954.

Schulze, Fred. *The USSR Today. Perspectives from the Soviet Press*. Columbus Ohio; Current Digest of the Soviet Press. 1985

Schutz, Edmond. "The Tat People in the Crimea." *Acta Orientalia, Academiae Scientiarum Hungaricae*. Vol. 31. 1977. pp. 77–106.

Scott, Charles. *The Baltic, the Black Sea and the Crimea*. London; Richard Bentley. 1854.

Seidamet, Djafer. *La Crimee. Passe-Present Revendications des Tatars de Crimee*. Lausanne; Imprimerie G. Vaney-Burnier. 1921.

Seitbekirov, E. "Sviashchennaia Bor'ba Krymskikh Tatar." *Golos Kryma*. Nov. 14, 1997. p. 5.

"Sessia po Istorii Kryma." *Voprosy Istorii*. No. 12. Dec. 1948. p. 148.

Sevdiyar, Memet. *Etiudy ob Elnogeneze Krymskikh Tatar*. New York; Fond Krym. 1997.

———. "FaLsifikatsiia Istorii." *Kirim*. Sept. 27, 1997. p. l.

Seydamet, E. "Eski Sehir Milletvekili..." *Emel*. May–June. 1994. No. 203. p. 10.

Seymour, H.D. *Russia and the Black Sea*. London; John Murray. 1855.

Shami, Seteney. *Ethnicity and Leadership: The Circassians in Jordan*. University of California. Dissertation. 1989.

Shaw, Stanford. *Between the Old and New. The Ottoman Empire Under Sultan Selim II, 1789–1807*. Cambridge; Harvard University Press. 1971.

Shcherban', N. "Pereselenie Krymskikh Tatar." *Russkii Vestnik*. 1860. Vol. 30. No. 11–12.

Sheehy, Ann and Bohdan Nahaylo. *The Crimean Tatars, Volga Germans and Meshketians: Soviet Treatment of Some National Minorities*. London; Minority Rights Group. 1980.

Shukman, Harold (ed.). *The Blackwell Encyclopedia of the Russian Revolution*. Oxford; Basil Blackwell Ltd. 1994.

BIBLIOGRAPHY

Shuster, A. *Krym*. Kiev; Ministerstva Kulturi U.R.S.R. 1961.

Skachko. A. "Vostochnye Respubliki na S. Kh. Vystavke v 1923 godu" *Novyi Vostok*. No. 4. 1923. pp. 482-484.

Slackman, Michael. "Displaced Peoples of the Former Soviet Union Living in Bitter Lands." *Newsday*. May 21, 2000.

Slezkine, Yuri. "The USSR as a Communal Apartment, or How a Socialist State Promoted Ethnic Particularism." *Slavic Review*, Vol. 53. No. 2. Summer 1994. pp. 414-453.

Smects, Rieks. "Circassia." *Central Asian Survey*, Vol. 14. No. 1. March. 1995. pp. 107-127.

Smirnova, la. S. et. al. *Nogaitsy, Istoriko-Etnograficheskii Ocherk*. Cherkesk; Stavropol'skoe Knizhnoe IzdatePstvo. 1988. Smith, Sebastian. *Allah's Mountains. Politics and War in the Russian Caucasus*. London; IB. Tauris. 1998.

Sobesednik. No. 29. 1989. p. 12

Soloviev, Sergei. "Istoriia Padeniia Pol's." *Sobranie Sochinenii*. St. Petersburg; Obshchestvennaia Pol'za. 1900.

Solzhenitsyn, Aleksandr. *The Gulag Archipelago. 1918-1956. An Experiment in Literary Investigation*. V-VII. New York; Harper and Row Publishers. 1976.

Soucek, S. "Kefe." *Encyclopedia of Islam*, Vol. 4. new ed. Leiden; E.J. Brill. 1978.

Soulotis, D. P. "A Greek Prelate in the Tatar Khanate of the Crimea in the Early Seventeenth Century." *Balkan Studies*, Vol. 31. 1990. pp. 269-282.

Spector, Shmuel. *Encylopedia of the Holocaust*, Vol. 2. New York; Macmillian Publishing Co. 1996.

Spektr. Informastionanno-Analiticheskii Biuleten. Simferopol; Crimean Center for Ethno-Social Investigation. 1996. No. 5 (13).pt. 2.

Spencer, Edmund. *Travels in Circassia, Krim Tatary etc*. London; Henry Colburn. 1839.

Spuler, Berthold. "Kirim."*Encyclopaedia of Islam*, vol. IV. New Edition, ed. by Bernard Lewis et. al. Leiden. E.J. Brill. 1978. pp. 136-143.

———. *The Muslim World. A Historical Surze): Pt. II. The Mongol Period*. Leiden; EJ. Brill. 1969.

St. Clair, Stanislas and C.A. Brophy. *Twelve Tears Study of the Eastern Question*. London; Routledge. 1877.

Stavrianos, L.S. *The Balkans Since 1453*. New York: Holt. Rinehart. and Winston. 1958.

Sukhareva, O.A. *Islam v Uzbekistane*. Tashkent: Akademii Nauk Uzbekskoi SSR. 1960.

Suliteanu, Ghizela. "Le Tabin dan la Tradition Populaire des Tatars Nogay de Dobroudja." *Turcica*, Vol. 12. 1980. pp. 95-111.

Sumarokov, Pavel. *Dosugi Krymskogo Sud'i ili Vtoroe Puteshestvie v Tavridy*. St. Petersburg; Imperatorskoi Tipograf. pt. 1. 1803.

BIBLIOGRAPHY

Suny, Ronald G. "Nationalist and Ethnic Unrest in the Soviet Union." *The "Nationality" Question in the Soviet Union*, ed. Gail Lapidus. New York: Garland Pub. Co. 1992. pp. 307–334.

Taheri, Amir. *Crescent in a Red Sky. The Future of Islam in the Soviet Union.* London; Hutchinson. 1989.

Tashkentskii Protsess. Amsterdam; The Herzen Foundation. 1976.

Taymas, Battal. "La Litterature des Tatars de Crimee." *Philogiae Turcicae Fundamenta.* Paris; Aquis Mattiacis Apud Francisum Steiner. 1974. pp. 785–791.

Tefler, J. Buchan. *The Bondage and Travels of Johann Schiltberger.* London; Hakluyt Society. 1879.

The Crimean Review, Vol. 1 No. 1. May 18, 1986.

———, Vol. 4. No. 2, 18. Dec. 1989.

———, Vol. 7. Special Issue. 1995.

Thunman. *Der Krimische Staat (Krymskoe Khanstvo).* Simferopol: Gosudarstvennoe Izdatel'stvo Krym ASSR. 1936. (Reprint).

Tillet, Lowell. *The Great Friendship. Soviet Historians on the Non-Russian Nationalities.* Chapel Hill; University of North Carolina Press. 1969.

Tishchcnko, Iuliia. *Povemennia Kryms'kikh Tatar. Khronika Podii.* Kiev: Ukrain'skii Nezalezhnii Tsentr Politichnikh Doslidzhen. 1999.

Todorova, Elisaveta. "The Greeks in the Black Sea Trade During the Late Medieval Period." *Etudes Balkaniques.* Nos 3–4. 1992. pp. 40–58.

Togan. Zeki Velidi. "Gaspirali, Ismail. *Encyclopaedia of Islam*, Vol. 2. Leiden; EJ Brill. 1960. pp. 979–981.

Totleben, E. I. "O Vvselenii Tatar iz Krvma v 1860 godv." *Russkaia Starina.* June. 1893.

Tropkin, Alexander. "Crimea. At the Crossroads." *Soviet Life.* April 1991, No. 4 (415). pp. 5–26.

Turkistan Newsletter. "Crimea Bulletin." Vol. 30:039 February 26. 1999. p. 7.

———. Vol. 3:019–05 Feb. 1999. p. 11.

Tzvetkov, Plamen. *A History of the Balkans*, Vol. 1. San Fransico. EM Text. 1993.

Tiituncii, Mehmet. "Why the Crimean Tatars Were Deported." *Bitig.* December 1992. Year 2, No. 5. p. 16.

Tystchenko, Julia. *The Repatriation of the Crimean Tatars. A Chronicle of Events.* Kiev. 1999.

Uehling, Greta. "Squatting. Self-immolation, and the Repatriation of the Crimean Tatars. *Nationalities Papers*, Vol. 28. No. 2. 2000. pp. 317–341.

———. Beyond Memory. The Crimean Tatars Deportation and Return. New York; Palgrave Macmillan. 2004.

Uralgiray, Yusuf. "Luzern Konferansmda Kirm'in Sesi." *Emel.* No. 105. March–April. pp. 7–26.

Urskaia, Ekaterina. "Berega Voselye Salgir." *Golos Kryma.* Jan. 13, 1996. p. 5.

BIBLIOGRAPHY

Vasiliev, Alexander. *The Goths in the Crimea*. Cambridge Mass; Medieavel Academy of America. 1936.

Vasiukov', S. *Krym i Gornye Tatary*. St. Petersburg; A.F. Devriena. 1904.

Veinstein, Giles. "La Population du sud de la Crimec au debut de la domination Ottomane" *The Customs Register of Caffa, 1487–1490*. Vol. 1. Cambridge Mass. Harvard University. 1996.

Veinstein, Giles. "From Italians to Ottomans: The Case of the Northern Black Sea Coast in the Sixteenth Century." *Mediterranean Historical Review*, Vol. 1. No. 2. Dec. 1986. pp. 221–238.

Vernadsky, George, et al. editor. *A Source Book for Russian History from Early Times to 1917*. Vol. 2. New Haven; Yale Univ. Press. 1972.

Vernadsky, George. *Kievan Russia*. New Haven; Yale University Press. 1948.

Vol'fson, B. M. "Emigratsiia Krymskikh Tatar v I860 g.'*Istoricheskie Zapiski*. No. 9. 1940. pp. 186–197.

Voloshin, M. "Kultura, Isskysstvo, Pamiatniki *Kryma*." *Zabveniiu ne Podlezhit*. Kazan; Tatarskoe Knizhnoe Izdatel'stvo. 1992. pp. 55–68.

Voroponov, O. "Sredi Krymskikh Tatar." *Zabveniiu ne Podlezhit*. Kazan; Tatarskoe Knizhnoe Izdatel'tstvo. 1992. pp. 162–194.

Vorozdin, I. "Soveremenaia Krymskaia Respublika." *Novy Vostok*. No. 19. pp. 99–120.

———. "Novye Dannye o Zolotoordynskoi Kulture v Krymy." *Xovy Vostok*. 1926. pp. 274–295. '

Vozgrin, Valerii. *Istoricheskie Sud'by Krymskikh Tatar*. Moscow; Mysl. 1992.

Vyltsan, M.A. "Deportatsiia Narodov v Gody Velikoi Otechestvennoi Voiny." *Etnograficheskoe Obozrenie*. No. 3. May–June. 1995.

Vysotskaia, T.N. *Pozdnie Skify v lugo-Zqpadnom Krymy*. Kiev; Naukova Dumka. 1972.

Waines, David. *A Sentence of Exile. The Palestine/Israel Conflict, 1897–1977*. Wilmette, Illinois; The Medina Press, 1977.

Wallace, Donald Mackenzie. *Russia*. New York; Henry Holt and Co. 1877.

Walpole, Robert. *Travels in Various Countries of the East*. London: Longman, Hurst et al. 1820.

Ware, Bruce. "Conflict in the Caucasus: An Historical Context and a Prospect for Peace." *Central Asian Survey*, Vol. 17. No. 2. June 1988. pp. 337–353.

Watt, W. Montgomery. *Muhammad at Mecca*. Oxford; Oxford University Press. 1953.

Weekes, Richard. *Muslim Peoples. A World Ethnographic Survey. (Maba-Toruk)*. Westport Conn. Greenwood Press. 1984.

Weisband, Edward. *Turkish Foreign Policy, 1943–1945. Small State Diplomacy and Great Power Politics*. Princeton; Princeton University Press. 1973.

Williams, Brian Glyn. "A Community Re-imagined. The Role of 'Homeland' in the Forging of National Identity. The Case of the Crimean Tatars." *Journal of Muslim Minority Affairs*, Vol. 17. No. 2. 1997. pp. 225–252.

Williams, Brian Glyn. "Bahcesaray." *The Modern Encyclopedia of Russian. Soviet, and*

Eurasian History, ed. Edward Lazzerini. Gulf Breez Fla.; Academic International Press. 2000.

———. "Central Asian Nationalism." *Encyclopedia of Nationalism*, Vol. 2. ed. Alexander Motyl. San Diego; Academic Press. 2000.

———. "Commemorating 'The Deportation' in Post-Soviet Chechnya. The Role of Memorialization and Collective Memory in the 1994–96 and 1999–2000 Russo Chechen Wars." *History and Memory*, Vol. 12. No. 1. 2000.

———. *"Hijra* and Forced Migration from Nineteenth Century Russia to the Ottoman Empire. *Cahiers du Monde Russe*. Vol. 41. No. 1. Jan.–Mar. 2000. pp. 63–92.

———. "Islam in the Crimea." *Modern Encyclopedia of Religion in Russia and the Soviet Union*. Gulf Breez Fla. Academic International Press. 1995. pp. 123–127.

———. "May 18, 1944. The Crucible of Crimean Tatar National Identity." *Turkestan Newsletter*, Vol. 3. 115. May 1999.

———. "Mustafa Jemilev." *Encyclopedia of Nationalism*, Vol. 2. ed. Alexander Motyl. San Diego; Academic Press. 2000.

———. "Mystics, Nomads and Heretics. The Dissemination of Heterodox Islam from Central Asia to the 13th Century Dobruca." *International Journal of Turkish Studies*, Vol. 7. No. 1–2. 2001.

———. "New Light on the Ethnogenesis of the Crimean Tatars." *Journal of the Royal Asiatic Society*. Forthcoming. 2001.

———. "The Cleansing of Muslims in the Russian and Soviet Borderlands." *Journal of Genocide Research*. Forthcoming. 2001.

———. "The Crimean Tatar Exile in Central Asia: A Case Study in Group Destruction and Survival." *Central Asian Survey*, Vol. 17. No. 2. June 1988. pp. 285–319.

———. "The Russo-Chechen War: A Threat to Stability in the Middle East and Eurasia?" *Middle East Policy*. Vol. 8. No. 1 March 2001.

Wilson, Ms. Andrew. *The Crimea: Its Towns and Inhabitants*. London; Partridge and Co. 1855.

Wilson, Andrew. *The Crimean Tatars*. Cambridge; International Alert. 1994.

Wittek, Paul. "Les Gagaouzes-Les Gens de Kavkaus." *Rocznik Orienlalisiyczny*. Vol. 17. 1952.

———. "Yazijioghlu Ali on the Christian Turks of Dobrudja." *Bulletin of the School of Oriental and African Studies*. 14/3. 1952. pp. 639–688.

Wixman, Ronald. "Manipulating Territory Undermining Rights." *Cultural Survival Quarterly*. Winter 1992. Vol. 16. No. 1. pp. 21–24.

Woods, Nicholas. *The Past Campaign. A Sketch of the War in the East*. London: Longman, Brown and Green. 1855.

Yalcinkava. Alaeddin. "Cedidcilerin Bilinmiyen Yonleri" *Tarih ve Medeniyet*. Oct. 1998. pp. 22–27.

Yavuz, Hakan. "The Patterns of Political Islamic Identity: Dynamics of National and Transnational Lovalties and Identities." *Central Asian Survey*. (1995) Vol. 3. No. 14. pp. 341–372.

ABOUT THE AUTHOR

Brian Glyn Williams is Professor of Islamic History at the University of Massachusetts-Dartmouth and formerly taught Ottoman and Central Asian history at the University of London's School of Oriental and African Studies. He earned his PhD in Central Asian History at the University of Wisconsin in 1999 and earned a Master's Degrees in Russian History and in Central Eurasian Studies from Indiana University in 1990 and 1992. He carried out his fieldwork for this book in the Crimean Peninsula and the Crimean Tatars' place of exile in Uzbekistan in the late 1990s. This fieldwork led him to write *The Crimean Tatars. The Diaspora Experience and the Forging of a Nation* (Leiden; Cologne, Boston 2001. 500 pages) which focuses on the ethnic genesis of the Crimean Tatars, their migrations and resettlement in the Caucasus, Ottoman province of Dobruca and Anatolia, as well as the Soviet exile period.

Dr. Williams has carried out fieldwork in Islamic Eurasia ranging from Kosovo in the west to Kashmir in the east. Most recently he has been engaged in fieldwork in Afghanistan and Pakistan. This research work has varied from living with General Dostum, an Uzbek anti-Taliban warlord, in the deserts of northern Afghanistan and working for NATO in Kabul, to carrying out fieldwork in the Pashtun tribal areas of Pakistan where Bin Laden previously found sanctuary. He has written four books on these experiences, including *Afghanistan Declassified. A Guide to America's Longest War* (University of Pennsylvania Press, 2010); *The Last Warlord. The Life and Legend of Dostum, the Afghan Warrior who led US Special Forces to Topple the Taliban Regime* (Chicago, 2013); *Predators. The CIA's Drone War on Al Qaeda* (Washington DC, 2013) and *Inferno in Chechnya The Russian Chechen Wars, the Al Qaeda Myth and the Boston Bombing* (Dartmouth College, 2015).

ABOUT THE AUTHOR

For his articles on Crimean Tatars, Chechens, Afghanistan, drones and Al Qaeda, as well as videos and photographs from his fieldwork in Eurasia (including the Crimea) see his website at: brianglynwilliams.com. He can be reached via email at: bwilliams@umassd.edu

INDEX

Abdül Hamid II, Sultan of the Ottoman Empire 50
Abdül Mecid I, Sultan of the Ottoman Empire 19
Abdülaziz I, Sultan of the Ottoman Empire 14–15
Abkhazia 59, 144
Ablaev, Reshat 135
"Action Groups" 130
Adalet Party 156
Adulhamitoglu, Necip 91
Ahir Zaman (apocalypse) 27
Ahiska 98, 150
Ahmet, Svetlina 129
Aikish, Crimea 24
Ak Hoja, Crimea 12
Ak Kaya (White Rock) 46, 147; *see also* Yalta
Ak Kogekskii, Crimea 24
Ak Mecit, Crimea 12, 74, 82, 111; *see also* Simferopol
ak sakals (white beards) 28
Ak Sheikh, Crimea 12
ak toprak (white soil) 14, 27, 28, 29, 46, 86, 116
Akchura, Yusuf 50
Akhmudov, Sham 105
Akiner, Shirin 85
akinjis (those who flow) xii
Aksyonov, Sergei 159
Albanians 29

Alexander II, Emperor and Autocrat of All the Russias 23, 25, 31
Algeria 29
Aliadin, Shamil 49, 53
All Crimean Muslim Congress 61
All-Union Resort 115, 128
Allahsizler (Godless Zealots) 78
Alma Ata, Kazakhstan 102
Alupka, Crimea 31
Alushta, Crimea 4, 31, 66, 94, 111, 112, 121, 141, 147
Ana Yurt (Motherland) 152
Anatolia xiv, 7, 30, 46
Andijan, Uzbekistan 88, 102, 107, 127
Andropov, Yuri 125
Angren, Uzbekistan 88, 106
apple orchards 142
Apskii, Crimea 24
Arabic 6, 34, 37, 40, 74, 76, 78
Ardahan, Turkey 97
Armenia, Armenians 46, 59, 73, 80, 88, 97, 98, 117, 137
Aromatnaya, Crimea 147
Asanov, Asan Sait 159
Asanov, Saniye and Seidjalil 146
Association of the Crimean Turk Americans 66
ata vatan (Fatherland) xiv, 12, 13, 31, 33, 45, 46, 50–2, 54–5, 79, 86, 108, 118, 121, 132, 139, 145, 155
Atatürk, Mustafa Kemal 81, 87

INDEX

Attila xi
Augsburg, Germany 95
Austria xiii, 29, 110
Autonomous Republic of the Crimea
  (1991–2014) 57–8, 141–60
Avcikoy, Bahcesaray 34
Avdet (Return) 154
Ayu Dag, Crimea 113
Azerbaijan, Azerbaijainis 34, 40, 41,
  59, 73, 117, 137, 146
Aziz Shehitler (the Great Martyrs) 3

Bacon, Elizabeth 122
Baharistan, Uzbekistan 132
Bahcesaray, Crimea xii, 4, 6, 8, 34, 41,
  43, 46, 52, 62, 66, 82, 87, 97, 111,
  115, 121, 130, 137, 145, 147, 148,
  159
Baidar Valley 4, 54
Baku, Azerbaijan 146
Balaklava, Crimea 112, 142
Balich, Abdulla 132–3
Balkans xiv, 7, 19, 29, 39, 58, 66, 67,
  68, 69, 84, 111, 155, 159
Balkars 97, 99, 108, 124
"Ballad of the Ancestral Home" 113
Baltic countries 61, 67, 137, 144
"Bantuzation" 73
Bariev, Haydar 129
Bashkirs 21, 73
Bashmak gang 141
Batu Khan xi
Bayramev, Reshat 129
Bekabad, Uzbekistan 127
Bekirov, Nadir 144
Belaya, Crimea 147
Belitser, Natalya 156
Bell Fialkoff, Andrew 114–15
Belogorsk, Crimea 112, 137, 145, 147
Belorussia, Belorussians 59, 82, 91
Bennigsen, Alexandre 11, 55, 80, 116
Beria, Lavrentii 97, 102, 104
Berkuts (Golden Eagles) 142
Berlin, Germany 92, 96, 97
bey (chieftain) 46

bid'at (innovation) 36
Bilal Agha, Crimea 100
Birobidzhan, Russia 84, 133
Bishkek, Kyrgyzstan 148
Black Sea xi, xiv, 1, 6, 7, 20, 26, 87–8,
  89, 97, 106, 111, 117, 139
Black Sea Fleet 64
blending (*slianiie*) 77, 127
blitzkrieg 91
blizhnee zarubezh'e (near abroad) 117
Blue Mosque, Istanbul 28
Bogatoe, Crimea 147
Bolshevik Party 64–6, 67, 68, 69, 70,
  72, 73, 78, 81, 130
Bosnia 58, 111
Bosniaks 29, 84
Brezhnev, Leonid 136
Briansk, Russia 112
bride price (*kalem*) 47, 122
Britain xiii, 17, 19, 20, 27, 133
Broshevan, B. 112
Buchanan, Meriel 6
Bugai, N. F. 101
Bujurova, Lilia 120–1, 131, 141, 152
Bukhara, Uzbekistan 102, 107, 132
Bukharans 40
Bulat the Pilgrim 12
Bulgaria, Bulgarians 9, 19, 29, 67, 46,
  82, 110
Bultaov, V. S. 96
Burliuka, Crimea 22
burma 118
Burundi 119
Buryats 72, 73, 144
Buytik Onlar, Crimea 112
Buyuk Goc (Great Migration)
  1860–1861 15, 23–31, 34, 82, 86,
  112
  1989–1993 xiv, 117–18, 137–46,
  152
Buyuk Lambat, Crimea 31
Buyuk Muskomiia, Crimea 142

Cadir Dag (Tent Mountain) 4, 121,
  152

INDEX

Campenhausen, Baron von 54
canals 10, 103, 107, 143
Caspian Sea xii, 146
Catherine II (the Great), Empress and Autocrat of All the Russias xiii, 1, 2, 7, 159
cattle (*tel'icah'ie*) cars 100–1, 104, 119, 146
Caucasus xiv, 7, 23, 35, 69, 72, 73, 80, 97, 99, 100, 101, 134, 137, 146, 153
Celebi, Aga 17
Central Asia xiv, 35, 36, 54, 56, 58, 65–6, 73, 87–8, 89, 101–110, 116, 118–34, 135, 138–40, 142, 144–6, 150–4, 155
chaihanas (traditional tea shops) 150
Chaktal Mountains 88, 127
chambuls (raids) xii
Charsou Bazaar, Tashkent 150
Chechnya, Chechens 21, 59, 69, 73, 89–90, 97, 99, 102, 108, 124, 153, 160
Cheka (Bolshevik secret police) 69
Chernigovsk, Ukraine 31, 112
Chernomorskii district, Crimea 111
Chervonnaia, Svetlana 107, 110, 133, 144, 174
Chimkent 113
China xii, 40, 68
chinovniks (Russian officials) 51
Chircik, Uzbekistan 88, 106, 127, 173
Chol (the Plains) 1, 2
chosen trauma 119
Christianity xi, xii, xiii, 3, 10, 24, 29, 37
Chubarov, Refat 142, 157, 158
Chukurdja Alim, Crimea 100
chums 73
ciborek 71, 118
Cihan, Numan Celebi 51, 57, 60, 61, 62, 64, 65, 66, 155
Circassians 21, 23, 29, 80
CIS (Commonwealth of Independent States) 148
Clarke, Edward 3, 8
Cobanzade, Bekir 75, 83

collective farms (*kolkhozes*) 70, 74, 81, 97, 107, 112, 137, 140, 141, 149
collectivization 45, 74, 83, 84, 93
Communism 56, 69, 70, 71, 74, 77–8, 79, 80, 81, 83, 84, 87, 91, 92, 102, 116, 137
Communist Party of Crimea 69, 70, 71, 72, 77, 79, 80, 83, 84, 96, 137, 142, 155
Communist Party of the Soviet Union 125
Communist Party of Ukraine 115
Communist Party of Uzbekistan 97
Communist Youth League 115
confiscation of land 7–10, 15–17, 21, 22, 24–7, 30, 47, 61, 144
Congo 119
Connor, Walker 123
"continue the race" (*prodolzhit rod*) 106
Cossacks 17, 20–2, 115, 159
"cotton *gulag*" 107
Council of Europe 143
Crimea
 1783 annexation by Russian Empire xiii, 1–2, 7–8, 155, 157
 1853–1856 Crimean War xiv, 15, 17, 19–23, 24, 28, 48, 112
 1860–1861 Tatar Great Migration 15, 23–31, 34, 82, 86, 112, 146
 1874 migration of Tatars after conscription decree 36–7
 1883 launch of *Tercuman* newspaper 35, 39
 1884 Gasprinsky launches Islamic education reform program 35
 1902 migration of Tatars to Ottoman Empire 42–6
 1906 Mehdi campaigns for return of Tatar land in Crimea 47
 1909 foundation of Tatar *Vatan Cemiyeti* (Fatherland Society) 51
 1912 organization of first Fatherland Society cells 51
 1914–1918 World War I 60, 61

INDEX

1917 formation of first Crimean *Kurultay* 61–6
1918 capture by Bolsheviks 64–6; German occupation and Russian Civil War 67–8, 93
1920 Bolshevik victory in Crimea 69
1921 famine 69, 90; creation of Crimean ASSR 56, 57, 70
1924 execution of Ozenbasli 83
1926 census 81
1928 arrest and execution of Ibrahimov 82
1931–1934 collectivization campaign; deportation of Tatars 83, 84, 93
1937 execution of Cobanzade 83
1941 German invasion 91
1942 formation of Tatar *Wehrmacht* legion 92–3
1943 partisan attack on German garrison at Stary Krym 94
1944 deportation of Tatars xiv, xviii, 58, 59, 83, 87–8, 89–90, 95–107, 109–10, 118–22, 146, 158–9
1945 converted into *oblast* of Russian SFSR 58, 59, 111, 115
1954 Crimean *oblast* transferred to Ukrainian SSR 115
1966 Tatars request repatriation at 23rd Communist Party Congress 125
1967 Tatars absolved of betrayal by Supreme Soviet 125; Tatars begin returning to Crimea 128
1968 re-deportation of Tatars 128
1989 return of Tatars xiv, 117–18, 137–9, 152
1991 dissolution of Soviet Union xiv, 57–8, 101, 116, 148; establishment of ARC 57–8, 141, 157–8; second Crimean *Kurultay* 66, 130, 144, 174; Ukrainian citizenship law 148, 155
1992 OMON units attack Tatar squatters in Krasnii Rai 141
1993 assassination of Yuri Osmanov 173
1995 removal of Yuri Meshkov from office 140; conflict between Tatars and Bashmak gang 141
1998 Ukrainian-Uzbek protocol on deportees 148
1999 firebombing of *Mejlis* building in Simferopol 156; Tatars protest at Simferopol parliament building 157
2000 Crimean militia raid *Mejlis* building 156
2014 annexation by Russian Federation xv, 157–60
Crimea, Autonomous Republic of (1991–2014) 57–8, 141–60
Crimean ASSR (1921–1945) 56, 57–60, 70–88, 89–101, 109, 110, 111, 119, 126, 128, 136, 139, 141
Crimean Council of People's Commissars 70
Crimean Khanate (1443–1783) xii–xiii, 4, 6, 10, 34, 46, 48, 55, 62, 67, 130, 136
Crimean Tatar National Movement (CTNM) 173
Crimean *oblast*, Russian SFSR (1945–1954) 58, 59, 111–12, 115
Crimean *oblast*, Ukrainian SSR (1954–1991) 115–16, 125–6, 128, 139–40
Crimean War (1853–56) xiv, 15, 17, 19–23, 24, 28, 48, 112
Croatia 111
cuisine 118, 151
Cuma Cami, Evpatoriia 66, 111

dachas (summer houses) 117
Dagci, Cengiz 100, 149
Dagestan 23, 59, 73, 153
Daniel, Saint 3
Danube River 19, 155
Dar al Harb (Abode of War) 12, 13, 26, 31

INDEX

Dar al Islam (Abode of Islam) xiii, xiv, 12, 13, 14, 28, 116
Dar al Kufr (Abode of the Infidel) xiv
Degirmen Koy, Crimea 94
Demerci, Crimea 94
Demir Kapi (Iron Gate), Khan's Palace 62
Denikin, Anton 68
Deportation (1944) xiv, xviii, 58, 59, 83, 87–8, 89–90, 95–107, 109–10, 118–22, 146, 158–9
Deportatsiia 88, 99, 119
Dere Koy, Crimea 31, 121
Derviza 3
destans (laments and songs) 14, 17, 28, 29–30
Detskii Mir (Children's World), Tashkent 150
Deutsch, Karl 41
Devlet-i Aliye (Exalted Realm) 14
dialects 40, 52–3, 75
diseases 106, 119
Dobruca 19, 46, 67, 82, 92, 95, 96, 110, 154, 155
Druzhinina, E.I. 9
Dushanbe, Tajikistan 150
dvorianstvo (nobility) status 16
Dzhemilev, Mustafa 66, 129–33, 135, 138, 142, 148, 156, 157, 158
Dzhemilev, Reshat 99, 102, 128, 129, 131, 135

"*echelons*" (cattle transport carts) 100–1, 104, 119, 146
Effendi, Sheikh Haci Bekir 44
effendis 37
Einsatzgruppen (mobile killing units) 99
Ekaterinoslav, Ukraine 21, 31
Elin, Saint 12
Emel 154
Eminev, Ruslan 129
endogamy 124
Engels, Friedrich 56
Eni Dunya (The New World) 75–6

Enlightenment, Age of 1
Eski Kirim, Crimea 75, 94, 111
Essays on the History of the Crimea (Nadinskii) 114
Estonia 61
ethnic blending (*slianiie*) 77, 127
"ethno-warriors" 66
European Union (EU) 143
Evenks 72
Evpatoriia, Crimea 20, 21–2, 24, 25, 66, 75, 111, 147

fanaticism 7, 11, 15, 17, 24, 27
Fatherland (*ata vatan*) xiv, 12, 13, 31, 33, 45, 46, 50–2, 54–5, 79, 86, 108, 118, 121, 132, 139, 145, 155
Fatherland Society 51–2, 54–6, 60, 61, 79, 110
Feodorov, F. A. 3
Feodosiia, Crimea 24, 141–2, 145, 147
Fergana Valley 72, 102, 106, 122, 150
Fergana Valley pogroms (1989) 138–9, 154
Fergana, Uzbekistan 88, 102, 107, 122, 127, 138
festivals 3, 5, 8, 127
fetwas 13
Finland 61, 72
Fire of Moscow (1571) xii
Fisher, Alan 79, 126
Fontany, Crimea 147, 159
Foreign Affairs 114
Foundation for Research and Support of Indigenous Peoples in the Crimea 144
"Fountain of Tears" (Pushkin) 116
France 17, 19, 20, 21, 39
freight (*tovarny*) cars 100–1, 119, 146
"Friendly Advice" (Gasprinsky) 44
Frunze, Tajikistan 150

Gafarev, Ridvan 129
GAI (*Gosudarstvennaya Avtomobilnaya Inspektsiya*) 146
Galiev, Mir Said Sultan 70, 80, 81, 82

INDEX

Gaspra, Crimea 31
Gasprinsky, Ismail 33–46, 47, 49, 50, 51, 57, 60, 83, 86, 155
Gaza, Palestine 119
Genghis Khan xi, xii, 1, 117
Genghisid rulers xii
George, Saint 3
Georgia 59, 72, 97, 98, 117, 136
Germany, Germans xii, 2, 39, 46, 47, 64, 67–8, 71, 79, 81, 89–97, 99, 100, 103–4, 109, 110, 114–15, 135–6
Gestapo 94
Giray dynasty xii, 34, 49, 55, 62
Giray, Hamdi 27
glasnost (openness) 120, 136, 138
"Godless Society" 78
Golden Eagles (*Berkuts*) 142
Golden Horde xii, 6, 75
Golos Kryma (Voice of the Crimea) 63, 154
Gorbachev, Mikhail xiv, 116, 130, 131, 134, 136
Goths xi, xiii, 2, 3, 75
Gozleve, Crimea 20
Grach, Leonid 157
Great Delimitation (*Razmezhevanie*) 58
"Great Friendship of Nations" 77, 87
Great Game 20
Great Migration
 1860–1861 15, 23–31, 34, 82, 86, 112
 1989–1993 xiv, 117–18, 137–46, 152
Greece, Greeks xi, xiii, 2, 3, 75
"green bands" 68
green isle (*yeshil ada*) 30, 119, 120, 137, 139, 146, 154, 155
Groder, Philip 79
Gromyko, Andrei 137
GRU (Military Intelligence) 140
Guboglo, Mikhail 107, 110, 133, 144, 174
Gulags 124, 131
Gulistan, Uzbekistan 88, 106

GUM (State Universal Shopping Mall), Tashkent 150
Gurzuf, Crimea 31
Gvardskii, Crimea 112

Habsburg Empire xiii
Hadiths 37, 49
Hagia Sophia, Istanbul 29
Haji Bulat, Crimea 12
Halil, Munire 129
Hambly, Gavin 122
Hanafi school 12, 13, 105
Hanoi 139
hard working (*trudolyubivii*) 134
helots 107
Hicret (Giray) 27
hijra (pilgrimage) xiv, 9, 13, 24, 27, 28, 33, 44–6
Hitler, Adolf 91, 92, 100
hiwis (helpers) 95
Holderness, Mary 11
Holocaust 99, 100, 119
Hungary 53, 69
Huns xi, 115
hyper-inflation 148

"I Pledge" 65
Iakutia 73
Ibrahimbeili, Haji Murat 27–8
Ibrahimov, Veli 68, 70, 78–83, 84, 110, 155
ihvan (countrymen) 45
ikinci surgun (second exile) 88, 89
Ilk Adim (First Step) 76
Illeri (In Front) 76
indigenousness (*korennoinost*) 58
Ingush 59, 72, 89–90, 97, 99, 102, 108, 124
"Initiative Group for the Defense of Human Rights in the USSR" 129
internal alien races (*inorodtsy*) 71, 80
internal passports (*propisky*) 84, 128
International Association of Workers 81
internationalists 154

206

INDEX

Iran 99
Islam xi, xii, xiii, xiv, 4, 6, 8, 9–14, 23, 24, 26–31, 33, 34–9, 41–2, 44–6, 48, 49, 54, 61, 62, 75, 77–8, 86, 103, 111, 116, 117–18, 120, 122
  Ahir Zaman (apocalypse) 27
  bid'at (innovation) 36
  Dar al Islam (Abode of Islam) xiii, xiv, 12, 13, 14, 28, 116
  Dar al Kufr (Abode of the Infidel) xiv
  Dar al Harb (Abode of War) 12, 13, 26, 31
  effendis 37
  fetwas 13
  Hadiths 37, 49
  Hanafi school 12, 13, 105
  hijra (pilgrimage) xiv, 9, 13, 24, 27, 28, 33, 44–6
  jihad 23, 118
  Kadimism (traditionalism) 38, 49
  kafirs (infidels) xiii, xiv, 37
  land laws 9–10
  madrasas (seminaries) 6, 16, 35, 37, 38, 49, 111
  mektebs (schools) 16, 35, 37, 42
  mosques 6, 7, 11, 12, 16, 28–9, 39, 46, 49, 66, 67, 69, 73, 74, 77, 100, 111, 112, 114, 156, 159
  mufti 23, 61
  namaz (public worship) 13
  Qur'an 4, 10, 26, 28, 37, 39, 86
  shar'iah (Islamic law) 9–10, 12, 13, 38
  Sunni Islam 12, 13, 105
  talaka (corvée work) 10
  ulema 13, 35
  umma (religious community) 10, 12, 28, 78
  ushr (Qur'anic tithe) 10
  Usul-i Jadid 35, 41 51
  zakat (alms giving) 13
Islam Terek, Crimea 12
Islamic fanaticism 7, 11, 15, 17, 24, 27
Ismail Bey, Crimea 147

Israel 80, 135
Istanbul, Turkey 28–9, 30, 43, 51, 54, 55, 64
Italy, Italians xiii, 2, 3, 75, 110
Ivan IV (the Terrible), Tsar of All the Russias xii
izmeniky rodiny (traitors to the homeland) 90, 97, 102, 103, 121, 134
Izvestiia 89–90, 139

Jadids (Modernists) 35, 83
Japan 39, 45
Jassy, Treaty of (1792) 10
Jews 6, 20, 82, 84, 92, 96, 99, 100, 119, 124, 133
jihad 23, 118
Jordan 80, 121
Joseph, Saint 3

Kadiev, Roland 129
Kadimism (traditionalism) 38, 49
Kadinlik Sotsializm Elinda (Women on the Road to Socialism) 76
Kadirov, Nariman 135
Kadiyev, Rollan 102, 135
Kaffa, Crimea 4, 8, 24
kafirs (infidels) xiii, xiv, 37
Kaiser, Robert 118
Kalamita Bay, Crimea 20
kalem (bride price) 47, 122
Kalmyks 72, 73, 77, 99, 108, 124
Kamenets-Podolsk, Ukraine 112
Kamenka, Crimea 147
Kara Gun (Dark Day) 99
Karachai 97, 99, 108, 124
Karagoss, Crimea 11
Karaims 96
Karangit, Crimea 53
Karanki, Crimea 46
Karapapakhs 98
Karasu Bazar, Crimea 4, 8, 46–7, 82, 112, 137, 145, 147
Karelia 59
Karimov, Islam 153
Karimov, Server 156

207

INDEX

Kars, Turkey 97
Kashga Darya, Uzbekistan 102, 107, 132
Kastel, Crimea 94
Katkov, Ivan 34
Kazakhstan, Kazakhs 14, 21, 34, 40, 41, 55, 85, 88, 99, 101, 102, 108, 113, 123, 134, 146, 150
Kebir Cami, Simferopol 111
kedays (traveling bards) 28
Kedreles 3
Kemal, Namik 50, 51
Kerch, Crimea 70, 91
KGB 87, 97, 125, 130, 131, 135, 140, 146, 158, 173
Khairov, Izzet 129, 131, 135, 153, 173
Khakass 73
khalats 122
Khalil, Maksumadzhi 43–4
Khan Cami, Bahcesaray 111
Khan Jami Mosque, Bahcesaray 6
Khan Saray (Khan's Palace), Bahcesaray 6, 62, 97, 115–16
Kharkov, Ukraine 31
Khazanov, Anatoly 73
Khemshils 98
Kherson, Ukraine 21, 134
Khiva, Uzbekistan 122
Khokand, Uzbekistan 72, 138
Khosh Geldi, Crimea 147, 160
Khrushchev, Nikita 108, 115
Kievsk, Ukraine 112
Kipchak Turkic 40, 52, 75, 150
Kipchak Turks xi, xiii, 1, 3, 40, 75
Kirim (the Fortress) xii
Kirim Adasi (Crimean Island) xv
Kirim Tatarlik (Crimean Tatarness) 50, 56, 118
Kirim Turkleri Amerikan Birligi 66
Kirimal, Edige 90, 92, 95, 96, 97
Kirimli, Hakan 13, 14, 50
Kirimoglu (The Son of the Crimea) 130, 131
kishlaks (villages) 88, 122
Kizil Krym (The Red Crimea) 76, 79

Kizil Kum desert 88
Kizil Tash, Crimea 31, 94
Kliachin, A.I. 54
Kok Koz, Crimea 53
Koktebel, Crimea 147
Kolay, Crimea 112
kolkhozes (collective farms) 70, 74, 81, 97, 107, 112, 137, 140, 141, 149
kolkhoznik (collective farm worker) 85, 102, 112
Kolstoe, Paul 76
Komis 59
kommandants 104, 106, 107
Kopurchi, Crimea 24
Koreans 134, 139
korenizatsiia (rooting) 71, 73–8, 79, 81, 84–6, 109, 110, 111, 116, 121, 123, 125–6, 132, 134, 136, 143
korennoi narod (native people) 58, 60, 71, 73, 74, 75, 76, 84, 85, 87, 107, 111, 141, 143
Kouz, Crimea 5
Koz Aydin (Greetings) 76
Krasnii Rai, Alushta 141
Krasnodar *Krai*, Russia 134, 135, 150, 151, 153
Kuban 87
Kubay, Mehmet 84
kubitye 118
kucuk vatan (little homeland) 54, 145
kulaks (wealthy peasants) 82, 84, 93, 102
Kun, Bela 69
Kurban Bayram 8
Kurds 98
Kurkchi, Aider 138
Kurotne, Crimea 141–2
Kursk, Russia 21, 31, 112
Kurultay 46, 60–6, 67, 68, 116, 122, 130, 143, 144, 174
Kutusovskii, Crimea 111
Kuvasai, Uzbekistan 138
Kyrgyzstan, Kyrgyz 34, 40, 69, 72, 73, 123, 134, 148, 150

Lada 146

INDEX

laghman (noodles) 151
Lake Biyuk, Crimea 100
land confiscation 8, 10, 15–17, 24, 47, 144
land laws 9–10
land reform 47–8, 69, 70
Lapland 144
Latvia 61
Lazovoe, Crimea 147
Lazzerini, Edward 41
Lebanon 119, 121
Lenin, Vladimir 48, 69, 70, 72–4, 81, 127, 130
Lenin Bayragi (Lenin's Banner) 123
Leningrad, Soviet Union 92, 95
Leninshchina 136
Levitskii, G.I. 15–16, 21, 22
Lewis, Bernard 12
Lithuania 61, 67
Lividia, Crimea 31
Luftwaffe 91

madrasas (seminaries) 6, 16, 35, 37, 38, 49, 111
mafia 138, 141, 145
mahallas (traditional neighborhoods) 123
Mahmut, Musa 128
Maksimov 21
malaria 106, 119
Mangup Kale, Crimea 75
manty (meat raviolis) 151
Marghilan, Uzbekistan 88, 107, 138
Mari ASSR 101, 102
Marino, Crimea 147
Marjani, Shihab al-Din 34
Markanda, The 151
Markevich, Arsenii 27
Markov, Evgenii 21
martyrs 65, 128
Marx, Karl 56, 72
Marxism 72, 78, 86
Mecca 13
Mehdi, Abdureshid 46–9, 51, 57, 148, 155

Mejlis 130, 131, 140, 141, 144, 145, 148, 152, 153, 156, 158, 159
mektebs (schools) 16, 35, 37, 42
Memalik-i Mahrusa (The Well Protected Realms) 14
Memetova, Susana 138
Memleket-i Islam (Dominion of Islam) 14
Meshketian Turks 97, 108, 135–6, 138–9, 150
Meshkov, Yuri 140
Middle East xii, 80
Middle Road (*Orta Yolak*) 75, 150
millenarianism 27
millet (nation) xiv, 45
Milli Firka (National Party) 62, 64, 67, 68, 69, 70, 75, 78–9, 83, 110, 173
Milli Shehit (National Martyr) 65, 128
Minority Rights Organization 143
mirza landlords 9–10, 16, 24, 34, 54, 62, 75, 82
Mittenwald, Germany 95
Moldova 117
Molotov *oblast*, Russia 101
Mongols xi–xii, 1, 2, 3, 4, 5, 6, 75, 92, 114, 117
Moors 24
Mordvins 59
Moscow, Russia xii, 34, 92, 95, 100, 125, 137, 138, 150
mosques 6, 7, 11, 12, 16, 28–9, 39, 46, 49, 66, 67, 69, 73, 74, 77, 100, 111, 112, 114, 156, 159
Mubarek Republic 132–4
mufti 23, 61
muhajir destans (religious-emigrant ballads) 14, 17, 28, 29–30
muhajirs (religious emigrants) 14, 28–31, 155
mullahs 6, 8, 11, 13, 27, 28, 36, 37, 38, 41, 48, 49, 52, 56, 61, 62, 75, 77
Muslim Committees 93, 95, 96
Mustafaev, Refat 94
Mustafayev, Rustem 160
Muzafarov, R.I. 58

INDEX

MVD (Ministry of Internal Affairs) 104, 105, 127, 141, 145, 173
"My Dear" (Ozenbashli) 45

Nadinskii, P.N. 114
Nagorno Karabagh 59
Nahylo, Bohdan 109
Nakhimovskii, Crimea 112
Nakichevan 59
namaz (public worship) 13
Namengan, Uzbekistan 88, 102, 107
al-Naqba (The Disaster) 119
Narkomnats (Commissariat for Nationality Affairs) 70
al-Nasiri, Abd al-Qaiyum 34
national identity 26, 33, 36, 37, 39, 41, 42, 48, 50, 51, 52–6, 57, 60, 61, 72–88, 118–23, 150–4
National Public Radio 159
Nationalism and Social Communication (Deutsch) 41
nationalism xiv, 12–13, 31, 33, 36, 39–42, 45–55, 59–70, 72, 75, 77–9, 82–8, 90, 92–3, 118, 121, 123–39, 142, 156–7, 174
native people (*korennoi narod*) 58, 60, 71, 73, 74, 75, 76, 84, 85, 87, 107, 111, 141, 143
natsional'naia rodina (national homeland) 89
Navoi Theater, Tashkent 150
Nazi Germany 89–97, 99, 100, 103–4, 109, 114–15, 159
Nekrich, Alexander 93, 96, 98, 108
Neu-Ulm, Germany 95
New Economic Policy (NEP) 81
New Jersey, United States 114
New Method (*Usul-i Jadid*) schools 35, 41, 51
New York, United States 66, 114, 128
nightingales 3
Nikolayev, Crimea 93
Nizami Pedagogical Institute, Tashkent 132–3
NKVD (The People's Commissariat of Internal Affairs) 87, 97, 99, 102, 106, 146
Nogai Tatars 1–2, 10, 19, 21, 24–5, 31, 40, 47, 52, 53, 54, 56, 66, 75, 82, 87, 122, 149, 150, 175
nomenklatura (bureaucratic elite) 131, 142, 145
Norway 144
nostalgia for Central Asia 150–2

Ogata, Sadako 95
Oghuz Turkic dialect 40, 52, 75, 150
Oiratia 73
Omerev, Riza 129
OMON (Special Police) 141
"On Migration" (Gasprinsky) 42–3
"On the Eulogy of the Crimea" (Toktargazi) 49
Orange Revolution (2004) 158
Oraza Bayram 8
Orenburg, Siberia 22
Organization of the Crimean Tatar National Movement (OCTNM) 130, 173
orgnabor (organized labor) 136
Oriental fatalism 7, 23
Oriental Institute 74
Oriental Romanticism 6
Orlovsk, Ukraine 21
Orta Turk Tili (Middle Turkish Language) 40
Orta Yolak (Middle Road) 75, 150
Orthodox Church 3, 10, 24, 75
Oskiuz Kapa, Crimea 67
Osmanov, Yuri 135, 173
Ostarbeiters (Eastern Workers) 94–5
Ostiak 73
otdel spetsposelenii (special settlement department) 105
Otouz, Crimea 5
Ottoman Empire xii–xiv, 7, 8, 9, 10–11, 13–14, 17, 19–31, 34, 42–6, 48, 50–1, 64, 75, 116, 155
1683 Battle of Vienna xiii
1711 Pruth River campaign xii

INDEX

1783 annexation of Crimea by Russian Empire xiii, 153
1792 Treaty of Jassy 10
1853–1856 Crimean War xiv, 15, 17, 19–23, 24, 28, 48
1860–1861 Tatar Great Migration 15, 23–31, 34, 82, 86
1874 immigration of Tatars after Russian conscription decree 36–7
1902 renewed immigration of Tatars 42–6
1908 Young Turk Revolution 50
oz sahipleri (true owners) 143
Ozenbash, Crimea 100
Ozenbashli, Ahmed 93
Ozenbashli, Seyit Abdullah 44–5, 83

Palace of the Friendship of Peoples, Tashkent 105
Palestine 80, 119, 121, 129, 135
Pamir Mountains 88
Pan-Slavism 34, 39
Pan-Turkism 39–42, 45
Panzers 91
paranjas (veils) 122
Paris, France 34
Partisankii, Crimea 112
partisans 93–4, 96, 100
People's Museum, Bahcesaray 115–16
Perekop, Crimea 2, 24, 46, 91, 108
perestroika (restructuring) 136, 138
Peter I (the Great), Emperor of All Russia xii, xiii
Peter, Saint 3
Pinson, Mark 22
Pipes, Richard 69
plov (rice) 151
Poland xii, 61, 92
Polovtsians xi
Poltava, Ukraine 21, 31, 112
polygamy 122
Pomaks 29
pomeshchiks (landowners) 7, 8, 9, 15, 21, 22, 24, 25–7, 30, 47, 61, 144
Poppe, Nicholas 101

Pravda 139
Pravda Vostoka (Truth of the East) 135
Primorskoye, Crimea 147
"Proclamation to all the Muslims of Russia and the Orient" (Lenin) 69
proletariat 70, 72, 77
Proliter Medeniyeti (Proletarian Culture) 76
propisky (internal passports) 84, 128
Pulatov, Temir 134
Pushkin, Alexander 6, 111, 116, 143
Pushkinskii, Crimea 111
Putin, Vladimir 157–60

Quelquejay, Lemercier 111
Qur'an 4, 10, 26, 28, 37, 39, 86

Radlov, Vasily Vasilievich 75
Raglan, Lord *see* Somerset, FitzRoy
Rashidov, Sharaf 133
Reagan, Ronald 130
Red Army 90, 91–2, 95, 97, 98, 103, 104, 120
Red Square, Moscow 137
religious identity 11, 13, 28, 31, 36–7, 45, 77–8, 116, 118, 120
"Return to the Homeland" movement (1957–1989) 124–37, 142
rodina (homeland) 10, 56, 77, 85, 86, 89, 105, 151
Romania xiv, 9, 19, 29, 46, 67, 82, 93, 95, 110, 154
Romanian Mountain Corps 91
rooted people (*korennoi narod*) 58, 60, 71, 73, 74, 75, 76, 84, 85, 87, 107, 111, 141, 143
rooting (*korenizatsiia*) 71, 73–8, 79, 81, 84–6, 109, 110, 111, 116, 121, 123, 125–6, 132, 134, 136, 143
Rorlich, Azade-Ayse 126
Rostov, Russia 112
Rumelia, Ottoman Empire 19
Rummel, Rudolph Joseph 110
Rus kafirs (Russian infidels) xiii, 37
Russia, Tsardom of (1547–1721) xii, 115

INDEX

1571 Fire of Moscow xii
1654 unification with Ukraine 115
1711 Pruth River campaign xii
Russian Civil War (1917–1922) 130
  1917 Russian Revolution 40, 46, 52, 54, 55, 60, 61; formation of first Crimean *Kurultay* 61–6
  1918 Bolshevik capture of Crimea 64–6; German occupation of Crimea 67–8, 93; Red and White Armies struggle for power in Crimea 68
  1920 Bolshevik victory in Crimea 69
  1921 famine in Crimea 69, 90; creation of Crimean ASSR 56, 57, 70
Russian Empire (1721–1917)
  1783 annexation of Crimea xiii, 1–2, 7–8, 155, 157
  1792 Treaty of Jassy 10
  1853–1856 Crimean War xiv, 15, 17, 19–23, 24, 28, 48, 111
  1860–1861 Tatar Great Migration 15, 23–31, 34, 82, 86, 112, 146
  1861 liberation of the serfs 50
  1874 migration of Tatars after conscription decree 36–7
  1881–1884 anti-Jewish pogroms 20
  1883 launch of *Tercuman* newspaper 35, 39
  1884 Gasprinsky launches Islamic education reform program 35
  1902 migration of Tatars to Ottoman Empire 42–6
  1904–1905 Russo-Japanese War 45
  1905 Revolution 41, 46
  1906 Mehdi campaigns for return of Tatar land in Crimea 47
  1909 foundation of Tatar *Vatan Cemiyeti* (Fatherland Society) 51
  1912 organization of Fatherland Society cells in Crimea 51
  1914–1918 World War I 60, 61
  1917 Russian Revolution 40, 46, 52, 54, 55, 60, 61
Russian Federation (1991–present) xv, 130–1, 148

  1994–1996 Russo-Chechen War 153
  1999–2009 Russo-Chechen War 153
  2014 annexation of Crimea xv, 157–60
Russian Muslim Corps 67
Russian Orthodox Church 3, 10, 24, 75
Russian SFSR 58, 59, 70, 101, 111
Rwanda 119
Rywkin, Michael 101

"sackmen" xii
Sakharov, Andrei 129
Salgir 154
Salgir River 4, 56, 121, 143
Saly, Crimea 94
Samarkand, Uzbekistan 73, 88, 102, 122, 132, 150, 151
Sami Lapplanders 144
samizdat (underground self-publications) 128, 133
Samoed 73
samozakhvat (self-seizure) raids 140, 147, 151, 155
Sancak-i Serif (Banner of the Prophet) 27
Sarabuz, Crimea 25
Sardinia 17, 19
sarma 118
Sarmatians xi
Sarts 69
Sary Su, Crimea 147
sblizheniie (rapprochement) 127
Scandinavia 2
Schutzmannschaftsbataillonen (police battalions) 93
Scythians xi, 75, 115
second exile (*ikinci surgun*) 88, 89, 101–16, 118–37
secularism 39, 78, 86
Seit Elin, Crimea 12
selbschutze (self defense) brigades 93
self-immolation 128
self-seizure (*samozakhvat*) raids 140, 147, 151, 155

212

INDEX

Serbia xiv, 29, 111
Sevastopol, Crimea 64–6, 70, 91, 95
  Siege of (1854–55) 15, 17, 20–1
Sevdiyar, Memet 70, 52, 135
Seydahmet, Cafer 51, 57, 60, 61, 64, 65, 67
Seyhislamova, Menube 103
Seytmuartova, Ayshe 125, 129, 131, 135
Shamil, Imam 23
shar'iah (Islamic law) 9–10, 12, 13, 38
Sheehy, Ann 109
Sher Dor *madrasa*, Karasu Bazar 46
Shevel, Oxana 156
Shirin *beylik* (chieftainship) 46
Shirinsky Cliffs 46
Shoah 99, 100, 119
Siberia xii, 22, 69, 73, 77, 83, 87, 101, 102, 109, 110, 124, 150
Simeiz, Crimea 31, 53, 74
Simferopol, Crimea 17, 24, 25, 48, 61, 64, 66, 70, 82, 90, 93, 97, 111, 137, 140, 141, 145, 147, 156, 157, 159
Sinan Pasha 66
Skalistoye, Crimea 147
slavery xii
Slezkine, Yuri 85
slianiie (ethnic blending) 77, 127
Smeets, Rieks 85
Sochi, Russia 150, 158
Socialist Party of the Workers and Peasants of Turkey 81
Soguk Su, Crimea 30–1
Solzhenitsyn, Alexander 76, 99
Somerset, FitzRoy, 1st Baron Raglan 20
Son of the Crimea, The 130, 131
Soviet Far East 84, 133
Soviet Union (1922–1991) xiv, 34, 45, 46, 53, 56–60, 70–88, 89–116, 118–40, 144, 145, 148, 154, 173
  1924 death of Lenin; rise of Stalin 81; execution of Ozenbasli 83
  1928 arrest and execution of Ibrahimov 82
  1931–1934 collectivization campaign 83, 84, 93
  1934 establishment of Jewish Autonomous Oblast in Birobidzhan 84, 133
  1937 execution of Cobanzade 83
  1941 German invasion 91; deportation of Volga Germans 99
  1942 formation of Crimean Tatar *Wehrmacht* legion 92–3
  1943 partisan attack on German garrison at Stary Krym 94; deportation of Karachais and Kalmyks 99
  1944 Battle of Crimea 95; deportation of Chechens, Ingush and Balkars 99; deportation of Crimean Tatars xiv, xviii, 58, 59, 83, 87–8, 89–90, 95–107, 109–10, 118–22, 146, 158–9
  1945 Crimea becomes *oblast* of Russian SFSR 58, 59, 111, 115
  1953 death of Stalin 108, 115
  1954 Crimean *oblast* transferred to Ukrainian SSR 115
  1956 Khrushchev lifts special settlement regime 108, 123, 139
  1957 deported nations return to home republics 108, 123, 124
  1966 Tatars request repatriation at 23rd Communist Party Congress 125; imprisonment of Mustafa Dzhemilev 129
  1967 Tatars absolved of betrayal by Supreme Soviet 125; Tatars begin returning to Crimea 128
  1968 Chirchik Riots 127, 173; re-deportation of Tatars 128
  1969 protests at May Day parade in Tashkent 128
  1973 imprisonment of Reshat Dzhemilev 129
  1987 Tatars protest for repatriation in Red Square 137
  1988 Mustafa Dzhemilev released from prison 130; imprisonment of Reshat Ablaev 135
  1989 foundation of OCTNM 130;

213

INDEX

Fergana Valley pogroms 138–9, 154; Tatars return to Crimea xiv, 117–18, 137–9, 152
1991 Crimean Sovereignty referendum xiv, 57–8; dissolution xiv, 57–8, 101, 116, 148
sovkhozes (state farms) 69, 70, 81, 97, 107, 112
Spain 24
"Speak" (Bujurova) 120–1
special settlement (*spetsposelenets*) camps 97, 104, 105–8, 119
spetsial'nyi uchet (special accounting reports) 105
spetskommandants 105
squatter camps 117, 128, 131, 141, 145, 147, 159
SS (Schutzstaffel) 96
St. Arnaud, Armand-Jacques Leroy de 21
St. George's Day 3
Stalin, Josef xiv, 70, 72, 81–3, 86–8, 91, 93, 96, 97, 98, 102, 107, 108, 110, 114, 115, 124, 134, 139
Stalingrad, Soviet Union 92, 95
Stary Krym, Crimea 94
state farms (*sovkhozes*) 69, 70, 81, 97, 107, 112
"State Program for the Return of the Crimean Tatars to the Crimean Oblast" 148
steak tartar xii
Stroganovka, Crimea 147
Studebakers 99
Sudak Valley, Crimea 4, 5, 31, 143, 145
Suleimaniye Mosque, Istanbul 28–9
Sulkiewicz, Aleksander 68
Sulkiewicz, Suleiman 67
Sultan Ahmed Mosque, Istanbul 28
Sunni Islam 12, 13, 105
Surkhan Darya, Uzbekistan 122
Svetochnaia, Crimea 147
swastikas 90, 159
Syria 29, 80

Taiwan 68

Tajikistan, Tajiks 72, 88, 102, 108, 110, 117, 122, 123, 134, 139, 148, 150, 155
talaka (corvée work) 10
Talat Pasha 64
Tambovsk, Russia 112
Tarak Tamgha crest 55, 62, 157
Tarak Tash (Comb Rock), Crimea 31, 121, 143
Tashkent, Uzbekistan 88, 101–2, 103, 105, 106, 122, 127, 132, 150, 173
Tashkent Ten 129, 173
Tass 94
Tat houses 3
Tat-Tatars 2–6, 16, 26, 40, 52, 53, 54, 56, 75, 122, 149, 150, 175
Tatar Autonomous Soviet Socialist Republic 59
Tatarness (*Tatalik*) 50, 56, 118
Tatars
canal building 10, 107, 143
confiscation of land by *pomeshchiks* 7–10, 15–17, 21, 22, 24–7, 30, 47, 61, 144
cuisine 118, 151
Deportation (1944) xiv, xviii, 58, 59, 83, 87–8, 89–90, 95–107, 109–10, 118–22, 146, 158–9
dialects 40, 52–3, 75, 150
Fatherland (*ata vatan*) xiv, 12, 13, 31, 33, 45, 46, 50–2, 54–5, 79, 86, 108, 118, 121, 132, 139, 145, 155
festivals 3, 5, 8, 127
Great Migration (1860–1861) 15, 23–31, 34, 82, 86, 112
Great Migration (1989–1993) xiv, 117–18, 137–46, 152
houses 3, 151
korenizatsiia (rooting) 71, 73–8, 79, 81, 84–6, 109, 110, 111, 116, 121, 123, 125–6, 132, 134, 136, 143
Kurultay 46, 60–6, 67, 68, 116, 122, 130, 143, 144, 174
land laws 9–10
Mejlis 130, 131, 140, 141, 144, 145, 148, 152, 153, 156, 158, 159

INDEX

mirza landlords 9–10, 16, 24, 34, 54, 62, 75, 82
muhajirs (religious emigrants) 14, 28–31, 155
nationalism xiv, 12–13, 31, 33, 36, 39–42, 45–55, 59–70, 72, 75, 77–9, 82–8, 90, 92–3, 118, 121, 123–39, 142, 156–7, 174
national identity 26, 33, 36, 37, 39, 41, 42, 48, 50, 51, 52–6, 57, 60, 61, 72–88, 118–23, 150–4
Nogai Tatars 1–2, 10, 19, 21, 24–5, 31, 40, 47, 52, 53, 54, 56, 66, 75, 82, 87, 122, 149, 150, 175
nostalgia for Central Asia 150–2
religious identity 11, 13, 28, 31, 36–7, 45, 77–8, 116, 118, 120
Return to the Homeland movement (1957–1989) 124–37, 142
second exile (1944–1989) 88, 89, 101–16, 118–37
Tat-Tatars 2–6, 16, 26, 40, 52, 53, 54, 56, 75, 122, 149, 150, 175
terrace farming 112, 147
tobacco growing 2, 5, 99, 107, 112
viniculture 2, 3, 5, 53, 74, 107, 112, 113, 147
Volga Tatars 34, 40, 41, 54, 56, 59, 70, 80, 82, 126, 172
Tauride Province 9–17, 19–31, 33–56, 61
Tauride University, Simferopol 74
Tav-Bodrak, Crimea 94
tchibouk (pipes) 5
Tepresh 3, 127
Tercuman 35, 39–42, 50
terrace farming 112, 147
Teselli (Aliadin) 53
Theodor, Saint 3
Tien Shan Mountains 36
tobacco 2, 5, 99, 107, 112
Toktargazi, Shamil 49
Topkapi Palace, Istanbul 28
Totleben, Eduard 15, 16, 21, 26, 28
Toulouk, Crimea 5

tourism 115–16, 117, 135, 145
traitors to the homeland (*izmeniky rodiny*) 90, 97, 102, 103, 121, 134
trudolyubivii (hard working) 134
true owners (*oz sahipleri*) 143
Tshei, Crimea 21
tuberculosis 147
Tula, Russia 100
Tunisia 29
Turan 41
Turgenev, Ivan 34
Turkenglocken (Turk Bells) xii
Turkestan 41, 69
Turkey 9, 24, 50–1, 59, 62, 64, 66–9, 80–1, 84, 87, 92, 93, 96, 97–8, 110, 135–6, 154, 155
Turki 40
Turkic Karapapakhs 98
Turkicness (*Turkluk*) 50
Turkish Communist Party 81, 87
Turkish Socialist Party 81
Turkmen 34, 40, 55, 72
Turkmenistan 146
Tutsis 119
Tygliiants, P. 112

Udmurts 59, 101
Uganda 119, 133
Uighurs 87, 134
Ukraine, Ukrainians xi, xii, xiv, xv, 1, 2, 11, 59, 63, 64, 70, 71, 81, 82, 84, 85, 91, 94, 96, 108, 112, 115, 134, 140–60
1654 unification with Russia 115
1881–1884 anti-Jewish pogroms 20
1954 Crimean *oblast* transferred to Ukrainian SSR 115
1991 establishment of ARC 57–8, 141, 157–8; second Crimean *Kurultay* 66, 130, 144, 174; citizenship law 148, 155
1992 OMON units attack Tatar squatters in Krasnii Rai 141
1993 assassination of Yuri Osmanov 173

INDEX

1995 removal of Yuri Meshkov from office 140; conflict between Tatars and Bashmak gang 141
1998 signing of protocol on deportees with Uzbekistan 148
1999 firebombing of *Mejlis* building in Simferopol 156; Tatars protest at Simferopol parliament building 157
2000 Crimean militia raid *Mejlis* building 156
2004 Orange Revolution 158
2014 annexation of Crimea by Russian Federation xv, 157–60
ulema 13, 35
Ulkusal, Mustecip Fazil 92
Ulu Uzen, Crimea 112
Ulu-Sala, Crimea 94
Umerov, Ilmi 148
umma (religious community) 10, 12, 28, 78
United Nations (UN) 95, 143
United States xiii, 39, 66, 99, 114–15, 128, 130, 135
Untermenschen (subhumans) 92
Ural Mountains 101, 102
Urus Kafirs (Russian infidels) xiii, 37
ushr (Qur'anic tithe) 10
Uskut, Crimea 31, 121
Usta, Selim 43
Usul-i Jadid 35, 41, 51
Uzbek Khan mosque, Eski Kirim 111
Uzbekistan, Uzbeks xiv, 34, 59, 72, 77, 85–6, 88, 97, 101–7, 108, 109, 117, 119–34, 122, 138–9, 148, 150–1, 153–5, 159

vakif estates 16, 47–8, 51, 61, 148
Vasili, Saint 3
Vasilievskii, Crimea 112
vatan xiv, 12, 13, 31, 33, 45, 46, 50–2, 54–5, 79, 86, 108, 118, 121, 132, 136, 139, 145, 155
Vatan 154
Vatan Cemiyeti (Fatherland Society) 51–2, 54–6, 60, 61, 79, 110

Vatan Hadmi (Servant of the Nation) 47
Vatan Party 156
Vatan yahut Silistre (Kemal) 51
veils 122
Veliibrahimovshchina 78
Verhnaya Ku-tuzhova, Crimea 147
Verkhovna Rada (Ukrainian Parliament) 143, 155, 156
Vienna, Austria xiii
viniculture 2, 3, 5, 53, 74, 107, 112, 113, 147
Vlasov, Andrey 92
Vol'fson, B. M. 27
Volga Germans 99, 108, 135–6
Volga River xii, 26
Volga Tatars 34, 40, 41, 54, 56, 59, 70, 80, 82, 126, 172
Volksdeutsche 136
Voronezh military academy, Moscow 34
Voronezh, Russia 31, 112
Vozgrin, Valerii 53, 55

Al-Wansharissi 13
Washington Post 158
Wehrmacht 91, 93, 95
West Bank, Palestine 119
White Army 68, 69
White Hoja, Crimea 12
White Mosque, Crimea 12, 74, 82, 111; *see also* Simferopol
White Sheikh, Crimea 12
white soil (*ak toprak*) 14, 27, 28, 29, 46, 86, 116
wine 5, 53, 74, 107, 113
women's rights 122
World War I (1914–1918) 36, 46, 50, 53, 55, 60, 61, 93
World War II (1939–1945) xiv, 83, 85, 89–101, 112
Wrangel, Pyotr 68

Yaila Mountains 2, 3–4, 31, 52, 54, 65, 66, 68, 70, 82, 84, 85, 87, 93, 94, 106, 113, 137, 145, 149, 150, 151
Yakuts 59, 73

INDEX

Yaliboyu coast, Crimea 4, 53, 54, 82, 84, 87, 106, 115, 121, 145, 149, 150
Yalta, Crimea 4, 31, 52, 53, 66, 75, 121, 145
yamas (underground grain storage bins) 21
Yangi Yul, Uzbekistan 88, 106, 129
yantyk 118
Yar Kaya, Crimea 147
Yas Kuvvet (Young Strength) 76
Yas Lenindzhiler (Young Leninists) 76
Yavuz, Hakan 49
Yaziciev, Ismail 129
Yekaterina II *see* Catherine II

Yemelianova, Galina 56
yeshil ada (green isle) 30, 119, 120, 137, 139, 146, 154, 155
Yildiz (The Star) 123
Young Tatars 48–50, 51, 55, 60, 70, 75, 78, 79, 83, 110, 148
Young Turks 50, 51, 62, 64
Yugoslavia 58, 84, 159
Yurter, Fikret 95, 135
yurts 1, 73

Zaire 119
zakat (alms giving) 13
zar zaman (difficult times) ballads 14